T0373915

MY GRANDFATHER'S KNIFE

By the same author

Berlin

MY GRANDFATHER'S KNIFE

And Other Stories of War and Belongings

Joseph Pearson

First published 2022

The History Press
97 St George's Place, Cheltenham,
Gloucestershire, GL50 3QB
www.thehistorypress.co.uk

British Library Cataloguing in Publication Data.
A catalogue record for this book is available from the British Library.

ISBN 978 0 7509 9739 3

Typesetting and origination by The History Press
Printed and bound in Great Britain by TJ Books Limited, Padstow, Cornwall.

Trees for Life

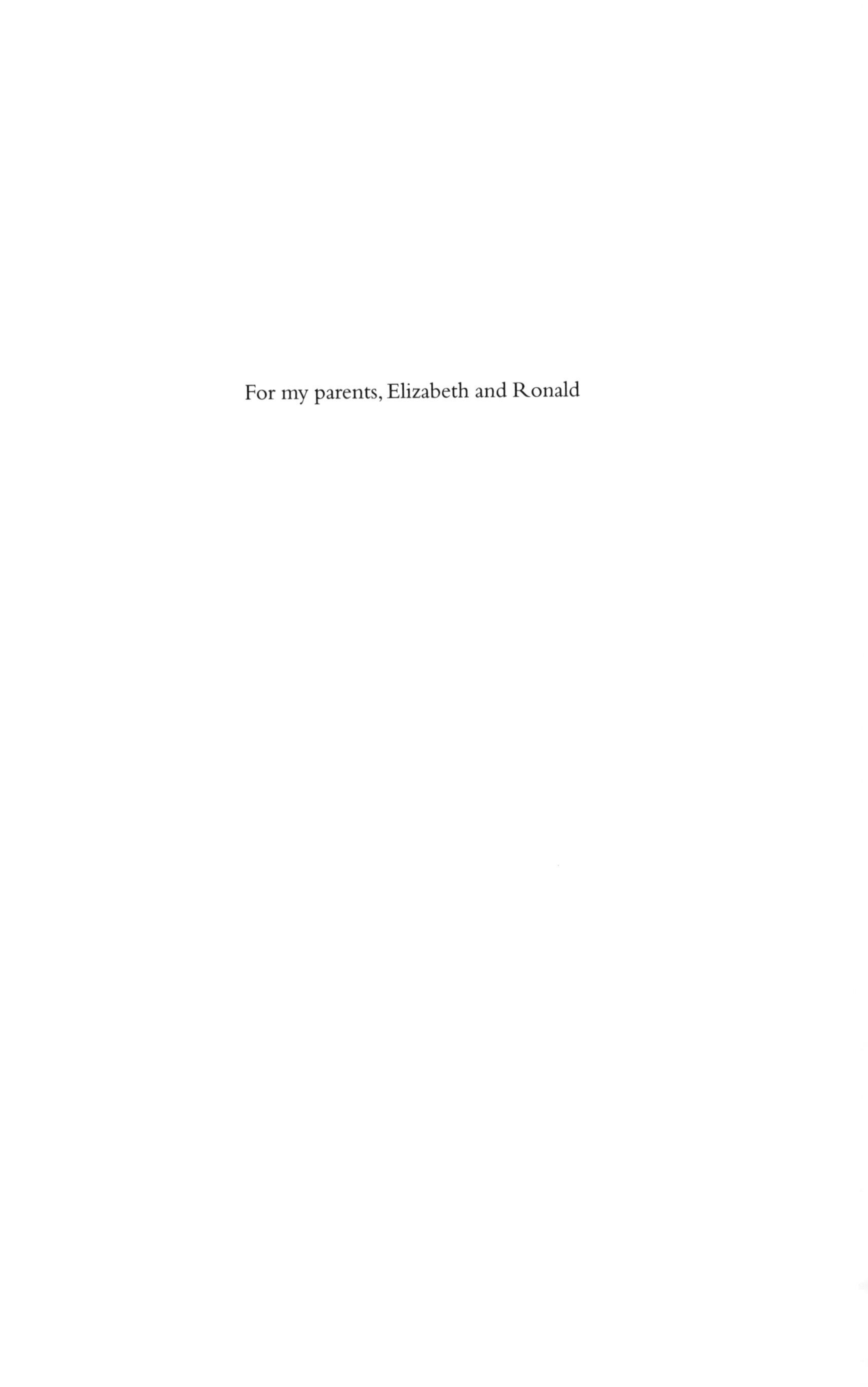

For my parents, Elizabeth and Ronald

Contents

Preface

A knife, a diary, a recipe book, a string instrument, and a cotton pouch. Each belonged to an individual in their twenties during the Second World War: a fresh-faced prairie boy, a melancholic youth, a capable cook, a musician wounded at the front, and a survivor.

Try asking your friends, over a cup of tea, what object they'd choose to represent their lives. The enthusiasm of their responses will give you an indication of how well objects anchor sprawling personal histories. I talked to elderly family members, friends, colleagues, and acquaintances – people drawn from everyday life – asking them the same question: is there a belonging that tells your wartime story? In most cases, I asked the question in reverse. Can I discover the Second World War story of a deceased person through an object they owned?

I had to make difficult choices to pare the book down to five objects. I found that even the most ordinary of them could tell a spectacular story; they are no less extraordinary or meaningful than famous examples.

Historians of material history – those who occupy themselves with what objects can tell us about the past – often divide their work into 'object-centred histories' and 'object-driven histories'. In the former, the objects are the focus of their owners' stories. In the latter, the objects might stand slightly left-of-centre but they nonetheless help us reveal something that would otherwise be hidden. In this book, I do a little of both; there are variations on a theme. Ultimately, in both cases, the belongings remain tools – even strategies – to draw out a witness's narrative. I think of them like attractors, dipped into the solution of history that then form crystals of memory.

Now, your neighbours may be more or less interesting than mine. I would never claim that my next-door objects are an uncomplicated sample from the pond of history. I'm a Canadian who moved to Berlin more than a decade ago – an outsider who teaches this material at a university in the German capital. But I am certain that almost any reader of this book – provided they have neighbours and family who remember the war – will make remarkable discoveries about the past if they start asking around. And I am also convinced that my everyday discoveries will resonate with people who never met my neighbours.

The most exciting aspect of writing this book has been the detective work. Unpacking these 'next-door' histories is at times inspiring, at others disheartening (and it's about the heart when you begin to know each individual intimately). But the step-by-step thrill of discovery was something I wanted to share.

As an unlikely mix of historian-meets-literary writer, I've often scratched my head at why history doesn't more often employ tools of creative writing to tell engaging but true stories – ones that capture the texture of the past. My response was to write the chapters as 'documentary short stories' of stumbling across Second World War witnesses, learning about their belongings and everyday histories, uncovering their secrets. The resulting book intentionally does not read like traditional history.

To reassure the general reader and the specialist: there is something here for you both. The former might spend more time with the stories, the latter with the concluding chapter of analysis and endnotes. To enjoy me at my most pedantic, you may read from the back, where I tie the theoretical problems to a dozen further objects to give context in the field of material history. Throughout, I argue how Nazi-era objects are especially vulnerable to opportunistic narratives – as screens for our fantasies, our projections – in the absence of their owners and careful detective work.

This 'object history of memory' is being written at an urgent turning point, one of generational change. The public health emergency of Covid-19 has disproportionately affected the war generation. Consider the following: a 22-year-old in the last year of the Second World War is 99 years old in 2022. Most of the witnesses for this book were about this age when interviewed. They are the last witnesses. I am worried what happens to their belongings when they are gone because, on their own, these things don't speak. Line them up on a table, try talking to them one by one, and I bet you won't get a word out of them. It's as if they were charmed, and their stories only summoned by those people who had direct experience of this most violent moment in world history. This momentary spell gives the objects value.

The line between the junkyard and the museum is a good story. Since knowing their stories – as you will – it's become difficult for me to see the objects as just flotsam. It pains me to imagine them collecting dust on the shelf of a second-hand shop or in a storage locker. But a generation that has not experienced war, whose members are unable to interpret the jetsam of the past, will more easily discard or misinterpret these things. Think of a belonging of sentimental value you own – an engagement ring, an admission ticket, a stone from a beach – which will become meaningless the moment you are no longer there to tell its story.

It is no coincidence that resurgent nationalism and xenophobia gain ground – and not just in Germany – as we lose those who saw their extreme consequences. Because many stories can be spun from these objects, but not all of them are true.

Berlin, December 2021

My Grandfather's Knife

The Knife

My grandfather kept a knife with a swastika on the wall in his basement. When I was small, he took me down to see it, and it frightened me. It hung cold from its hook, surrounded by other weapons the veteran had collected or inherited. There was the riding crop and sword of my great-great-grandfather, a colonel from the Boer War. The colonel's sword was imbued with positive feelings: the material was bright and shiny and silver, and I had read enough fairy tales to want a sword.

But, even at the age of 6 or 7, I knew to distrust the knife in its scabbard. I did not have the words then – nor really now – to describe its negativity. Was it the silver eagle's head, decorated with carved feathers? That it was bolted with a layer of bone – human? – below the elaborately carved hilt of laurels? Was it the scabbard, of worn leather, for the ferocious blade that had brushed against some trouser leg?

When my grandfather took it down from the wall and unsheathed it, the knife made an efficient sound – a slide and a click. This was so unlike the elegantly resounding ring of the colonel's sword. And when he lowered it into my hands, I looked into the blank eye of the eagle. I examined all the Xs carved into the silver of its hilt. I turned it over, fascinated with the insignia of the eagle, wings spread, also wreathed with laurel leaves, all surmounting the swastika.

My grandfather told me that he had liberated the knife as a captain in the Canadian forces in 1944 or 1945 in the Netherlands. My father told me a different story – perhaps to protect me – which was that he 'found it in the mud somewhere'. At that age, the word 'liberate' was a positive one. I did not for a moment think that it could be a euphemism for capturing or killing the enemy.

Many years later – after my studies and time spent living in many places, with possessions scattered between college storage, my parents' house, and lockers in Cambridge, New York, Nottingham, Vancouver, and Edmonton – I settled down and ended up living in the capital of my grandfather's enemy. I have been living among the defeated in Berlin for more than a decade now.

My grandfather died in 2005, and I never paid much attention to his will, except for a couple of details: he left me both my great-great-grandfather's sword and his Nazi knife. The sword was outside normal baggage restrictions (it's still in my parents' basement and I wonder if I should transport it with golf clubs one day). But the Nazi knife had vanished; no one knew what had happened to it. 'Thank goodness,' my aunt told me. 'It was so horrific. Stuff like that should just disappear.'

A few years ago, my family shipped many of my books to me in Berlin. Surrounded by boxes in a new apartment, I started to go through the stacks of historical tomes. It was then, at the bottom of one box, that I was surprised to find a long object wrapped in a cloth. I unpacked it and – to my horror – discovered that my grandfather's Nazi knife had somehow slipped through German customs and ended up back in the fatherland.

Nazi symbols are, of course, illegal in Germany. I was lucky that the knife had not been discovered during a customs search. I shivered at the idea of a metal detector passing over what was declared as a box of books and documents. But I also felt helpless, and exposed, holding this object from a villainous regime, in the country that had murdered so many of its citizens. I honestly went to pieces, not knowing what to do with it: whether to turn it in to a museum or to call the police, or to hide it deep somewhere in my apartment, under a floorboard, or else try to destroy it somehow. Because the knife, which had merely been terrifying back in Canada, had a completely different set of meanings in the country that had produced and used it.

I could not risk sending the knife back to Canada through customs. But I wondered if it could stay in Germany either – a country haunted by its past, where almost any object emblazoned with a swastika causes panic and ends up being put away. I remember how it was only with a great deal of fuss that the German Historical Museum finally exhibited everyday objects – such as a Nazi doll's house and SS action figures sporting tiny swastikas – in their collection. They were afraid that visitors including, at worst, neo-Nazis on pilgrimage, would tell their own stories about these objects instead of the carefully researched ones of historians. If the knife went to a museum, it would end up in a crate in the basement, not used as a tool for examining the barbarity of the regime's executors.

With the knife in my hands, I was stuck. Would I be reduced to taking it out at dinner parties to horrify my German guests? Or had the knife followed me to Germany for a purpose? Had my grandfather left me this knife so it could find its way back to the continent where he had fought? Nonsense: a good historian would rubbish this kind of superstition. Rather, the knife provided me not just with an opportunity, but with an imperative to tell its story and justify its presence.

Perhaps I could, too, learn something, as a descendant of the victorious powers. In Berlin, they tell the story of war differently than we do in Canada or Britain, where we are often uncritically patriotic about the deaths of so many men who were too young to die. Perhaps the ugly object would speak in the absence of the man who owned it: it would tell me a darker story about a loved one I had only ever known as sweet and gentle.

The obstacle was that I had almost no context to understand the object. I did not know why it was made, who owned it, who used it, against whom – all I knew was that it was *German* and vaguely represented to me the evils of the Nazi regime. The object should be a key, but to what door?

The object itself did provide clues: the crosses etched into the silver by some hand, perhaps a death count. Engraved letters and numbers: 'S.Sch. II.421.' crossed out and replaced with '47'; 'W80' stamped on the skinny edge of the blade; the crest 'ACS' adorning the image of a weighted scale and then, on the obverse, the name of the person who had made the blade, 'Alexander Coppel'; the name of the city of Solingen. There was, too, the knife's model, which I imagined was one of many.

Apart from these physical clues on the knife – archaeological evidence – there was what my grandfather might have told me: information about the battle in which he captured it from the Nazis. I might still find details in his military file, the regimental war diary, the twenty-minute recording he left of his memories.

I imagined discovering two journeys, the knife and a young soldier moving inexorably towards one another. I expected fascination in the detective work. History is usually presented as conclusions, sparing the reader hypotheses, wrong turns, revisions, and fudges. The historian shows the front of the rug to the reader, neatly sewn up, not the messy back with the knots and corrections. The back of a rug is more interesting.

Charting the knife's journey would require a visit to the company that produced the knife in Solingen; an understanding of the history of the knife's iconography; an explanation of the etchings on the object itself. From these, I hoped to find out how it came to be in the Netherlands. My grandfather's journey to the knife would be a war narrative focusing on that country where he found the knife and where it had been used. The stories, naturally, interwove. I hoped that the journeys would speak to and illuminate one another, like colours in a single woven fabric.

Letters, numbers, code, documents – but would they be enough? Could a whole story be told with so little? Seventy-five years had passed since my grandfather had 'liberated' the knife. Who was left who could make the object speak and tell its story?

Or could the knife tell its own story after all?

The Makers

The knife's maker was etched directly on the blade, with some pride, I imagined. Alexander Coppel, with the location Solingen, and the crest of the company, ACS with a balanced scale. It was the only other insignia on the knife besides the swastika. A cursory look on the internet showed me that Alexander Coppel's company still operated out of Solingen, had done so since 1821, and was even using the same insignia.

The prospect of travelling to Solingen made me nervous. What, was I going to bring the knife and confront these people with the proof of their complicity? Ask them, 'Where were your grandfathers during the war?' Say, 'Look, I have this ugly object and your family name is right on it.' This object was presumably mass-produced for the Nazis. Pointing fingers at perpetrators was uncomfortable business. Victims were easier to talk about: often they were no longer around.

Blade city, or *Klingenstadt*, as Solingen is nicknamed, is four and a quarter hours south-west from Berlin via Wuppertal. I read in a downloaded travel brochure the slogan *Solingen macht scharf*, an unsuccessful wordplay Germans might expect from the denizens of the Rheinland, popularly thought to be oversexed. *Macht scharf* means 'turns me on' but is literally 'makes me sharp'. This was not a feeling I had as my high-speed Intercity Express train cruised towards the industrial heart of western Germany.

Solingen had a hint of the Wagnerian to it. The craftspeople of this small city (today's population is 160,000) were not masters of singing but specialised instead in blades. In the Middle Ages, they made swords and knives among their half-timbered houses, amid wooded hills, holly, and streams of the Bergisches Land. The castle and smithy, established in the twelfth century, benefited from waterpower and nearby coal fields. Solingen blades, engraved with the insignia and names of their makers, grew famous at approximately the same period that Sheffield blades in England gained renown. By 1571, a quality seal was created with the Latin words *Me fecit Solingen* ('Solingen made me'). Some of the oldest trademarks in the world originated in Solingen, such as Zwilling J.A. Henckels knives, registered with Solingen's Cutler's Guild in 1731. Until the middle of the nineteenth century, all work was done by hand. Then steam engines arrived and specialised foundries were established. Solingen, which had been part of the Kingdom of Prussia, grew in prestige and power with the industrial revolution in a united Germany. Workshops and factories were no longer just making swords, forks, and knives, but also automobile and bike parts, and the kind of tools my grandfather would later sell from a warehouse in Canada (as the entrepreneur of a distribution business for

industrial supplies). For the Nazis, Solingen was a stage set: a paradigm of salt-of-the-earth German handwork and industrial prestige, as showcased in photographs of the Solingen working class *(opposite)* produced for the Nazi Ministry of Propaganda in 1937.

This Wagnerian fantasy – a quintessential German half-timbered town peopled by industrious craftspeople – no longer exists. Solingen Hauptbahnhof, the main station, is an unlovely rust-painted box. From the persuasive tourist brochure, I expected a city of sloping grey roofs topped by cupolas and shaded walks into the hills. I did not reckon that Solingen is in the belly of the Rhine-Ruhr metropolitan region, 3,000 square miles of industrial sprawl crowded by 10 million inhabitants. Neither bucolic nor architecturally distinguished, Solingen was flattened by bombs in the Second World War. I followed a grid – of 1950s and 1960s commerce, storefronts of familiar German brands such as Rossmann, Lidl, Aldi – to my destination, the location of the Coppel foundry. Situated just east of the centre, it was on a corner between Werwolf and Malteser Straße.

Here, I found a *Stolperstein* or 'stumbling stone'. More than 75,000 of these bronze remembrance plaques have been drilled into the ground all over Europe, in front of the last known residence of a Holocaust victim. Passers-by *stolpern*, or 'trip', over these fist-sized blocks, jolting them out of habitual thoughts to reflect on someone murdered by the Nazis. This

one was engraved to Dr Alexander Coppel, born in 1865, and deported in 1942 to the Nazi concentration camp at Theresienstadt, where he was murdered on 5 August. Alexander Coppel, the man who produced the knife, was Jewish, and himself a victim of the Nazis.

Most Jews in Solingen, arriving from Central Europe in the early eighteenth century, were not involved in blade production, but rather in textiles. By the end of the nineteenth century, of the 800 blade producers in the city, sixteen were Jewish. Alexander Coppel was one of the largest producers in the industry. He was also a community leader: a philanthropist, an active member of his synagogue, a city councillor for the progressive left-wing Democratic Party in the Weimar Republic period. He funded his social activism with profits from his knife business. In 1936, the company was 'Aryanised'. After Nazi persecutions ramped up and the Solingen synagogue burned during *Kristallnacht*, the Night of Broken Glass, on 9 November 1938, his family fled to Switzerland. One brother committed suicide. Alexander Coppel remained.

In July 1942, on learning of the transit of Jews to Theresienstadt concentration camp, Coppel wrote in a letter to his grand-nephew:

> I never expected that I would have to leave the place of happiness where my parents have lived since they were married in 1856, and where I was born, before I die. It is a sanctuary to me ... I have enjoyed a rich and beautiful life.

Indeed, many Jews of his time were acculturated and thought of themselves as German. They were stunned to be rooted out from society.

One month later, he perished from hunger and exhaustion, standing at the well in the camp where he went to wash, according to a fellow prisoner. His body was burned and the ashes disposed of in a cardboard box. Today a street and a school in Solingen are named after Alexander Coppel.

On 23 May 1943, twice as many incendiaries were dropped on nearby Dortmund and the surrounding region than would be dropped on Britain in the first six months of that year. It was a very early example of the firestorm that consumed German cities such as Hamburg two months later. Bricks melted in the 1,000-degree heat. Steel deformed. The first major bombing of Coppel's 'sanctuary' Solingen occurred a week later, on 30 May, and the city would sustain almost 100 aerial bombardments. On 12 September 1944, almost 2,000 people were killed in an RAF attack, leading to a total evacuation. The old city was completely wiped out on 4 and 5 November 1944.

After the war, the surviving members of the Coppel family were compensated – at least, monetarily – for their losses. The knife foundry went through a series of new owners and bankruptcies. Today, it no longer makes blades that can be used on human beings. Instead, the firm has turned its production entirely towards products for animals: shears, trimmers, clippers, and scissors.

A Nazi knife made by a Jew is a grisly irony. If Alexander Coppel's firm made this knife, how tragic that it forged a military eagle for its hilt and put a swastika on it. If the Aryanised company made the knife, how hideous that it bore the name of a persecuted Jew. Meanwhile, the knife survived the war, but its city of origin burned to ashes. Its maker was killed by hands that wielded weapons engraved with his name.

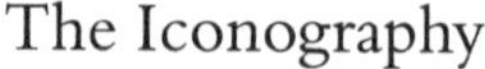

The Iconography

For years, my grandfather had nightmares that woke the house. When asked about the knife and his wartime memories, his three children mentioned being roused recurrently by the man screaming. My grandmother did not recognise the recruit who had proposed to her during the war. An anxious but kind creature of habit, she made her children decide what they would eat for breakfast in the evening, setting the table before going to bed. Not a word about the disturbances was said over the morning meal. The veteran, in step with his generation, and its distrust of psychiatry, brought an officer's stoicism into civilian life. Wartime memories of France and the Low Countries were difficult to explain among the well-mowed lawns and bungalows of a northern Alberta city. My grandfather went for long walks with his Labrador retriever and busied himself with his tool company – distractions from the mousetrap of an unhappy marriage.

Soon after the knife arrived in my Berlin apartment, I also started having bad dreams. I tried to be pragmatic like my grandfather. Dreams are a sieve for daytime thoughts; sorting, putting things right, and the knife had been on my mind. But I could not help but think the knife caused the nightmares.

In these dreams, soldiers were dressed in animal costumes. Wild things slipped from behind one tree to the next with machine guns on their backs. Because they had animal faces – but on human bodies, with human weapons – their hunt in the darkened wood was all the more terrifying. An expressionless tiger, a silent wolf's snout, the hollowed eyes of a lion, showed not human fear, or hesitation, but indifference.

Unnerved, I sat with a cup of tea in that sensitive atmosphere rooms have when the city is asleep. The knife was hidden behind a shelf of books. I examined it in the reflection of the opaque windows. I was quick, in my vulnerable state, to identify what was most malevolent about it: the eagle's head. The knife was half animal.

The ancients understood the power of zoomorphic weapons. They were meant to transform their wearers and impart animal qualities. An iconic example is a sixth-century BCE Athenian bronze by Antenor. His statue group *Harmodius and Aristogeiton* represents the two tyrannicides, or rebels, about to murder the dictator Hipparchus in 514 BCE. Four years later, when democracy came to Athens, the young men were celebrated as heroes and their image went into mass production, preserved on coins, and numerous copies of the statue that travelled around the Mediterranean world. When I visited the two warriors in the Archaeological Museum in Naples, I took two steps back in surprise.

The men are frozen, in a moment of action, like a paused film, each brandishing weapons in both hands. Harmodius attacks with one knife above his head, while his lover Aristogeiton lunges. Aristogeiton's second knife (today missing its blade) is ready behind his back.

Conspicuous is the eagle hilt of this knife: a similar beak, rounded crown, the same eye as my grandfather's weapon. One knife was inspired by the other; it was modelled on examples from antiquity.

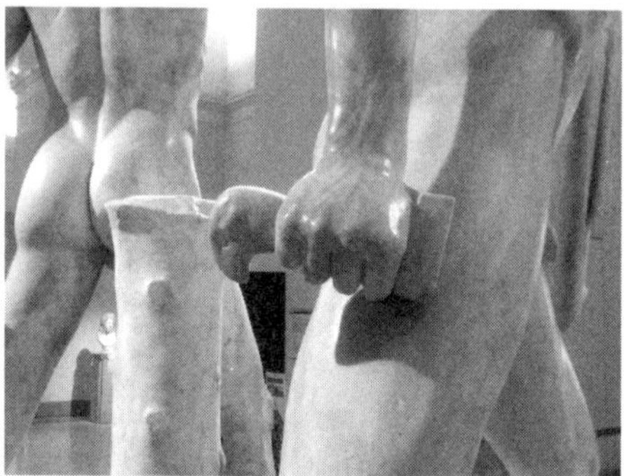

The Romans subsequently crafted eagle-hilted daggers, *parazonia*, were meant to give their bearers courage. Four Roman emperors, in the fourth-century porphyry statue in the façade of St Mark's in Venice, embrace, their hands ready on eagle-hilted *spathae*, or long swords, that demonstrate their power.

Why the Third Reich, or other military regimes for that matter, modelled their weaponry on classical examples is easily explained. The Nazis, upstarts that they were, were concerned with legitimacy. Hitler graspingly employed motifs from antiquity – imitating Mussolini in his stripped-down neoclassical architecture and use of the Roman *fasces* – to claim his Third Reich descended from the Roman Empire and was destined for greatness (although it lasted a mere thirteen years instead of the promised thousand). What the ancients gave the Nazis was *ethos*, or authority and credibility. They needed, as a classical rhetor would put it, to project an aura of power.

What is the *ethos* of an eagle? The Greeks and Romans zoomorphised the valour of their heroes. For the Christians, the eagle was the symbol of St John: the animal that could look directly into the sun. The Romantics celebrated the beast's indifferent nobility. Tennyson's eagle 'watches from his mountain walls, and like a thunderbolt he falls'. Nietzsche's birds of prey are judged by the slavish as evil because they bear off sweet little lambs. The eagles themselves have a different opinion (imagined the German philosopher), viewing the herd morality 'a little ironically …:"we don't dislike these good little lambs at all. We even love them! Nothing is tastier than a tender lamb!"' The eagle soars above our moral concerns, then swoops and kills: the ideal pattern for the efficient soldier.

Strength, courage, remorselessness, indifference, nobility: all these qualities gave the eagle a particular resonance in German history, with an iconographical use that far predated the Nazis. The heraldic origin in Central Europe was military: the eagle was consolidated as the standard for the legions of the Roman Empire in the second century BCE. The standard was passed on to the Holy Roman Empire and adorned the sceptre of King Otto III in the tenth century. From the thirteenth century – single and double-headed – the eagle became widespread as the Empire's emblem. When Germany unified in 1871, the *Reichsadler* (imperial eagle) was the state's coat of arms and remained so into the period of the Weimar Republic. The Nazis embraced the Roman symbol as both the emblem of the party and of the state (the *Parteiadler*, or 'party's eagle', looks over its left shoulder and the *Reichsadler* looks over its right, as on my knife). Today, the beast is stamped on Euro coins and hovers over the floor of the German Bundestag, neutered as a *Bundesadler* (federal eagle) but with origins in the Roman armies that trampled Europe.

The eagle can evoke a multitude of images and associations but the animal on my grandfather's knife, produced in Germany, draws from this particular heritage. It is steeped in military heraldry and classical imagery. Historians argue teleologically about the *Sonderweg*, or 'special path', in German history: that the atrocities of the Nazi period have a long, explanatory prehistory. Other European countries had liberal revolutions, whereas Germany followed a rigidly military and authoritarian path. In this deterministic way of telling history writ large, Germany had followed the Roman standard for centuries – the eagle not just a symbol but a continuity of war.

In peacetime, being civilised means not acting like animals. In wartime, that logic is inverted: young people are encouraged to engage in dark possibilities, to grow wings and talons, and be rewarded for it.

The eagle was a potent, terrifying symbol whose military history would dovetail with Nazi racial theories. The indifferent killer would separate, to use Primo Levi's phrase, 'the drowned and the saved'. I found it tempting to assume the knife belonged to an SS officer and was used on Jewish victims. But I did not yet know the job entrusted to its owner – whether it required an indifferent, remorseless kill. I could not yet imagine the indistinct face of the one who buckled the knife to his hip, who – in an instant – was transformed into an animal, focusing distantly on his prey, clawing the precipice with his crooked hands.

Perhaps my grandfather could have told me where, on his wartime path, he had met him.

Sources

The knife travelled to my grandfather and my grandfather travelled towards the knife. I sat in my Berlin apartment with sources for my grandfather's journey on my desk. An envelope with Canada's emblem, the maple leaf, on one corner had arrived with the morning's post, containing the regimental war diary and his service file. The former was an official daily account of the Calgary Highlanders by a company diarist, constrained to write about tragedies in chipper, patriotic language. Two-thirds of the latter – a tidy abstraction of the man's recruitment, health, disciplinary record, and deployment, compiled by the military authorities – had been

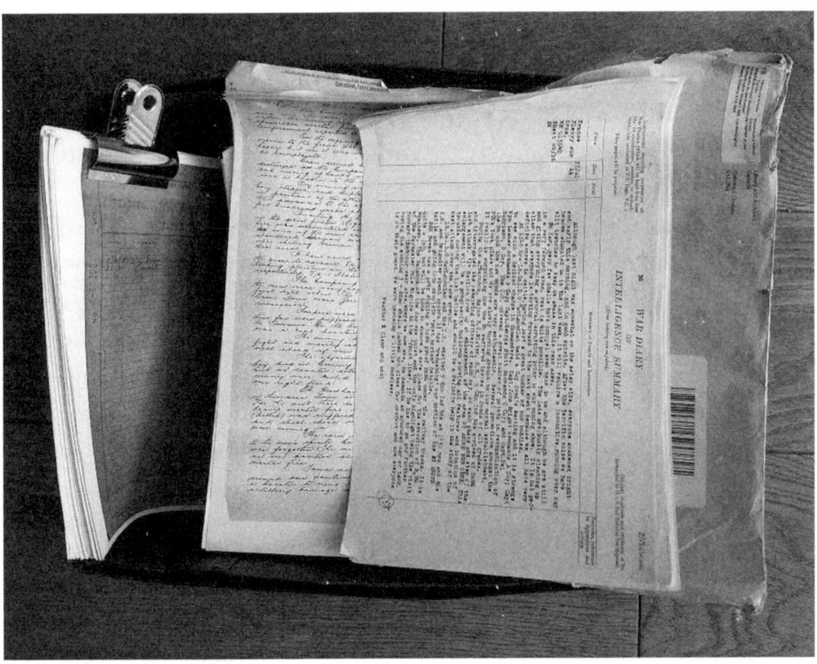

redacted for privacy. In addition, I had a cassette tape, various family letters, photos, testimonies, and newspaper clippings. From these, I hoped to pinpoint exactly where my grandfather had been and to catalogue direct contact with the Germans, the taking of prisoners of war and their possessions, to narrow down possible locations for the discovery of the knife. I trusted my grandfather's explanation that he 'liberated it from a Nazi' in the Netherlands and not that he found it randomly in the mud somewhere.

The story of Captain Hugh John Sanders 'Sandy' Pearson, born on 9 September 1921, was that of his regiment. The Calgary Highlanders, part of the 5th Infantry Brigade and 2nd Canadian Infantry Division, was composed of volunteer soldiers from the western Canadian provinces. On recruitment, the Highlanders were still wearing kilts from the First World War. They did not have battle-dress uniforms, or matching hats, or collar badges. They wore yellow armbands bearing the words 'Calgary Highlanders' to identify their regiment. They were not ready.

Travelling by train to the Maritime provinces, my grandfather embarked on 27 October 1942 from Nova Scotia to Scotland. By the standards of British Army training, the regiment was deemed below average. It waited two years in Britain before landing in Normandy on 6 July

1944, to march north-east along the coastal belt through Belgium and the Netherlands. My grandfather spoke often of the city of Groningen, in the far north, partly because it was here that he had been promoted to command 'B' section as an acting major, but also because of the intensity and proximity of the fighting.

I hoped for my grandfather's war story to be encapsulated in his military file, but it was low on personal detail and heavy on abbreviations – TOS, MFM2 & 2A, CIRU, SOS to 'B' Bn, AEF – which had a distancing effect, as if itemising the individual, as if he were an inventoried weapon. I looked for 'poetry' in the file – a glimmer of the individual, a striking detail – but there was precious little. I found humanity in my grandfather's photograph. 'He's good-looking!' I thought, with that inability grandchildren have to believe their forebears could ever have been younger than they are now. Here he was at the age of 22: the oval head, the high forehead, the small, rounded ears, the thick eyebrows, and pursed lips. He stared out and his eyes told me … absolutely nothing, except perhaps that they were dutiful. But I already knew about his loyalty to the empire. In his enlistment report, words jumped out: his complexion was marked as 'fresh'. *Fresh* for battle. He was evaluated as 'immature' but would 'make a good officer'. He knew how to march. Later, he would be mentioned in dispatches.

But the military file gave me one document I needed: his service and casualty form. It provided the dates when he had been on duty, on leave, and injured. The war diary, meanwhile, gave me the locations of his regiment. Cross-referencing, I knew day by day where he had been. Again, I hoped to find a date, with my grandfather serving at the front, when a German battalion carrying this knife – perhaps it was particular to the dress code – crossed the Highlanders' path. Or perhaps I would find some mention of confiscated weaponry in the war diary. It was a long shot, but I'd try.

I turned to the cassette tape he left to his descendants six decades later. I was lucky that my grandfather, knowing he would die soon, wanted his story told – an unvarnished story.

OFFICER RECORD OF SERVICE

No.: G.S.
No.: NRMA

1. CHRISTIAN NAMES HUGH JOHN SANDERS SURNAME PEARSON

2. Date of Birth 9 SEP 21
3. Date of enlistment NRMA
4. Date of enlistment G.S. 10 July 1942.
5. N. of Kin LT. COL. H.E. PEARSON M.C.
Relationship FATHER
6. Address of N. of Kin: 12507 STONY PLAIN RD EDMONTON ALBERTA
7. Marital Status: S
8. Occupation on enlistment: STUDENT CADET R.M.C.

9. RANK, ACTING OR CONFIRMED | WEF | AUTH.
LIEUT
B/CAPT.
A/Major
Capt.

10. SERVICE (Country) | FROM | TO | DAYS
CANADA
U.K.
N.W.E.
U.K.
N.W.E.
U.K.
N.W.E.
W.H.
O.S.

11. HONOURS AND AWARDS | WEF | AUTH.
Cdn. Vol. Service Medal & Clasp.
AWARDED THE 1939-45 STAR
Awarded France and Germany Star
AWARDED THE DEFENCE MEDAL
52/45

12. QUALIFICATIONS AND COURSES | PLACE | WEF | RESULT | AUTH.

13. HOSPITALIZATION | WEF | UNIT | DO or CL

14. PUNISHMENTS | WEF | UNIT | PLACE | D.O. | POINTS:

15. TRANSFERS, POSTINGS etc. | WEF | UNIT | DO
Wounded (Remained on duty)
Embarked AEF
Disembarked UK
Embarked in N.W.E.
Disembarked in U.K.
Att'd fap to 10 Cdn.
Repat Depot (Trans Str)
Granted 11 days P.L. with M.A. to 12 Oct 45 (incl) | CH
Granted leave from 20-10-45 to 28-10-45 with M.A. (8 days) | 20-10-45 | Repat
Granted 7 days P L with M A to 8 Nov 45 (incl) | 2-11-45
S.O.S. Cdn. Army O/S and C.T.S.A. fap to 10 Cdn. Repat Depot (Trans Str.) (XUK-239)

16. MED CAT OR PULHEMS | YOB | P | U | L | H | E | M | S
17. M.D. PREFERENCE:
18. RE-ALLOC. PREFERENCE 1. 2. 3.

13/248

My grandfather sat in a room alone and recorded himself. I somehow knew which room: the den of their house in Edmonton, with the window over the lawn sloping to the crescent. I could not hear the dogs, who were no doubt penned in the back yard, jumping up against the gate at arrivals and departures. The narrow den – with its chintz loveseats, the rotary telephone on the ledge, the bookshelves with a leather-bound set of Kiplings, the landscape oils of the Rockies and wobbly watercolours he painted himself – was a place where we would sometimes go and have a drink before a meal or where the men would go after a formal dinner and drink whisky. He and my grandmother would sit there and eat on TV tables, not talking much to one another.

Alone and taping himself, he said what he would not have told others if they had been present, even though he made this tape for others.

He pressed record and said next that he 'learned about living with other men and leading other men' and that he had:

> admiration for private soldiers who had to negotiate horrible situations, as opposed to officers. It was much easier for an officer to be brave. Because everyone is looking to you to be brave and lead. For a private soldier, it was much more difficult.

On the war dead lists, 430 Calgary Highlanders were named, more than half the size of the full regiment. Most of these were privates and most private names were not Anglo-Saxon. Every single commander name was British: MacKenzie, Wilkes, McQueen, Robinson. If you found a name – French, Italian, Slavic – such as Bissonnette, Campagnolo, Gorgichuk – they were almost always the lowest possible rank and listed among the dead.

My grandfather went on to provide an account of his movements through the war and key memories that I could compare to the war diary – an intimidating stack of paper – cross-checking with the dates in the service and casualty form.

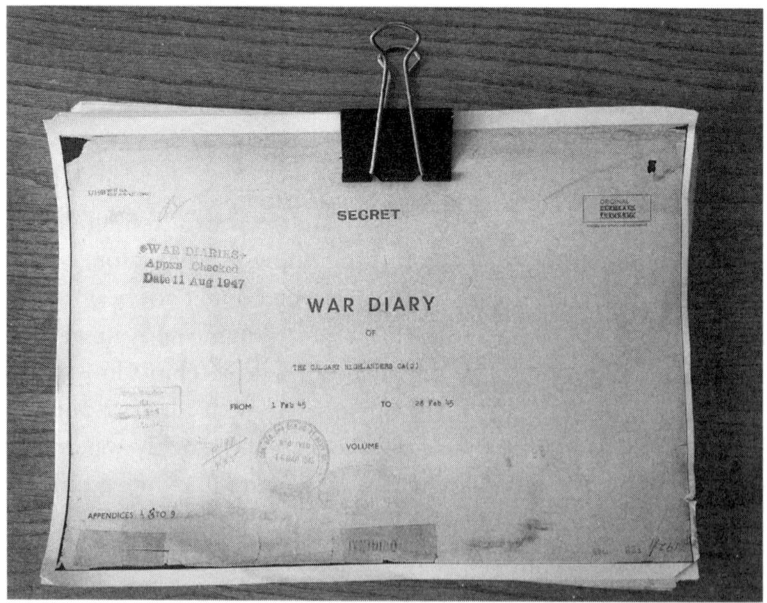

Whenever my grandfather spoke about someone who died, he suddenly stopped the tape, waited, then resumed. Was he holding back tears in these moments? I see him instead sitting very still. My family told me that he got more emotional as he grew older, memories bubbling to the surface. At the very end of the tape, he was interrupted. I knew immediately – by the space in the room, the kind of mousy humming that accompanied her – that it was my grandmother. 'What are you doing?' she asked. And he turned off the tape.

German Family

I spent the next weeks reading the regiment's war diary. Following the Highlanders from the Normandy landing on 6 July 1944 (50 per cent of their fighting force fell as casualties in the region), I learned how my grandfather was shot through both thighs and evacuated on 30 July to a hospital in Uxbridge, England; after spending two weeks convalescing, he was allowed to visit family in Dorset before being redeployed on 10 September. But my focus was on the entries in the country where the knife was discovered. The Highlanders crossed the frontier of the Netherlands on 7 October 1944. As they approached the soggy fingers of the Scheldt Estuary, a key battleground against the 70th Infantry Division, part of the 89th German

Corps, an unusual line of enquiry presented itself – please bear with me – that turned out not to be so far-fetched. 'Maybe the knife belonged to one of our German relatives?' my Aunt Kit, a children's novelist, proposed. I dismissed this idea as fanciful but was happy to travel along.

My great-great-grandfather, Colonel Gilbert Edward Sanders – the owner of the 'noble' sword in the basement and a mentor to my grandfather – had a British uncle residing in Germany. Howard Oakley Sanders had fought in the Austro-Prussian war of 1866 and was decorated with the Iron Cross. His daughters married soldiers.

I sat down at my kitchen table to letters about the Teutonic Sanders that my aunt unearthed from a basement. One was difficult to decipher because of the cross-writing, in two directions, saving space on the page to reduce expensive postage to the west coast of British North America. Another describes how one daughter, Amelie von Sanders, married in 1877 the then Lieutenant Otto Liman von Sanders (who took his wife's last name to promote himself in the German Army). He would prove important to European history as a rare example of a German general of Jewish descent, heading the Ottoman campaign in the First World War, including the operations at Gallipoli, where countless soldiers, especially from Australia and New Zealand, were slaughtered.

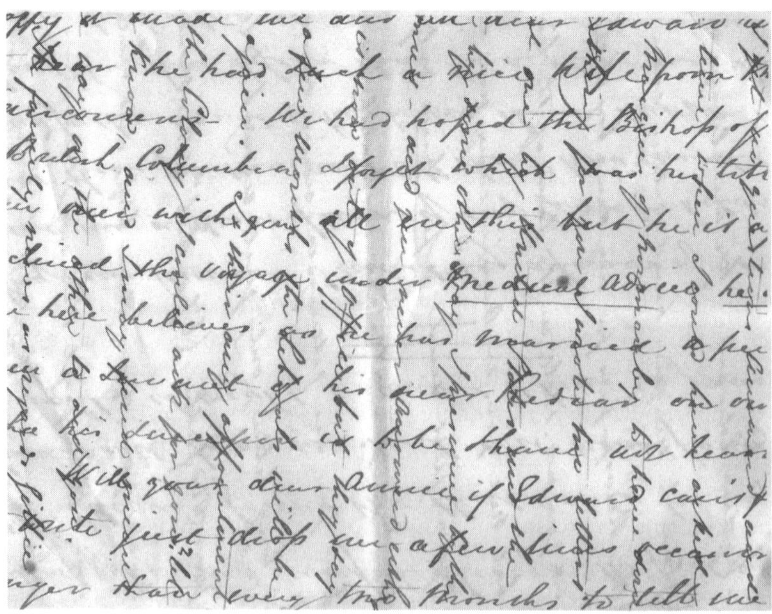

[illegible] Edward [illegible]
hear she had such a nice wife from [illegible]
[illegible] We had hoped the Bishop of
British Columbia [illegible] which was his title
[illegible] with you all [illegible] but he is [illegible]
declined the voyage under medical advice he
[illegible] believes as he has married [illegible]
[illegible] of his dear [illegible]
[illegible]
Will your dear Annie if Edward can't
write just drop me a few lines [illegible]
[illegible] than every two months to tell me

The Sanders families also exchanged images. I examined a yellowed daguerreotype of three of Howard's little girls, seated on a large armchair in the early 1860s. The children looked like dolls. In the foreground, a little black dog reached up to them, and in the back was a folded curtain. In the centre of the chair, and the picture, was the smallest, Bertha Karoline von Sanders, perhaps 5 years old, astride the leg of the oldest. She had pudgy arms, legs, and cheeks, and she stared softly at the photographer. She would marry in 1879 a Freiherr (baron) from Hessen, Felix Eitel von und zu Gilsa, whose family name would later become famous in the Nazi project.

The Sanders family in Germany would eventually be split between Nazis and Jews. The transatlantic Sanders relationship would be broken as the soldiering lines fought on opposing sides of the First World War. My great-great-grandfather re-enlisted and saw brutal service in France, while his daughter, my great-grandmother, was a nurse in England. They lost close friends and family members to the war – animosity may well have put an end to family correspondence.

As the twentieth century progressed, the von und zu Gilsa family rose in the military ranks. Werner von Gilsa was made the Nazi Commandant of the Olympic Village in Berlin in 1936 and was later a Second World War general in the *Wehrmacht*, taking his own life after leading the Battle of Dresden in 1945. I have since looked up the descendants of the Gilsa family, and find, to my surprise, that some also live in Berlin. One current Freiherr even sells real estate. Perhaps his castle is for sale.

I have little truck with titles or ranks and am grateful to have been born in the New World. But, for our purposes, the genealogy is important as a mirror for European conflict. One military family was split between Britain, its Commonwealth, and Germany. Historians name opposing camps in wars 'German' or 'British', but conflicts between nations were often individualised to the family members caught behind opposing lines, especially at the level of the officer corps. I had considered the knife as only 'German' but found it was made by a Jewish-German family. Did objects also have nationalities? Likewise, it was difficult to speak uncomplicatedly about the 'Germans', the 'British', or the 'Canadians' when explaining the warring Sanders. Mine could not be the only family so mixed up. The lofty epitome of this fratricide, of course, was the British and German royal families during the First World War. I began to imagine a story of the knife in this light.

Walcheren Island and the Scheldt Estuary, armed with the world's most fortified coastal defences, saw the most important battles of 1944 in north-west Europe following D-Day. Here, in the race north, is where my grandfather had his first major confrontation with German troops in the Netherlands. He saw brutal fighting, especially in the struggle for the Walcheren Causeway between 31 October and 2 November 1944. I am astonished Walcheren is so often overlooked, especially in Canada.

As my grandfather recounted on his tape: 'There was an island called Walcheren, across the bay from Antwerp …' He explains that the island had an ideal offensive position facing the city's harbour and that 'the Germans were determined that they were not going to allow any supplies into that'. It was joined to the mainland with a causeway and dykes that the Germans had flooded. All the fields were underwater. 'Taking Walcheren was very tough fighting. There was no place to go except a straight line on either side of the dyke, along the water, and people were shot in the chest and the head, with really awfully heavy casualties.'

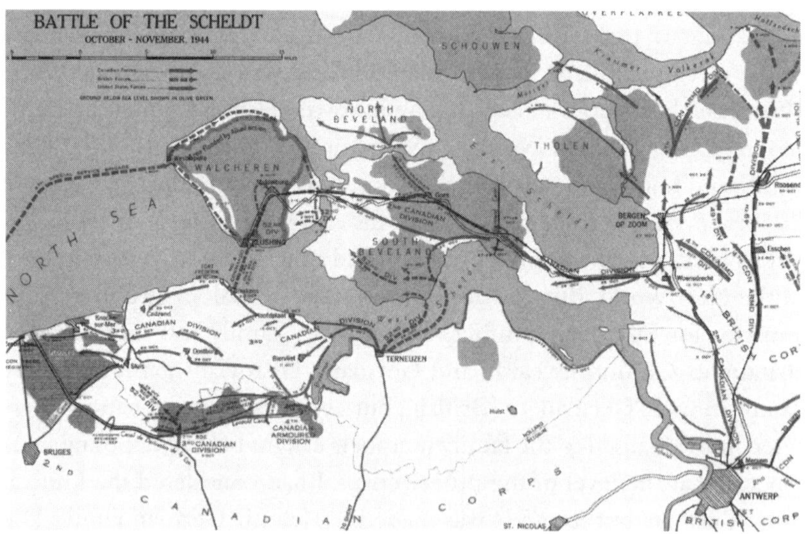

I imagined my grandfather walking across the causeway, that tightrope, exposed on all sides to enemy fire, to the watery island where he found an enemy officer, a body gunned down on the ground. Removing the Nazi knife – with its eagle's head – from the man's belt with a victorious gesture, he would stand over him before turning the face of the defeated general with one hand, to look at him. And then, perhaps, he would start back with surprise. Because he recognised the same high forehead, the same oval face, the same rounded ears, that he had. Just perhaps the nose and eyes were different. But I imagined he stared at someone who looked alike as a brother.

I laughed at this reverie, amused by my aunt's suggestion that the knife might have been acquired this way. I returned instead to my box of Canadian archival documents, books, and the actual movements of my grandfather's regiment across the treacherous wetlands stretching into the sea of South Holland, where the army divisions and regiments were clearly marked by national uniform. And I read, for example, that when the 2nd Canadian Infantry Division met the Germans in October 1944, in the Battle of the Scheldt, they fought the 70th Infantry Division, commanded by the 89th German Corps. Reading further, I explored the chain of command and discovered that the general of the German forces stationed in precisely the same areas where my grandfather was fighting – such as on Walcheren Island – was one General Freiherr Werner von und zu Gilsa, his relative through marriage.

I rethought my aunt's suggestion, the image of the man wounded on the ground. For a moment, it became clear how the knife might have belonged to him after all.

The Swastika

Goa Lawah ('Bat Cave') Temple, Bali, Indonesia

When my grandfather's knife, with its swastika, arrived from Canada by freight, Section 86a of the German Criminal Code was briefly violated. The law states it is illegal to 'import or export' symbols of unconstitutional organisations, such as the Nazi party. A violation can be punished with three years in prison.

The swastika, or *Hakenkreuz* ('broken cross'), has at least a 12,000-year history and is considered auspicious in many South Asian religions. But in Germany, the thirteen years of Nazi rule overshadow millennia of use. Nazi 'flags, insignia, uniforms, slogans and forms of greeting', such as the Nazi salute and saying '*Heil Hitler*', pose a danger for the prankster tourist and the hardcore fascist alike. A photograph of a deplorable great-uncle, displaying a *Hakenkreuz* on his SS uniform, may be legally stored in a box at home but it cannot be shown in public. The far right in Germany relies on modified symbols that resemble swastikas to avoid imprisonment. Critics argue that making the swastika illegal gives it mystery and importance, increasing a lurid and pornographic quality. Many more believe a symbol really can be that dangerous.

I knew I was in a sticky situation when my knife was unwittingly imported but also that the law would not be applicable under a 'social adequacy clause', provided I used the knife 'to further civil enlightenment' or 'promote art or science, research or teaching' (which is why a swastika can appear in a scene of *Inglourious Basterds* but not hang from a Munich apartment window). Giving the knife a historical, literary, or anti-fascist purpose was a protection. Nonetheless, treading at the edge of the law was an alarming feeling and I did not want to draw attention to myself.

Surfing the internet for 'Nazi knife' or 'Eagle-hilted swastika', in the end-of-privacy era, was drawing attention – a little like a gay man googling for pornography in Saudi Arabia. I imagined that the moment I clicked on a page devoted to Nazi paraphernalia, a light would illuminate in an office on Chausseestraße in Berlin, where the headquarters of the Federal Intelligence Service is located. Fear, self-preservation, self-censorship, restrained me from research on even respectable sites, let alone those of collectors, visited by neo-Nazis, profiteers, and the naive.

I needed, nonetheless, to look for Nazi knives that resembled my grandfather's. Two solutions: I could take a trip outside the country, or I could talk to my friends at c-Base.

C-Base is, in the popular imagination, a space station that crashed to Earth and was buried under the city of Berlin. Only its antenna, the iconic television tower at Alexanderplatz, is reputedly still visible above ground. Through an airlock in Berlin's former East, a visit to remnants of the spaceship is difficult to describe: part nightclub, techno bar, event space, and non-profit agora for coders and transhumanists, as well as hardware, software, privacy, and data geeks. C-Base is unsurprisingly the hangout of the Chaos Computer Club, Europe's largest community of hackers. In short, you wouldn't be surprised to meet Edward Snowden at the bar, if he could crawl out of Russia. Perhaps he's dug a tunnel. At c-Base, I was directed to encryption software and came away with some pointers – obvious to many readers, but I'm non-technical and needed help – on how to stock an armoury of private browsers, end-to-end stealth messaging, VPNs, and other layers to keep out the chill of privacy violation, without letting on to these noble lefty Germans that I was looking up swastikas on the internet.

With a gulp of dread, I opened my open-source anonymous browser and typed my search phrases. The internet of Nazi collectables – akin to visiting the dark web when you live in Germany – was every bit as miserable as one would imagine. Nazi mementoes – uniforms, weapons, propaganda, busts, toys, you name it – fetch large sums in online auctions. Countless forum threads are populated by grim avatars and aliases (ironeagle666, darkcross33, and so on). Some acquire clothing for fetish purposes, sex parties. I did not know why most of the sites displayed in dark mode, perhaps to exalt the illicitness of where one had landed. I sent out encrypted messages and received suspicious replies, but also came closer to solving the mystery of the knife's use and its journey.

The Markings

My trawling quickly brought me to an auction of a knife that looked almost identical to my grandfather's: '750 USD', 'private purchase', 'for casual dress', 'little to no wear', 'excellent detailing', 'only one available', 'outstanding example', 'very rare object'. The knife was described as a 'Short Army Dress Police Bayonet'. A Nazi police bayonet! The Nazi police, under the umbrella of SS Chief Heinrich Himmler, was no ordinary police force. Armed as soldiers, they were cast across Europe to implement the Nazis' ideological programme.

I had thought of the weapon up to now simply as a 'knife'. But a bayonet is an offensive weapon, meant to be used intimately. Snapped to the end of a rifle, it is employed at close range in hand-to-hand combat. The auction mentioned a 'blood channel' and I saw that the blade of my grandfather's knife had a long groove. Some sellers claim the macabre detail was functional. It prevented the knife from getting stuck. It reduced suction and channelled fluid away.

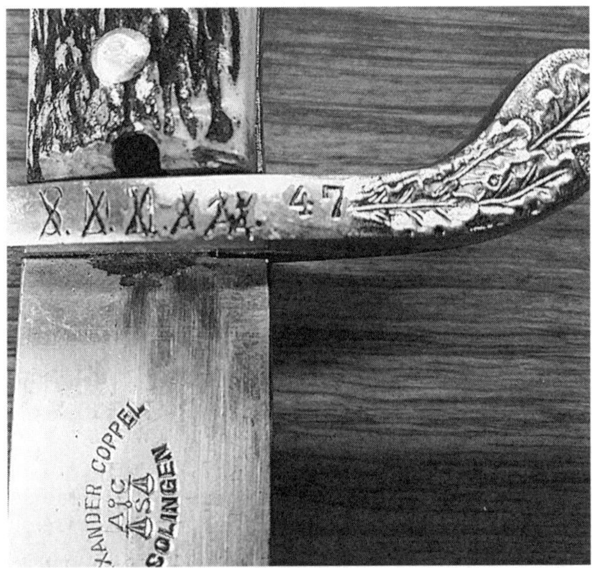

With some clarity on the type of bayonet, I turned to the markings on the object. Code, I thought, as it turned out they would be. I should mention that my language had not been exact and my collector audience were quick to correct me. The eagle head should be referred to as the bayonet's 'pommel'. The series of letters and numbers appeared on the 'reverse quillon', or cross-guard, and upper scabbard.

A series of crosses – was the knife's owner keeping track of kills in the tens? – deleted the original letters and numbers still readable on the blade.

But why did S.D. II. 912 not match the S.Sch II. 421 marking on the scabbard? I originally thought 'SD' might mean *Sicherheitsdienst* – or the Nazi Secret Police, the Gestapo – and 'S.Sch' might be an abbreviation for *Schutzstaffel*, the SS, but that hypothesis went by the wayside knowing the object belonged to that other branch under Himmler's control, the police.

A forum obsessed with police classification markings (yes, this exists) led me to a catalogue dedicated to them. The struck-out letters indicated the police unit – SD is for the Düsseldorf District and S.Sch. for Schleswig in the far north of the country – and the subsequent markings identified the item: an inventory system so that the police armourer could keep track of public property.

Why these markings were crossed out – both on the quillon and scabbard, and replaced with a '47', which did not abide by the original classification system – I had no idea. Two other numbers on the weapon's edge – W80 (bayonet) and W29 (scabbard) – also remained a mystery.

A mention of a professional source, *History Writ in Steel: Police Markings 1900–1936*, lured me (with relief!) off the shady web. Its author, L. Don Maus, was based, as many of these experts and collectors seemed to be, in the belly of all weapon knowledge, Texas. I was intrigued and alarmed that people wrote whole books about the markings on vintage sidearms … but, then again, what was I doing?

Don Maus kindly accepted my encrypted photos of the knife and confirmed that it had been assigned to 'SD II', the *Schutzpolizei* command of Wuppertal district not far from Düsseldorf and a twenty-minute journey from Solingen. The scabbard's 'S.Sch II', however, indicated Kiel near the Danish border in Schleswig-Holstein.

'What did this "47" mean?' I asked my man in Texas. Did it refer to the police battalions sent to occupied Europe, numbered 1 to 325? He replied that the wartime police battalions did not number their weapons, as the classifications were terminated in 1937. The number 47 referred instead to something of 'a second marriage'.

Let me explain. After the police forces were centralised in 1936 by Himmler, the Nazis decided to reuse the eagle design of the Weimar-era Prussian police force bayonet. Old bayonets and scabbards were transformed into Third Reich weapons in facilities. The reassembled weapons were given new serial numbers, in this case 47. The W80 and W29 markings likely indicated the *Werkstätten* (workshops) that had made those modifications. In all likelihood, the knife had belonged to the Weimar-era police in Wuppertal before it was remade in such a workshop by the Nazis.

Traces of these changes were visible on my knife. A decorative clamshell over the blade had been removed and the nickel starburst Weimar insignia replaced by the swastika, leaving holes around the insignia. After 1938, the long blades of the Weimar era were shortened to bayonet length (13in, precisely the length of my grandfather's bayonet): easier to carry when on foot and useful when the victim was shot and already down. A rivet hole from this modification on the grip was also visible.

Maus suggested I get in touch with George T. Wheeler, author of *Seitengewehr: History of the German Bayonet 1919–1945*, to see what he might add. He confirmed the knife had been a municipal Prussian police bayonet, removed from Prussian service, and reworked and re-issued under the Nazis. He also told me that a brown scabbard would normally indicate it belonged to the *Gendarmerie* (rural police, as opposed to the *Schutzpolizei*, or municipal police). In the context of occupied European countries, however, it may have been issued to the *Ordnungspolizei* (ORPO, or order police), as ORPO were 'authorized to wear these bayonets ... Thus, members of the Police Battalions could have been issued this bayonet.'

Wheeler suggested I look at archival photographs of ORPO and their police battalions stationed in occupied Europe to confirm whether they were issued eagle-pommelled bayonets. After viewing hundreds of blurry photographs, I found a 1941 poster celebrating the 'Day of German Police', of the SS and the armed police battalions working side by side *im Kriegseinsatz*, or 'war deployment', with the laurel-leaved insignia stamped in one corner, and a familiar weapon under a left arm.

What were the ORPO and their police battalions doing in occupied Europe alongside the SS? And would they have been stationed in battle locations in the Netherlands, confronting Allied troops and risking capture?

The ORPO had a key role in the Holocaust. Known as the 'Green Police' because of their uniforms, they first formed battalions with the invasion of Poland in 1939. While the *Wehrmacht* and *Waffen-SS* focused on military war against the Allies, the ORPO formed the *Einsatzgruppen* in the East that carried out racial war against the local population. Christopher Browning's classic study *Ordinary Men* describes how Reserve Police Battalion 101 assembled middle-aged functionaries, many with no wartime experience, and had them massacre tens of thousands of Jews in the Lublin district of Poland. There were overlaps in duty, such as when the ORPO joined the SS, forming '*Waffen-SS*-Police' divisions, but this was a rare occurrence in the West, where they mostly fulfilled duties as part of the *Staatsschutzkorps* or 'State Protection Corps' with the SS.

The chief of the SS and police in the Netherlands was an Austrian engineer and soldier, Hanns Albin Rauter. He recruited the Dutch for Germanic 'Dutch SS' units and deployed the ORPO to root out Jews, Jehovah's Witnesses, homosexuals, Dutch communists and resistance, and other undesirables. The work and transit to purpose-built concentration and death camps from Holland were run mainly by Dutch Nazis, with victims after 1942 sent on to Auschwitz and Sobibor. Some 80 per cent of the country's 140,000 Jews perished. 300,000 additional Dutch were brought into forced labour, in a country where a quarter of a million would be killed. Rauter was particularly radical and intent on protecting the Dutch designated Aryan gene pool and his name was synonymous with his programme of summary arrests, detention, reprisals, and the establishment of the Dutch concentration camp of Herzogenbusch, which held 30,000 prisoners.

As the Allied troops battled their way north, Rauter did not retreat but formed his division, known as the *Kampfgruppe Rauter*: a combination of the 34th SS-Volunteer Grenadier Division *Landstorm Nederland*, drawn from Dutch volunteers, and, unusually for the Netherlands, an ORPO regiment. They massed in September 1944, during the Arnhem campaign, in the area of the Veluwe, between Arnhem and Utrecht, the northern corridor leading to Groningen.

Rauter and his men continued operating in the region into the spring of 1945. On the night of 6–7 March 1945, Dutch resistance dressed in German uniforms hijacked a vehicle at Woeste Hoeve, a village near Apeldoorn, just north of Arnhem. They were surprised to find Hanns Albin Rauter inside. He was wounded and left to die. Unfortunately for the resistance, he survived. Two days later, on 8 March, the ORPO, with their eagle-pommelled bayonets, bussed in hostages to Woeste Hoeve as a reprisal, and 263 were killed by firing squad. Four days later, the Calgary Highlanders arrived at Berg en Dal, 19 miles from Woeste Hoeve, where the ORPO had shot their victims.

A Campaign in Chiaroscuro

My grandfather did not make it across the Walcheren Causeway, where his fellow soldiers were shot to bits. He did not meet a *Wehrmacht* officer on the island to whom he was related by marriage. Nor were the ORPO organised into the battle divisions in the Scheldt; they were further to the north-east. Instead, my grandfather was wounded. Walcheren, meanwhile, was a wholesale defeat for the Calgary Highlanders and a senseless loss of life. Lt Col Ross Ellis, the Highlanders' commanding officer, later commented: 'The main accomplishment was that we got as many as we could out alive.' Walcheren was taken in November by a British amphibious assault.

Walcheren Causeway, October 1944, painting by Robert Johnson

My grandfather was shot in the side. A friend of his – 'from Banff, no, from Cochrane, Alberta', he recounted on the tape – came and helped him out of the dyke. He was taken back to a hospital in Antwerp and evacuated to England. On 7 February, at Groesbeek, a suburb of Nijmegen on the German border, close to the Rhine, he rejoined 'B' Company.

'Not one [from my previous duty] was left. And I mean it. We had very heavy casualties. I think the Calgary Highlanders had the heaviest casualties of any of the Canadian regiments,' he told the tape. Numbers suffering battle exhaustion in the regiment were also second highest of all Canadian regiments on the Western Front.

The Highlanders ploughed through the territory of the knife: the road from Nijmegen, to Doetinchem, onward to Groningen, a route precisely where the ORPO division had been. Groningen was the largest city in northern Holland, which they attacked from the east.

I read the war diaries of these weeks, between February and April, looking for specific confrontations with the ORPO and notes on prisoners who were police, as the diary regularly catalogued the number of POWs. I did not find what I was looking for. I found instead chiaroscuro: alternating descriptions of hellish fighting and debauchery to compensate. These entries in the diaries suggested to me the knife's mythology. And I wondered how easily the soldiers shifted from the violence to days of feasting. Had they grown sufficiently inured to the violence to enjoy themselves even as their boots were splattered with blood? Had they become indifferent birds of prey or were they frightened lambs passing through extreme states?

Crossing into German territory, the infantry began to use Wasp flamethrowers which 'did a marvellous job of enveloping Jerry's entire Pl dug-in locality. This was too much for the supermen, and they left their holes discharging their burning clothing.' The diary spoke of piles of bodies, rotting livestock, continuous fighting with small arms, heavy shelling, burning buildings. And 'on every side, the devastation of war proved to us that the Germans were now receiving their share of what invasion means to a nation'. The Canadians too faced friendly fire ('one of those unfortunate incidents that are very hard on the morale of the troops'), enemy snipers ('movement became a case of run and pray'), and then suddenly found themselves back in Nijmegen for ten days (between 14 and 25 March) of picture shows, company dances and carousing.

Locals saw the Allies as taller, larger than life even, with better teeth and better skin, even if they were filthy. The soldiers reminded them of luxuries denied to them: white bread, real tobacco, real coffee, real chocolate, real gasoline instead of ersatz fuel. In Belgium, it was recorded that women of all social classes threw themselves at the men in a way that shocked moral authorities, so much so that people were dragged under the tanks in the emotion, and buttons were ripped off uniforms, even though the men were slimy with sweat and caked with dirt.

The halls in Nijmegen were decorated with old Dutch chandeliers, flags, and welcome signs. The nights would start with cocktails or punch.

The pipers played, drums rolled, toasts were made. There was singing and cigars. Music was supplied by the Nijmegen orchestra. On a good night, there were women: both Canadian nurses and local girls (if not, the dances could turn into 'somewhat of a stag party', as the boys rolled the 'last barrel of beer down the highway'). The war diary recounted the men were gripped with 'spring fever'. My grandfather later joshed, at the end, when dementia had loosened his tongue, that it was a good thing his kilt was so heavy because it kept down his erection.

The joke went like this: there would be no need to send Canadians to a future war in Holland; they only needed to send uniforms to all their illegitimate children. Servicemen, encouraged to balance duty and pleasure – and better fed than their competition, the remaining local men – were a source of resentment. There were 7,000 illegitimate births in 1946: the highest number per year in Dutch history. Many of these children are still looking for their fathers, a reminder that the relations between men in uniform and starving women was a troubled romance.

From punch and sex, the men were soon plunged in battle: bridges being blown 'up in their faces' in Doetinchem, a town where the Germans had barricaded themselves between 1 and 2 April into the main square, using railcars filled with cement. The adversary was impossible to flush out until they brought in the flamethrowers, 'which proved too much for the Jerry'. From here they raced north, to the canal city Groningen, the denouement of the Dutch campaign.

The Battle of Groningen

Groningen, a city of 110,000 people, had strategic importance as the north's communication and transport hub, close to the port of Delfzijl, key to the access of U-boats to the North Sea. It had been correspondingly fortified by the Germans, with trenches and bunkers, who made strategic use of the Hanseatic canal ring and its sixteen bridges and the narrow streets, which led to the market square, its cathedral and tower. The claustrophobia of Groningen's ancient canal houses made for intimate conflict, often hand-to-hand – the kind for which bayonets are made – under the watch of snipers on rooftops. The Allies had decided not to bombard the city wholescale because of the civilians.

The operation began on 13 April. The war diary, on 15 April, reported my grandfather's experience of house-to-house fighting, 'the Company objective [being] a series of blocks consisting of apartment houses each with three stories and each apartment having about four rooms containing several civilians and many snipers … the Companies smashed through one after another'. My grandfather remembered entering a Dutch woman's living room with his Bren gun. He used her hardwood table to set up the bipod, so he could shoot at the Germans in the street. His bewildered host got to making ersatz coffee, which she brought to him in a porcelain cup. She also handed him a cushion to put under the legs of the gun, so that he wouldn't destroy her table. He alternated between sips of coffee and machine-gun fire.

War in a civilian-filled city created chaos. Hundreds of Dutch residents raided a German liquor depot and got drunk. 'Great throngs' stood and watched. My grandfather attacked the old post office with flamethrowers and 'the Germans tumbled out in a hurry to surrender'. The prisoners were lined on the street and the Highlanders began to loot. My grandfather observed: 'The boys very illegally took the watches off their wrists, and some of our troops had eight or ten watches on each arm. Probably not a very ethical thing to do, but we didn't care.' Altogether 2,400 Germans were taken prisoner in Groningen; some were remnants of the *Landstorm Nederland*, who had been led by Albin Rauter and had fought with the ORPO.

If I were to imagine why my grandfather had bad dreams after the war, I would think it was not the knife but rather the memory of flamethrowers. The Wasp, mounted on a carrier, was much more precise than the incendiary aerial bombs that fell on Solingen. It had a 120ft range that increased if the wind was working in your favour. He told the tape that in Holland, 'We used portable flamethrowers, a vicious darn weapon, you could burn a house and clear the way in a hurry.' My grandfather requested them to be brought in again that Sunday afternoon. Men scattered the apartment windows with machine-gun fire to keep the snipers at bay, as the flamethrower was brought into range. Its incendiary materials were like 'glue; it would hit and it was stuck there and it was on fire'. My grandfather in an interview stated that the manoeuvre was 'extremely effective and horrifying … as soon as you would start to use them prisoners would just pour into the streets'. Terrified screaming men must have run to the canals, on fire. The use of flamethrowers was later restricted by the UN, as part of the 1980–83 Protocol on Incendiary Weapons.

The Calgary Highlanders' journey through the Netherlands initially read to me like a Tolkienesque episodic quest. Not to a ring but to a knife that would transform its bearer from a 'fresh', 'immature' prairie boy into a killer. I was aware that my providential reading was nonsense; he did not go to Europe to find the knife. But the Canadian advance – from the massacre on Walcheren to the flamethrowers of Groningen – was nonetheless episodic horror. It would not be a knife, with a negativity akin to Bilbo Baggins and Frodo's ring, that would transport my grandfather into a world of shadows. It would be the journey. Bilbo too had trouble sleeping.

In Canada, history is often treated as an edifying as opposed to cautionary craft. This is why I could be nostalgic and ascribe positive feelings to my great-great-grandfather's sword – the one with the beautiful sound – used in the Boer War. Even a necessary war, like the campaign against Hitler, required killing. A 'good war' – but war is never good. The horror is not suggested by the titles – such as *Battalion of Heroes* – given to the carefully researched, but official patriotic histories of the Canadian advance in the Low Countries. War cannot be convincingly explained with the euphemistic language of 'clearing' or 'cleaning up' Germans, Canadian forces being 'depleted', or by the editing out of images of Canadian bodies or Dutch civilians whose property was devastated by Canadian artillery. This was something that my grandfather understood, like so many veterans who saw war up close. Did this make him quite unlike the eagle on his knife, sensitive as he was in his testimonies to horror? He knew exactly what the knife did to people.

After the victory, the regiment was sent back to the area around Apeldoorn where the ORPO had had their reprisal: 'We lived in tents … which became the headquarters for the Canadian armies, awaiting transportation to get back to Canada.' 'The hardest part of the war came with the conversion from wartime soldiering to peacetime soldiering,' my grandfather said.

In Apeldoorn, he crossed paths with a housemaster from his boarding school, Trinity College School in Ontario, discovering that he outranked him. My grandfather advised his former teacher that 'he didn't need to call me sir. He didn't think that was very funny.' I wonder what the housemaster had observed, how the pupil had changed.

On leaving the Continent, on 29 September 1945, the men were told that anyone taking weapons back to England would be sent back to the

occupation force. 'Pistols and whatever must have filled the bottom of the Channel,' he told the tape. Nonetheless, my grandfather admitted smuggling weapons back: 'Two small pistols at the top of each boot.' And, as we know, he had a third weapon.

A few weeks were spent in England, saying goodbye to family cousins in London and Dorset, whom he had visited during pre-deployment and when he was injured. He later happily recounted many anecdotes of Britain: how he shot a pheasant on a cricket lawn from a windowsill (feathers everywhere) or caught pneumonia on the way to a pub and met Lady Astor when she visited his hospital (he learned to 'lie to attention' in his bed), or how much British girls liked their North American visitors (very much). My grandfather left the UK behind, 'embarking again on the Queen E, back to Canada', arriving on 19 November 1945. It was a five-day trip by train, across a country that had not been invaded or bombed during the war, for which the devastation was distant. The Highlanders were greeted by the entire population of Calgary.

A little over two weeks later, on 7 December 1945, he married his fiancée, Kay Hastie, a 24-year-old Scottish Canadian whose family had emigrated from just outside Glasgow. He had not seen her since the early autumn of 1942.

Slaves to Objects

I stop waking in the middle of the night. The knife is on a table in the sun. The more I study it, the less it frightens me. The bright light suggests both distance and scrutiny. Perhaps my grandfather was capable of hanging it on a wall, instead of putting it in a drawer, because he had a context for its story. After everything he had seen, it had become … maybe not ordinary, but disempowered.

While the knife was not inherently evil (perhaps only in its function as a bayonet), it was very seriously tainted by its transformation into a Nazi object and its subsequent use. Working from the artefact, the way an archaeologist might, brought us to the Coppels and its police classification and modification. It is ironic and tragic that the knife was used in the Netherlands by the ORPO, where they were complicit with a particularly radical implementation of Nazi race ideology and mass murder against victims like the family who made the knife.

From the blade, I imagine a voice: metallic, distorted by faraway cables. In the absence of living witnesses, the object had indeed spoken, but not unmediated: it required conjurers, such as collectors, diarists, and historians. While its markings had led to this Jewish family's story – and by extension many family stories like it – it was my grandfather's journey to the knife that provided the context and meaning for the knife's use. I cannot know for sure whether my grandfather 'liberated' the knife in the area north of Arnhem, the region where the ORPO had been grouped into the *Kampfgruppe Rauter* in 1944 and were active during the reprisal massacre at Woeste Hoeve in March 1945. The knife might have been taken from any one of the German prisoners captured daily during the Dutch campaign. However, the proximity of the Calgary Highlanders to where the ORPO had operated in a military capacity – a rare example of such engagement in the north-west military theatre – made this explanation of discovery at least plausible.

An inanimate object invites readings. Not only as a child did I craft a romantic narrative of the knife's negativity, its association with heinous acts, its cinematographically lurid side. Iconography features so strongly in the films of figures as diverse as Leni Riefenstahl and Steven Spielberg because of the powerful and expedient way symbols convey *ethos*. The knife is, simply, a scary-looking object that one immediately assumes came from a Nuremberg rally or an SS officer in a death camp ... or a Shakespearean scene involving an evil twin, who by some chance happens to be facing off against my grandfather in the same battle. Revising assumptions is salutary, as is taking the reader by the hand through the detective work that will challenge such cinematic hypotheses. When I paid more attention to the back of the rug – the method, prejudices, and dead ends, and of course false assumptions – I arrived not just at more nuanced history, but also the hermeneutic sense of it too, of how interpretation comes together.

I worry that readings from popular culture have arguably replaced such documentary readings. Most people today learn about the Second World War through film. The Nazis are in *Indiana Jones*, *Valkyrie* or – God help us – *Iron Sky* and *Jojo Rabbit*. The Holocaust is *Son of Saul*. Or *Schindler's List* with its soulful soundtrack and scenes in high-contrast black and white. Keeping the public aware of the Holocaust is vital, in a time of generational change and lost memories. But doesn't the gripping evidence of the period – from archival footage to everyday belongings – correct the larger-than-life version of the Second World War and bring us closer to comprehensible everyday figures? Doesn't it dismantle an elaborate stage set, similar to the one the Nazis fabricated in their propaganda to obscure their everyday brutishness? The knife's ordinary connection to heinous events is a much more meaningful story than the one told in cinemascope.

The romantic iconography of the bayonet must have also spoken to the lowliest police officer, the most visible face of the occupation, ennobling him with the indifferent remorselessness embodied in the knife's symbols. But the knife has mundane qualities: its cataloguing, circulation, its on-and-'walking-off' duties. The knife is only an amalgam of metals. The knife's eye is nickel. The eagle was cut alongside forks and spoons in a workshop. The knife cannot be entirely extracted from the meanings that necessarily unfold from its symbols. But a de-romanticising of Nazi symbols, in the end, is what robs them of their power – the power that militarists have searched for in the eagle since Roman times, and that neo-Nazis still hope to gain from the swastika today. As Epictetus, the Stoic, said: the moment we start to give the inanimate a special aura or imbued importance, we become slaves.

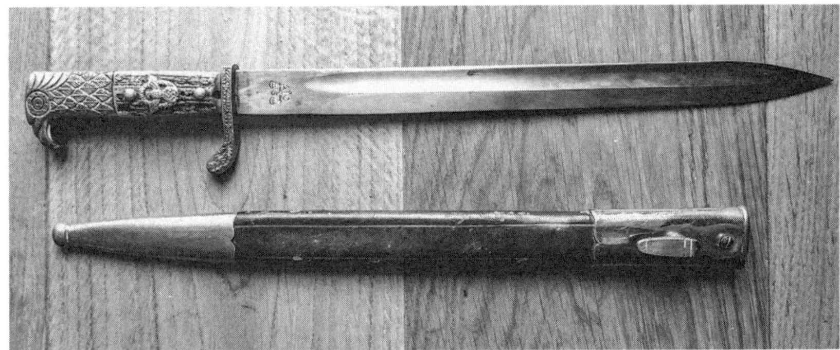

A Diary in Code

Generation Z

It starts with a post on social media: 'Does anyone know a historian in Berlin? I can't read a World War Two diary that's written in code.' I reply on the forum to the creator, a woman from Marseilles named Flora Giuliani: 'I'm a historian, I'm interested in objects, let's see about this code.'

For a brief moment – in a flight of self-regarding fancy and excitement – I imagine myself an object detective, called on to crack a mystery. The next minute, as I trip down the stairs, I hope Flora's not going to be disappointed.

From her profile picture, she can't be much older than 23 years old, the age of my grandfather when he was fighting in Groningen. Do young people today actually care about what happened to those their age eighty years ago? I suspect the answer is yes.

We meet in a coffee shop in Friedrichshain, a student neighbourhood. The establishment's name is μ. How Berliners search for a Greek letter on Google maps is a mystery. I can't find it coded on my phone. I think of how the generations are lettered: X, Y, Z. I'm Generation X and Flora just sneaks into Z.

Once inside, I'm clueless about what to order. The coffee shop serves cold brew and pour-overs. Young people are wearing tie-dye and specs – what I parse as a throwback to 1970s fashion – and here I am, bearded, all in black. The speakers play a mix of experimental ambient and Mahler. I feel the latter tug at me, with sympathy. I'm in the kingdom of the next generation. But even they want to talk about the Second World War.

I'm surprised when I see Flora in an elegant shift dress, striding from a back room into the industrial space, with its second-hand furnishings. She notices me immediately – am I that conspicuous? – and greets me with a big smile. Tall, poised, bright-eyed, she retrieves a package from behind the bar; she must work here. She cradles it, wrapped in tissue. I can't help but think of a new parent.

She directs me near the window. There is plenty of light and a repurposed bedside table. Flora brings me a hot drink, a pastry. We start with chit-chat. Everything is easy. She tells me how she came to Berlin last year to be with her German boyfriend, a medic whom she met on his Erasmus year in France. 'French people don't understand why I moved here. Everyone asked me why I was going to a country with such an ugly language.'

'Even young people? I thought Berlin was cool – '

'No, that happens a lot with French friends,' she sighs. 'Why are you moving in with your boyfriend "*le boche*" [the kraut, the jerry]? Ah. The French don't know a lot about Germany except for the war. They always go back to that.'

Flora sits across the bedside table and places the object carefully between us, unwrapping it softly. Between the folds of tissue is a volume. The book has a cloth-bound cover – a fine burlap, rough to the touch, hard enough to have the words *Tagebuch*, or 'Diary', printed across it in frilly letters. It has a small clasp, which is broken. 'Here, open it,' she instructs me, and – careful of flakes of pastry, the hot chocolate on my fingers – I do.

The pages are thin but stiff. But what is immediately apparent is the fine, educated cursive that covers every page. It's almost completely indecipherable but I recognise it. What Flora calls a code is *Sütterlin* script. A handwriting taught in Prussian schools a century ago, it is already illegible to today's Germans, even when written clearly, rather than in this author's idiomatic, poetic hand.

I have a sinking feeling: I can't even decipher the signature on the inside cover of the diary. The most I can make out is *Karl B------* in a flourish. There's a hurdle before us.

Flora looks at me, expectantly.

Where's my Rosetta stone? The diary is an object from a lost writing system, except frustratingly in a language we speak every day in Germany! Flora's description is not that far off: it really is in code.

'There are things I've figured out,' she tells me, and I realise just how many hours she has spent with the object. She has examined its every surface. Dates are decipherable: 1941, 1942. She indicates a recurring place name: Le Havre. I suspect now that this diary belonged to a German soldier in occupied France. On one page are water stains, drops that smear the ink. I wonder if it was raining when this Karl wrote his diary. But Flora looks at me and says, 'He was crying, wasn't he?'

'Look here.' She turns to the back of the journal. The final twenty or so pages have been torn out, in an act so violent that it bruised the spine. 'Who did this?' she implores, a look of disbelief on her face.

I shake my head. I don't have any answers, yet.

'To protect someone?' she asks.

'Why do you think that?'

'There's something else I need to show you. A love letter. It was in the diary.'

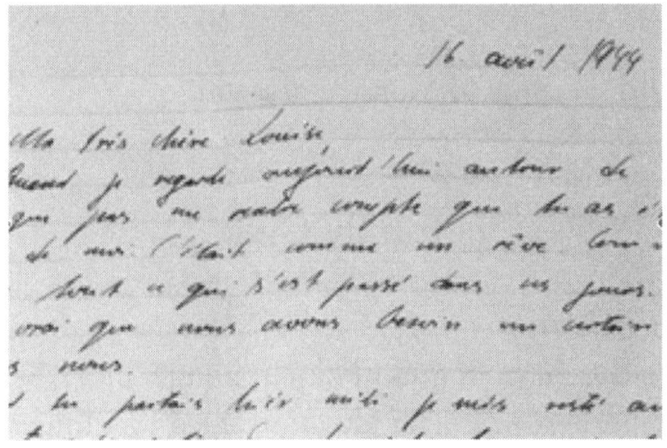

16 avril 1944

Ma très chère Louise,

Quand je regarde aujourd'hui autour de [illegible] me rends compte que tu as [illegible] de moi. C'était comme un rêve [illegible] tout ce qui s'est passé dans ces jours. [illegible] que nous avons besoin [illegible] [illegible] [illegible]. [illegible] tu partais hier [illegible] je suis resté [illegible]

From between the pages, she takes out a letter from an envelope. It is dated 16 April 1944, written in the same angular hand as the diary's author, but in French. It is – a relief! – in letters I can read:

My very dear Louise,

When I look around me today, I can hardly imagine that you were still here, close to me.

It is like a dream. A dream too everything that has happened these past days.

It seems true that it will take time before we are together again. When you left yesterday at midday, I stayed a long time by the side of the road to watch you go. You looked like a boy on your bicycle, like a good loveable comrade. Because I love you not only as a woman but also as a comrade. You are so good and courageous. We two, we will get through things together.

Soon after you left, it started raining. I thought of you, hoping you found shelter. Tell me that you arrived safely. Did Monsieur Arnaud find a room for you? I need to know you are safe.

Do not worry about me. When the time comes, I will know what to do. Everything will be as we said.

I slept well last night, going to bed at a good hour and waking at 8 am. I hope you slept as well as I did. You must be tired after your trip, no? Above all, promise me you will take good care of your health. You know we both need to be strong. I have a lot of work at the moment but there will be less over time.

My love, write to me a lot about your life in your letters. Be always strong and careful. I hold you, strong.

As strong as I love you,

Karl

PS My cordial greetings to Monsieur Arnaud

Family Guilt

'When I read this letter, I started to cry,' Flora says, putting down the paper. 'It is written in such good French: simple, short, beautiful. There is so much tenderness in it. The love story is so touching. I imagine the scene when they leave each other. I want to know what happens to them and what happened before. Who was this German man? How could such a relationship exist between enemies? Was he a Nazi and how did he fall in love with a French woman? And was he killed because of his arrest?'

Here, I start back: 'Killed?'

'I feel somehow responsible – ' She pauses. 'Not personally responsible. But *connected* to the responsibility … of ending this relationship. My family did this.'

Flora tells me the unlikely journey of how the diary came into her hands. She takes out yet another letter. This one is from her grandmother, who received the volume from her father in the French Resistance. It reads like a teaser:

C'est dans ces circonstances que mon
père, le maréchal des logis chef de gendar-
François Louis Rumin
merie, affilié aux Forces françaises de l'Inté-
rieur, a fait prisonnier un déserteur alle-
une femme française
mand qui se cachait avec, une certaine
Louise, dans une ferme des environs de Blaye
Mon père lui a pris ses papiers, et parmi
eux, son journal intime. Ce journal, conser-
vé dans notre famille n'a jamais été tra-
-duit. Présente-t-il un intérêt ? Historique ?
psychologique ?

> It's in these circumstances that my father, the marshal of lodgings [a sub-officer rank], chief of the Gendarmerie [in Blaye, Bordeaux], François Louis Rumin, affiliated with the French forces of the Interior [FFI], took prisoner a German deserter who had been hiding with a French woman, a certain Louise, on a farm near Blaye. My father took his papers, among which was this diary. This diary, kept in our family, has never been translated. Does it have any interest? Historical? Psychological?

In the letter, Flora's grandmother also indicates that her father told her that the deserter had been in the *Kriegsmarine*, or German navy, and that he was arrested in August 1944, at the time of France's liberation, four months after the love letter was written.

'You see,' Flora tells me, 'I was about to leave for Germany to be with my boyfriend. I visited my grandmother in her kitchen in Brittany. She loves to cook. But the kitchen is also where she has her office: all her papers and her chair. It's her spot.'

'This is when she gave you the diary?'

'Yes. She had prepared a package for me and put it to one side. She told me that her father had arrested this young German. And then she said: "I have something to give you."'

Flora's grandmother had done her best to decode the diary, without success. 'Perhaps in Germany, they will know what to do with it,' she told Flora.

Flora saw the interest of the mission right away. 'I had no idea it existed before. I was struck by how, even when two countries are at war, there can be love. I also thought there was historical merit in the story of a deserter. But the diary was so personal. I didn't feel I had the right to possess it. It was someone else's intimacy. But then I thought: no, this is also my family's story. My grandfather arrested this young man. I was already mixed up in the story.

'I wrapped up the diary in tissue and took care of it. Eventually, I took it to the family of Simon, my boyfriend, here in Berlin, in Spandau. But they couldn't read it. His mother had some notions of the script but only a word or two jumped out at her. Simon was studying in Heidelberg, so when we went there, I visited the university, the Department of History. They showed me the door. I went home disappointed because I thought it was enormously interesting. *Et voilà*, now here we are – '

I considered what we had. A diary we cannot read. One that had spent seventy years on a family bookshelf. Flora's great-grandfather, no longer with us, as a witness. So many pages torn out. The frustration of being unable to read the name of the owner. A letter suggesting a tragic love story without much context. Was it a lost cause?

Yet, Flora's family had not given up for three generations. Flora had come to live in the country of the enemy, which made her family's unresolved guilt even more acute. She certainly wasn't going to quit now.

Where to go with this story of love in wartime? Was it especially tragic only because we knew so little? Or could we – from the object itself, and the few clues it presented – go deeper and unlock some truth? I realised, like Flora, I was captivated because the clues we did possess exhibited such sincerity: the yearning and hope of a man determined to see his lover again.

I tell her, 'Let's see what we can find out.'

The 'Code'

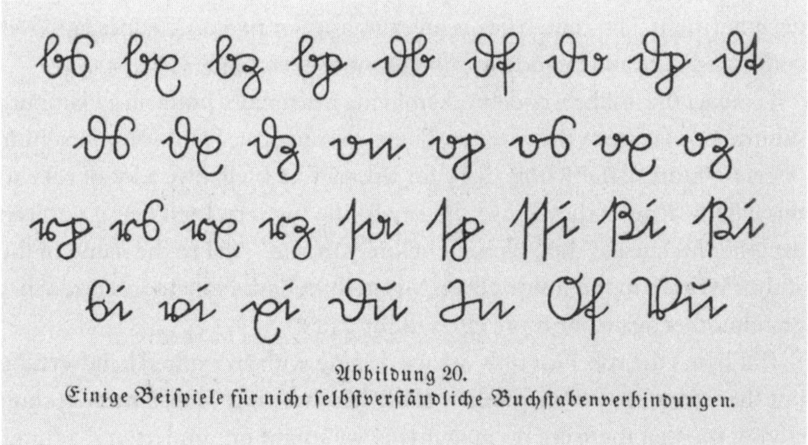

Abbildung 20.
Einige Beispiele für nicht selbstverständliche Buchstabenverbindungen.

The script was invented in 1911 by Ludwig Sütterlin, introduced to Prussian schools in the 1920s, and imposed on the rest of Germany between 1935 and 1941. *Sütterlin* is a modified form of *Kurrent*, based on late medieval German cursive. This flash-in-the-pan 'modern handwriting' was abolished in 1941 by the Nazis, who wanted to make German more legible in occupied Europe. Only one generation of Germans learned *Sütterlin*, precisely those now dying with the skill.

Sütterlin was taught widely for only six years. Only a handful of archivists and specialists nowadays have much proficiency. A friend from Cambridge, now a pre-eminent historian of modern Germany, tells me *Sütterlin* 'gives him the shivers' when I explain my dilemma. Although he had to learn it in graduate school, he says most scholars have trouble with the handwriting of private individuals and 'often give up'. The hand of public officials is more forgiving. Generally, only doctorands working on earlier periods will dedicate any time to old handwriting, and in that case to *Kurrent*. So, I send samples of the diary to an early modernist, a former professor of German at Princeton University, who replies with four possible variations of Karl's last name. 'His handwriting is too idiomatic.' Great. I ask a German friend to bounce it off her mother who was born in Silesia before the war. Again, no joy. Trained historians and laypeople alike don't seem to be getting anywhere.

But then I discover the existence of *Sütterlinstuben*, or 'Sütterlin Lounges', at a handful of care homes across Germany. Unable to read correspondence from grandparents and other relatives, people can send in their letters for decipherment. The centenarians meet an hour or two on Wednesdays over coffee and cake and decode for donations to the cookie jar.

I contact the unlikely codebreakers living in a seniors' home in a Hamburg suburb, not far from the airport. Their coordinator, Frau Sommerschuh, offers to translate the whole diary for a donation. I will owe a lot of cake to this elderly army if they prove the key to the mystery. I tell her: if you can decipher his cursive, then please – before you start – tell us the name of the author written in the inside cover. Meanwhile, I ask Flora to interview her grandmother again, for more clues to the story.

But here's the rub. Not only are we dealing with an expired handwriting but that extra layer of illegibility: *Karl's* handwriting. Frau Sommerschuh advises me that there are no guarantees; we might not understand a thing.

Papyrus

What is the difference between an object and a document? Legibility: you interpret an object but you can also read a document. When Flora asked me to look at the war diary, I did not expect an object; I expected to be able to read a document. But since an almost illegible object is before me, I go through the same motions as with my grandfather's knife. I examine the surface of this object – cloth and paper and metal and glue – for clues because inside there are only squiggles.

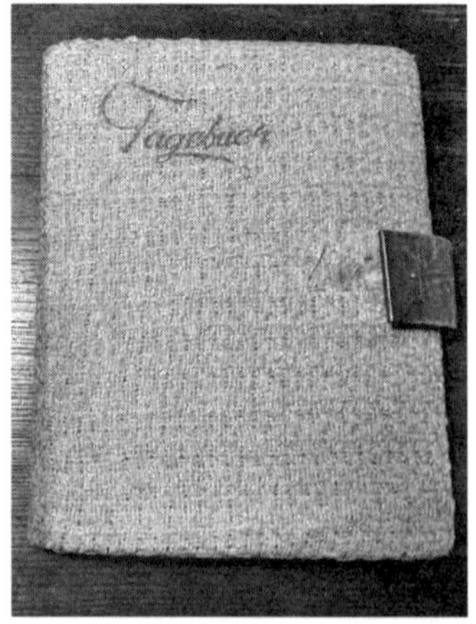

I touch the object's burlap cover. The material is rustic and recalls farmyards, straw, and sack races. The embossed script, '*Tagebuch*', is romantic: the serifs of 't' and 'g' fly away, into the air, flights of fancy. The font contradicts the prejudices I have of the hardened Teutonic soldier. If this object were in a painting, it would be in an oeuvre of German Romanticism, a pastoral by the artist Ludwig Richter. The fine clasp, fashioned to look like a small envelope, is broken: a sign of an invasion or betrayal.

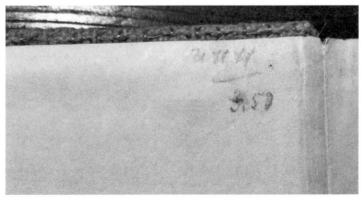

I open the object. The paper's weight is twice that of today's photocopy paper, perhaps 150gsm. In the inside cover is a price: 3.50 Reichsmarks. In 1939, 1 Reichsmark was worth 4.10 euros. In today's coin, the diary would cost 14.35 euros – not an insignificant purchase for most people. The book was an investment: more a Moleskine diary than a spiral notebook. Except this object feels artisanal; it's not a mass-produced confection. Karl leaves many pages blank, decoratively. Perhaps he can afford to. Or were his thoughts so valuable? He concludes most entries with a decorative swirl, or perhaps the infinity sign.

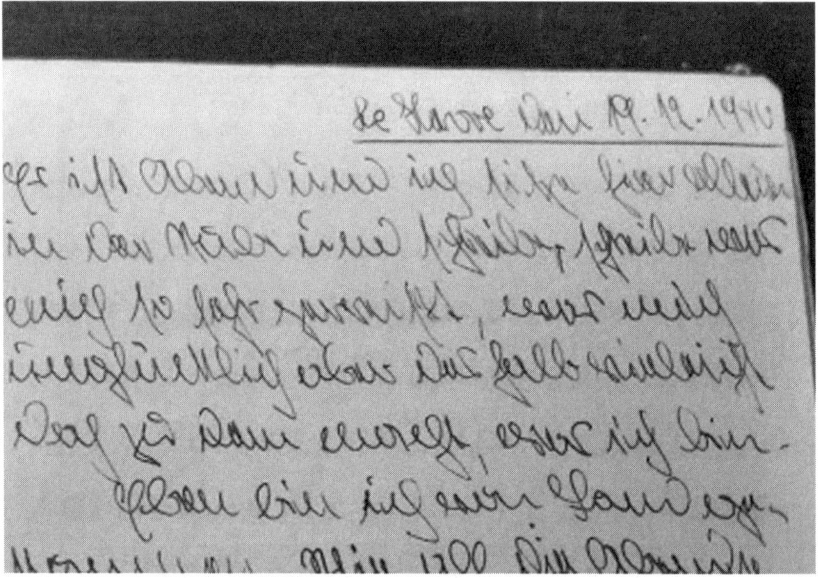

I turn to the next page, which has the name of the owner of the diary in that almost indecipherable script. Karl B – – . Opposite is the first entry. What partial legibility is there in the *Sütterlin* script? I scan the first two pages carefully for any words I might recognise:

Le Havre 19.12.1940

I alone
I

unhappy but
that I am.
am I
the previous
evenings I always
bring and
whorehouse

But I always go
there

[page 2]
is there woman
that I I
letter immediately in
love with this woman; but
feelings

but I love
love
a
I
that

I
of

The sentences are riddled with holes. I recall the poet Anne Carson's method while translating fragments of Sappho, preserved on badly damaged papyrus rolls. Carson relishes the drama of solving the puzzle, negotiating the voids on the damaged surface: 'As acts of deterrence, these stories carry their own kind of thrill.' Karl never intended for his writing to be a code, but the contemporary reader confronts deterrence. It's astonishing that a script from the twentieth century, after just three generations, can become just as challenging to decipher as poetry originating in the seventh century BCE. Time, that devours all things. *Tempus edax rerum.*

What is legible? A vision: of a young romantic, clutching his diary on the deck of a German navy vessel, swelling with loneliness. The word *Bordelle*, or 'whorehouse', was perhaps not the obvious place to start, especially after the intimacy of the love letter. But I have read enough fourth-wave feminist theory to have a nuanced view on the subject. I'm sure it's late at night. Karl feels the fleeting, guilty pleasures of the brothel; they only pique his isolation. His most intimate thoughts are gathered from a broken language. This is the beginning of our love story; we know the tragic end from the letter. Already here, we glimpse the passion he desperately wants, to be eventually found in the arms of Louise, someone he truly loves. A few broken words belie the longing of a sensitive man. They even foreshadow the coming tragedy. All this sounds quite convincing, I persuade myself.

But as I continue through the second half of the text, I wonder how much I've really gleaned from these tatters. I pore over the repetition of that word: 'love', 'love', 'love'. More conspicuous are the ellipses, the brackets. Who is this Karl? He could be a womaniser. A criminal. But would someone like that curate such a diary, write in such a fine hand, and use the semicolon correctly? Perhaps the brackets omit his pragmatism about sex and exchange. I am left indecisive: at first, I thought I had solved a puzzle – seen his face in the fragments – but perhaps I don't recognise him at all.

Le Havre

Flora read into this diary a romantic story, and the few words I deciphered confirmed her suspicion. The account passed down in Flora's family that he was a sailor is also probably correct. Le Havre is a seaport in Normandy

192 LE HAVRE. Ensemble de la Place Gambetta, du Bassin du Commerce
et du Bassin du Roy

that became a primary naval base for the *Kriegsmarine*, or German navy. When I flip forward through the diary, I conclude that he spent two years there. Only three other place names jump out: two I cannot read; the other is Kristiansand, a port on the southern tip of Norway.

Le Havre suffered during the Second World War. On 10 May 1940, the Germans launched their offensive on the Western Front. On 13 June 1940, the same day French troops abandoned Paris, Le Havre was occupied by the German forces. The armistice happened on 22 June and the formation of the Vichy government on 10 July. The strategic coastline, including the places relevant to this story – Le Havre, and Blaye in Bordeaux – were under German occupation. Four German divisions gathered in Le Havre, building enormous military fortifications. The port was one of the most important staging points for Operation Sealion, the planned invasion of Britain. Some 40,000 German soldiers occupied a city that had only a population of 120,000, saturating it with young men in uniform.

The inhabitants, *les Havrais*, adapted to censorship and a spartan life under the German authorities: strict food rationing, shortages of necessities, parachutes used to make clothing. Civilians were requisitioned to defuse unexploded Allied bombs and 900 Jews were deported from Normandy, including the mayor of Le Havre, Léon Meyer, who would survive Bergen-Belsen and then Theresienstadt.

Relationships between German soldiers and the French were discouraged. In January 1942, the field commander for Le Havre proposed that soldiers be forbidden from dealing with the local population. Bordellos were the officially sanctioned release valve for sexual energies. The *Wehrmacht* requisitioned existing brothels and also established new ones; there were 500 such places across Europe by 1942. These policies subjugated many local women to an often-ignored side of the occupation.

On 5 and 6 September 1944, the RAF, to expel the Germans, dropped almost 50,000 incendiary bombs on Le Havre, destroying more than 80 per cent of it and almost wiping the city from the map. Six days later, the city was the last to be liberated in Normandy.

When Karl began his diary, at Christmas 1940, only six months of occupation in Le Havre had passed. What was it like for a young man – even a soldier of the enemy – to live for several years in a foreign city, shielded from the battle lines, with time on his hands? Is it a surprise that he fell in love?

I turn to the last pages of the object and I am confronted again by its most dramatic traces: the final third of the book's pages torn out with a force that left visible shreds of paper. The violence has ruptured the book's spine. What would have compelled Karl to damage his cherished belonging this way? Did the love affair go sour? The diary has provided an enormous canvas on to which I can imagine, just like Flora, a grand romance – one that might actually be true. I see those words from the first pages again: love, love, love. Are they telling Karl's story? Or is his story coming more from *me* – the voids of those brackets tugging at my longing, imposing it on an undeserving subject, a German soldier participating in a brutal occupation, and in the subjugation of women? How much of this puzzle can – with so little – be solved?

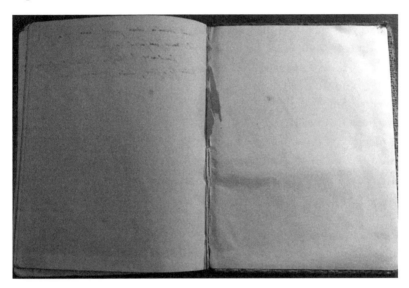

The Grandmother's Story

Karl Biedassek. Or perhaps Biedaseck. Or Biedasek. Frau Sommerschuh writes with possibilities for the name encoded on the inside cover. At least she has narrowed them down. I will now contact the German Federal Archives and ask if they have the file of a sailor named Karl plus all the variations. If simply his name is causing the *Sütterlinstube* so much trouble, how can they possibly translate 120-odd pages?

Then Flora returns from a holiday back home in France with an audio file. It's a long interview with her grandmother, Jeannette Thomé, about events she witnessed when she was a girl. Madame Thomé may have been born in Paris (and her father in Finistère, western Brittany), but she grew up in Blaye during the Second World War.

Blaye is a little port, population 4,000, on the Gironde Estuary, 30 miles from Bordeaux and not far from the Atlantic. It is known for its enormous citadel, a UNESCO site, with expansive views to the river from its walls. Surrounding Blaye is Bordeaux red-wine country, producing a cuvée of Cabernet Franc and Sauvignon with Medoc from hills of clay soil. Sun, a great river, lush countryside, and superb wine: I can think of few better places to wait out a war. Except that it was in the zone of France occupied by the Germans.

Flora asks her grandmother, 'How did you get the diary?'

She replies that she found the journal on a bookshelf. Her father had been dead for some years. Only her mother was still alive. 'I can't tell you how many times I opened it and looked for words I might understand. My brother, who studied German in high school, also tried, but he couldn't translate it. Still, I wanted to know what was in it. So, in the '60s, I took the diary from that bookshelf and kept it, thinking: if I don't take care of this, the memory of this story could just disappear. For years, I asked colleagues who were teachers. I asked a German who told me the diary had no interest. Well, not everyone knows how to use documents. Something going against me, in those days, was that Germans were hated by the French.'

Finally, in the 1990s, after trying for decades, Madame Thomé gave up on translating it, even though she was 'sure it had greater interest'. Nobody could read it. This broke her heart because she thought that there must be a story worth telling locked inside.

'Why did you care so much about this story?'

'It was the letter that touched me. It was in excellent French. I knew this man was someone cultivated, someone sensitive, and I was curious. What were the impressions of a German in France in 1940? But I was also wary. Did he participate in atrocities?'

Madame Thomé tells the details that her father recounted. He had been a gendarme in occupied France, and he hated the occupation. 'He had 1,200 kilograms of plastic explosives in the garden!' she exclaims.

At the time of Karl's arrest, in August 1944, her father was on extended medical leave because of tuberculosis. 'Nonetheless, he put on his uniform and he arrested this young man in a farmhouse.'

'Why did he do this?' asks Flora.

'Because it was their mission: to go on raids, arrest Germans, take their belongings. My father found him by chance at a farm north of Blaye.

I think the farm was at Saint-Ciers. It's a place where we used to go swimming in the woods. This Louise was not there at the time. No one else was at the house except for a farmer, in whose house he had been lodged. A couple lived there. I don't know who the farmer was. Perhaps Monsieur Arnaud from the letter.'

I have located Saint-Ciers-sur-Gironde on the map, some 12 miles north of Blaye. I find that Arnaud is a common name there. One Arnaud is a wine producer. Just up the road from the village is an auto shop owned by another Arnaud. I write query letters to both of them. The enclosed 'wanted posters' must have struck these addressees as odd: have you seen this man from the 1940s? We don't even know his exact name. Perhaps unsurprisingly, we do not get a reply.

'Why did you suppose he was a deserter?' asks Flora.

'Karl wasn't in uniform. My father took him from the farm and he interrogated him.'

'Do you think Karl pulled the pages from the back of the book?'

'I don't know anything about that,' she replies.

'What do you think happened to Louise?'

'I picked out Louise's name in the diary, from their time in Le Havre. I thought she must have been from Normandy. They must have had a plan, the lovers, to find each other. She risked a lot too, you know, as a collaborator. I know of many people who married Germans during this time: even our neighbour across the street. I am sure that Karl was so worried about her. It must have been obvious that he was German. At the end of the war, many of those who resisted took vengeance on the women who had been with Germans. My father refused to do this: it shocked him. I remember how terrible I found it. But I also understand: many young men in the Resistance were tortured while French women went with Germans. It's not good but I understand why they took revenge.'

Flora asks her grandmother, 'What do you think happened to Karl after the arrest?'

'The Germans were taken to the Citadel of Blaye, and then to Bordeaux. I guessed Karl was a sailor not only because he was in Le Havre also – something I discovered later, on reading about the Resistance in Blaye – because the last prisoners of the Citadel in Blaye had been German sailors. That is where he was taken.'

'Do you remember what happened when your father came home that day?'

'You see I was a little girl at the time, twelve years old, so I don't remember exactly what happened. Only that he had found a German and that he was pretty satisfied with himself for having arrested him. I was surprised by this. I don't remember if he was holding the journal; he certainly didn't talk about it at the time. A couple of years later, when I was fourteen, I saw it. I became aware of it.'

'What about the love story? Didn't it matter to the family that Karl was a deserter?'

'Care that he was a deserter? No, we weren't interested. There were no particular family sentiments about that. A relationship between a French woman and a German was looked on poorly. We used to say: poor girls marry for money, ugly girls collaborate! I'm not saying that Louise denounced people. Perhaps it was just for love.'

'Why did you give the journal to me then?' asks Flora.

'Because you are in Germany. Because you are with a German. Maybe you will manage to get it translated: I saw a chance for this journal.'

'What would you say if you met someone from Karl's family today? Have you thought about that?'

'You mean, would they be angry at my father? I would understand if they were. But I would try to help them understand that he was not anti-German. He was anti-Nazi. In my family, we are not racist or xenophobic: this is a Breton tradition. It would be a relief to talk to them.'

'What do you think happened to Karl?'

'I don't know the end of this story, Flora. But it's an intriguing story. It could have historical interest. Even the everyday is interesting. I see a tendency in history to look for who was extraordinary, not who was ordinary even when that's what touches us. More than the exploits of Napoleon. I think it's unsurprising that a German would love a French woman. The Bretons have always flirted with the Portuguese and the English sailors. That has always been the case with young people who love each other.'

Was a man named Karl Biedassek – or perhaps Biedaseck, or Biedasek – among the prisoners taken to the citadel? The citadel had a long history of housing enemy combatants. The First World War POWs were German, but the prisoners during the Second World War were French Resistance. Flora's grandmother takes this task on and promises to keep us informed about whether he appears on a POW list. And I investigate whether German mariners were later kept in the citadel in the days of the August 1944 liberation. I find that it was probable, since from 1940 the German navy had been operational in the Gironde.

What of Karl's fate at the hands of the French Resistance? 'What French Resistance?' Albert Speer, Hitler's chief architect, and later armaments minister, famously opined. Most French kept their heads down. But in the last year of the war, occupied France saw a marked rise in resistance activity. Acts of sabotage played an important role in the denouement of the occupation. For that, many French civilians paid the price. The Germans used brutal reprisals against the Resistance – or *Maquis* as it was called in the countryside – as a deterrent. As late as 25 August 1944 in Maillé, on the road between Paris and Blaye, the SS systematically killed 124 of the 500 residents, including 48 children, as a payback for a *Maquis* ambush. After weeks of violence, on 28 August 1944, Bordeaux was officially liberated and the streets filled with those celebrating and Resistance fighters, also from Blaye.

Madame Thomé is correct to worry about Louise. It was not only Karl in danger. The term 'horizontal collaboration' described French women's relations with the enemy over the four years of occupation. The most visual punishment was head shearing, occurring in public squares as spectacles, followed by parades through the streets. Prostitutes and young mothers alike were shaved, stripped naked, tarred, publicly humiliated in a frenzy of liberation, celebration, sexism, revenge, and scapegoating. At least 20,000 – who often lived better than other French, under the protection of their soldiers – were targeted and some 6,000 were killed. One-third of women identified as such collaborators in Brittany were killed by the mob, which only months earlier had accommodated itself to the occupation.

And what of Karl? If he was indeed a deserter, he had taken an extraordinary risk. The crime was a capital offence; already in *Mein Kampf* Hitler articulated that deserters must be put to death. Around 30,000 German soldiers were court-martialled and sentenced during the war, and more than two-thirds of them executed. Although 100,000 German soldiers

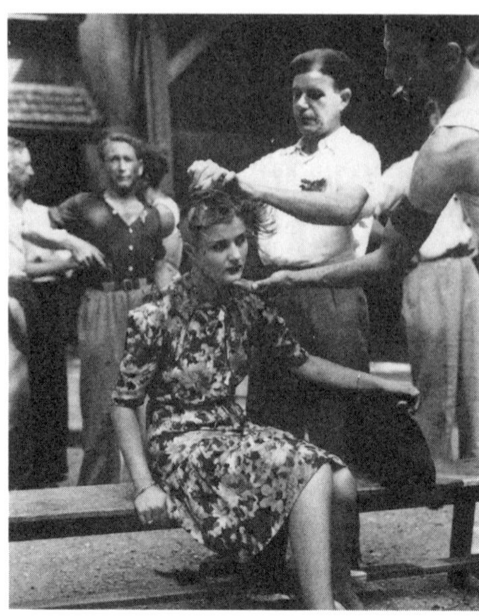

abandoned their posts in the denouement of Germany's defeat, this disobedience was not congratulated. Post-war, there would be no legal amnesty for deserters. A stigma of cowardice tailed these men back home, to towns and villages where other men had remained in service, despite the dubiousness of the cause. It took more than sixty years, until 2009, for the German parliament to revoke the convictions against 'war traitors'.

This stigma would have followed a deserter to wartime France. Even his captors in the Resistance, styling themselves as military units, might have considered him a traitor to his rank. Soldiers were officially protected under international conventions. France put a million German soldiers into prisoner-of-war camps in 1945. But when Karl was found, he was not in uniform. Even by the standards of the 1949 Geneva Convention, deserters had only 'debatable' claim to the rights of a POW. In the Netherlands, on 13 May 1945, a Canadian-led tribunal sentenced two German sailors to death for desertion. They were shot by a firing squad composed of German POWs.

Is it so surprising that desertion was a worse sin than the enemy's ideology? Desertion questions hierarchy and undermines authority, the foundation of military discipline. And it was not uncommon for the Allies to respect the rules of the German military: Nazi officers in Allied POW camps, after all, were afforded more privileges than ordinary infantry.

Karl may have forfeited the protections of his rank in the eyes of his captors. And in the carnival of death which was the endgame of the war in France, I cannot help but see him hanged from a tree in the vineyard as Louise was paraded through the streets.

Codebreaking

An email from Frau Sommerschuh at the Sütterlinstube Hamburg e.V. explains that she showed the diary to the seniors and they can decipher it. It will just take a great deal of time. I imagine them in a circle of reading and transcribing, and the number of cups of coffee or tea and biscuits or cake the marathon requires. How many of these older people – also of Karl's generation – will take his story to heart? Will they wake up the morning of their meetings excited, wanting to know what comes next? Not that I had evidence that the contents would all be interesting. Perhaps I had inflicted on these pensioners hours of drudgery, as they translated banalities, which made them relieved to return to their other aches and pains.

I once examined my great-great-grandfather's diary in the archive. He was a horseback inspector for the Northwest Mountain Police in western

Canada in the 1880s. Later he was a colonel in the Boer War and owned the 'noble sword' that hung on the wall of my grandfather's basement next to the Nazi knife. Such an exalted personality must have heroic tales to tell, I figured. I was jittery with anticipation as the librarian brought the archival storage box containing my forebear's most private thoughts. But the entries, such as one from 23 September 1886, were devoid of personal detail. One read: 'Much the same as yesterday. Did nothing in particular. Drill. Official duties. Slept at 8 pm.' Each entry ended scintillatingly with the weather, such as 'fair and clear'. Those seniors in Hamburg could end up hating me.

In late December, three months after our first contact, Frau Sommerschuh writes again. The diary has been transliterated. It took the group of seniors forty hours of labour over three months. They must have worked through Christmas: I hope they were drinking mulled wine. The transliteration is in a Word file in German: something I can read, unlike the encoded object, this canvas for so many projections: Flora's, Madame Thomé's, mine. I try not to get my hopes up.

Even those of you without a little school German might find the following exercise of fill-in-the-blanks as exciting as I did. First, I open the belonging, Karl's coded diary, to the first pages of writing. The object itself is tactile; it has traces of the moment – even perhaps, as Flora suggested, the man's tears. Then I open the decoded transcription on my computer. Microsoft Word doesn't reveal any spilt *Glühwein* or crumbs of *Spekulatius* cookies. Karl began his diary eighty years ago; it's been almost as long since anyone else has understood his words. I feel something miraculous as his thoughts reappear – the fascination of inserting the final pieces of a jigsaw puzzle. I am witnessing the transformation of the object into a document.

You might also compare the words in typed German to Karl's *Sütterlin* handwriting; I have underlined the words already deciphered (and omitted the words I misread):

Le Havre, 19 December 1940
Now the air-raid siren, and **I** sit here **alone**
in the parlour and write, write what
tears me so terribly apart, what
makes me **unhappy but** in the end perhaps
makes me who **I am.**
I just came from shore.
Like all the **previous**
evenings, **I** was at the 'Moon', one of
those famous **and** questionable
whorehouses in France. The hustle
and bustle there sickened me, and
sickens me still.
But still **I always go**
back **there**. Why? Because Md.

[p. 2]
is there. Md., the most beautiful **woman**
that I have ever seen. **I** know that
I was foolish to **fall** ~~in~~ **immediately in**
love with this woman; **but** those who
account for their **feelings** can account
for what is the very essence
of Man. She is married,
but I still **love**d her,
loved her despite her age with
a platonic, if not also
passionate love. **I** believed
still **that** she would be faithful,
to her husband at least.
Well, this evening **I**
have been convinced **of**

[p. 3]
the exact opposite.

Le Havre den 19. 12. 1940
Es ist Alarm und **ich** sitze hier **allein**
in der Stube und schreibe, schreibe was
mich so sehr zerreißt, was mich
unglücklich aber deshalb viel[l]eicht
doch zu dem macht, was **ich bin.**
Eben **bin ich** von Land ge-
kommen. Wie all **die Abende**
zuvor war **ich** im Mond, einem
jener berühmten **und** berüchtigten
Bordelle Frankreichs. Das Leben
und Treiben dort ekelte und
ekelt mich noch immer an.
Aber trotzdem **ging ich immer**
dorthin. Warum? Weil Md.

[S. 2]
dort ist. Md. die schönste **Frau,**
die ich bisher je sah. **Ich** weiß, daß
es töricht war, sich ~~in~~ **gerade in**
diese Frau zu verlieben; **aber** wer
kann für seine **Gefühle**, kann
für das, was ureigenstes des
Menschen ist. Sie ist verheiratet,
aber trotzdem **liebte ich** sie,
liebte sie trotz ihres Alters mit
einer platonischen, wenn auch
Leidenschaftlichen Liebe. Glaubte
ich doch, **daß** sie treu wäre,
ihrem Manne wenigstens.
Nun, heute abend habe **ich**
mich **von** dem glatten

[S. 3]
Gegenteil überzeugen können.

Karl coalesces like a figure from a cloud, and becomes a human being. He is no longer a caricature but someone with fickle emotions. I cannot yet imagine his face, but I am struck by the bubbling, susceptible sensibilities of a young person who easily falls in love. He is a romantic, determined to confront his emotions honestly, even though he confuses love with lust. His sexual drive overwhelms his judgement – not surprising at, what, 18 or 19 or 20 years old? Meanwhile, he blames a prostitute's lack of 'faithfulness' for his transgressions.

Do we see Karl now? Do we now know who he is? What is clear is that this diary is not going to read like a dry report.

I compare the decoded contents to the papyrus fragments. Had a few words been able to suggest the whole? They captured Karl's loneliness and his love but lost all the subtle fickleness. How much meaning would have been lost had that word 'whorehouse' gone unnoticed? I also cannot ignore how I was primed. Flora, Madame Thomé, and I all expected the diary to have a love story in it. But was this suggested by the object, or by the legible letter determining our approach to the object? Certainly, the latter.

Now, our expectations are being satisfied, with Karl's salacious heart-brimming prose. The story is full of raw and exposed emotions, as we expected it would be. I shake my head and try to remain critical, not drawn into conclusions. Was this Karl – this man found four years later in a farm in France without his uniform, whose capture by Flora's great-grandfather probably put an end to his love affairs – a brutal occupier? A deserter? A criminal? And what of Louise?

One thing I do know, this Md. – Madeleine? – would be forgotten.

Lord of the Lonely

'And so, disillusionment and disappointment came to me. Perhaps it is better this way … I've never been able to keep a girl I loved …' Karl sits alone in his quarters and enumerates his former affairs.

Gertrud: a childhood adoration that left him feeling stale. Even the strongest loves will die without reciprocity. Ushie: a girl from school, whose rejection drove him to become a sailor, 'on the vastness of the sea I wanted to forget'. During his nautical training, he met Irma: for the first time, it's purely lust not love. Their encounter lasted 'only a few wonderful hours'. But Karl was too inexperienced to follow up his erotic urges. Irma grew impatient with him and found someone else. There was another girl, but Karl did not love her either. Now, having remembered all these other women, he feels rather better about Madeleine.

It's Christmas 1940. Karl is nostalgic for holidays at home in East Prussia, at the far edge of Germany in what today is eastern Poland. He thinks about a Christmas tree, carols, about when his father was still alive. Now, his mother is lying on her deathbed and Karl is far from home. He loves her so much, owes her everything. Her death will break him. Downstairs is the hustle and bustle of his fellow soldiers celebrating. Their songs, jokes, laughter, are all frivolities. Sharing them would make him sadder than being alone, up in his quarters. What he truly loves is 'the great loneliness'. It gives him peace and the strength to bear his past and future troubles. He will remain lonely, even at Christmas 1940.

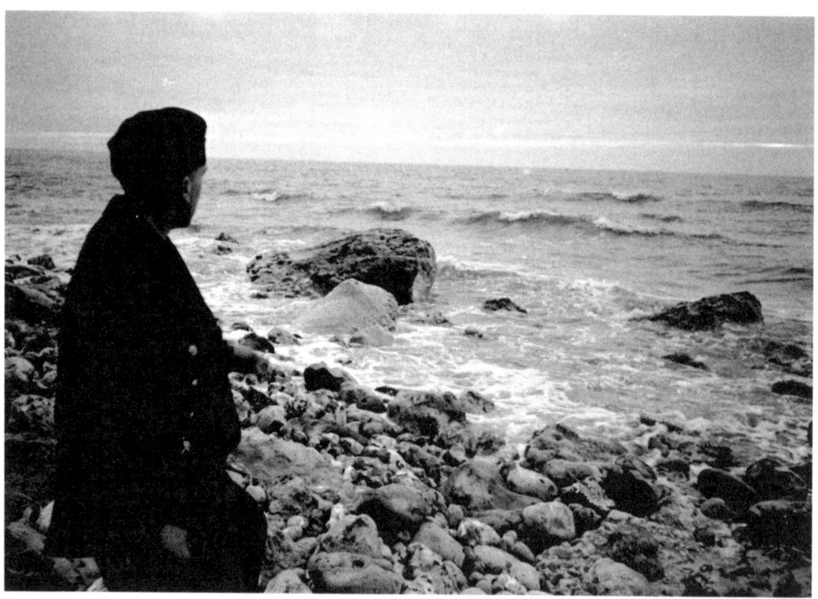

Le Havre, German navy sailor, 1940

Karl is in love with the darkness. He is also in love with Germany. His first seven months of diary entries are steeped in tropes of *Heimat*, victory, and the superman.

Heimat is a German expression that indicates the land where one is born or grows up, a place that feels like it has sunk into your bones and become part of you. *Heimat* thus is an emotional word to describe attachment to place.

Sieg, or 'victory', is more obvious; *Sieg* was, of course, part of the *Hitlergruß* or Nazi salute: *Sieg Heil*, or 'hail victory'.

Finally, *Übermensch*: Karl calls Friedrich Nietzsche, who also loved loneliness, his 'great role model'. The philosopher urged a superhuman detachment from the great herd of humanity.

Neither *Heimat*, *Sieg*, nor the *Übermensch* is intrinsically, ideologically Nazi. Nietzsche's ideas come from a classical aversion to the profane multitude. But all three tropes had been usefully turned to the service of the Nazi project in public education, justifying *Lebensraum*, or 'living space', and the victory of a German racial community of 'superior beings'. I read into Karl's writing this education and these Nazi tropes – and also the Nazis' sexism. The question will be whether Karl can shape these tropes or whether they will form him.

It is 31 December 1940 and Karl looks forward to the New Year. The outcomes for himself and his country are linked: 'What will it bring? For me, for Germany?' Already, he sees himself losing his mother, then being stripped of his inheritance, the family farm, and thus losing the 'victory', losing his 'homeland'. He could only with difficulty overcome the loss of his *Heimat*, just as the loss of his mother would be unbearable.

His *Heimat* – the family farm on the edge of Prussia – is a garden which, in spring, is splendid with the colour of new green, with tall lime trees that surround the property like walls, in whose crowns birds sing. Under them, in the grove, are a table and bench, a place where he has spent 'longing hours'. Behind, the land is expansive: billowing cornfields, a blinking lake. Karl, in this landscape, is a boy with dark eyes, open to beauty. He follows quiet paths to see the sunset: the mist a white veil over the meadows, the western sky a sea of flame. Then, he spends quiet winter evenings in the familiar light of a kerosene lamp, with his mother to whom he can say everything. She understands him so well. Karl wants nothing more than to be a farmer, working his land – in direct contact with his *Heimat*.

At the end of January, Karl is called home from France to Talten, East Prussia. The unbearable has occurred. He is unable to see his mother before she dies: 'I cried like a little child … we are orphans now.' 'Why have I not died? Why did you have to die?' Karl prays, he invokes angels. 'Mamma! I don't know how I'll bear it without you! I pray to you and ask you to remain in my life as a good, protecting angel!' He is obliged to sign a contract to relinquish the farm: 'It flickered before my eyes as with trembling hands I put my name on that document. In doing so, I forfeited every right to the piece of earth that I love so much. No parents, no relatives, no *Heimat*! Can it get worse?'

For months despair overwhelms Karl, especially in the quiet evening hours. Only work numbs him. Or the longing for perhaps another woman, with something 'motherly in her'. 'Everything beautiful attracts me but also makes me sad, I don't know why,' he writes. Increasingly desperate and alone, he 'comes to realise how difficult it is to have no one and how bad other people are … there is no one who understands me'. He writes that the men on his boat conspire against him in intrigues behind his back. He is 'torn apart searching for the meaning to existence' and asks: 'What do we actually live for?' 'These hours, they gnaw at my life. Maybe I will be killed in battle. It would be a release.'

Out of this utter dejection, Karl turns to philosophy. 'Out of pain and suffering, I have begun to search for knowledge and truth.' A philosopher 'feels more deeply than others'. He is always the 'unhappiest of people', willing to 'perish' in his search. Karl's hard-nosed philosophy, born of his adversity, is a mix of Nietzscheanism, social Darwinism, and Nazi race theory. 'Life is struggle and sacrifice and action!' It hates inferiors: 'The fat and self-satisfied bourgeois … I despise these petty ones, the all-too-comfortable ones.' It is only for a 'caste of higher-thinking people' and not the 'herd man' with his 'worries and weakness and cowardice'. The 'Superman' – a 'master' who is proud and unbowed – condemns pity and weakness towards himself and others. 'Egotism is desirable.' Karl will transform into a man of the wilderness, a bird of prey resembling the eagle on my grandfather's knife, ascending northwards, with the 'rough air around him', ever lonelier and more silent. At these altitudes, he will breathe a philosophy that 'the world has so far not yet read or heard. My philosophy will be a German philosophy.' Germany will be 'its power, its sharpness, its fire, its impetuosity, astringency'. This philosophy will be forged from the 'violence of the German soul'. Karl rejects religion, all his prayers, and his guardian angels. His 'master race … will burn everything that comes near them' and will laugh as they 'dance over the graves of the dead'. I see Karl in a high castle, wrapped in the 'austerity and sweetness' of sadness and detachment.

On 24 July 1941, in Le Havre, Karl writes:

> Loneliness! You were always my companion, always with me, in me, around me. Lord of the lonely. You – my loneliness – are my life, are my lover, are my father and mother, my friend, my brother and my sister. I will live my loneliness, which will deny me lovers and the company of women. It will not tolerate others. I praise my loneliness because my life seeks eternity.

Three days later, on 27 July, Karl meets Louise.

Louise

Karl sees her three times on the same Sunday.

The beach is busy. A group stands out: three German soldiers with French women. One in particular, 'delicate and soft and sensitive like a beautiful butterfly'. He reads into her both a woman's experience of love and a child's innocence. Under her simplicity, and cheer, there's another perceptible, volatile quality – something impetuous in her manner, 'fluttering in its impulses and effects'.

21. LE HAVRE. La Hève, la Falaise et la Plage.
C. M., Le Havre

Karl strolls along the wide boulevards of Le Havre in the evening. The atmosphere of sun, sea and land is 'godly in its harmony'. Suddenly, he sees her again: a group of three French women and a sailor. He writes that 'my second look went right to the soul of this girl'. But Karl is overwhelmingly self-conscious: his interest has been too obvious. From one look, she must have understood all his 'hours of loneliness'.

Karl perhaps does not expect to cross her path again. But as he turns into a small, lonely lane at the end of the evening, he discovers himself alone with her. That third glance that passes between them 'brings knowledge'.

Karl's diary now explodes in a fury of unsettled emotions. I imagine a shovel turning over the embers he thought had gone dark. From that look, he reads Louisette's soul like 'an open book'. It is a revelation: of life, of beauty, but also 'an abyss of horror'. In her soul, he sees chaos, a storm of feelings resulting from their exchange. Karl is not attracted to a simple beauty. Louise promises lust, sorrow, and 'renunciation'. The combination is fatal to him: he falls for her immediately.

The young soldier struggles to understand why this happened, after all his efforts to remain supremely and untouchably alone:

> Why? Why? What for? Many questions and only one answer: Because I love her, this soul that lives in a beautiful body! … I saw debris, saw tears and saw laughter. It was, for me, an evening of sublime ideas. On the ruins of a broken passion, something new will arise. A new world will open up to me, new insights flow through me, new destinations will reveal themselves. *Wohlan!* Well then! Standing tall I will stride, directly towards her.

Zweisamkeit

Two weeks later Karl is delirious with passion: 'The 9th of August! What an evening! A harmony of clouds, water and earth. Louisette, me, and our love.' Karl wants to confess his love. He describes it as a wild animal in a cage snarling and jumping against the bars. Louise's dark tousled hair, her pensive eyes, her face 'charming in its irregularity', all drive him crazy. 'Your body is a revelation, Louisette!' He admits too that when he looks into her eyes, 'I see myself! Sadness, expectation, and happiness.' 'Fulfilment and renunciation in your eyes.'

That word *Entsagung*, or 'renunciation', is always on his lips. A month passes and he ponders: 'Our love is a singular renunciation that requires fulfilment, just as spring finds fulfilment in summer.' Rich in desire, pure in innocence, a single path of 'suffering and tears … dark and deep is our love … our love is suffering, our suffering is our happiness'.

Entsagung. I look for explanations for the repeated use of this word. Is it that Karl anticipates the end of something beautiful? Hanging over the romance is the harbinger of hard times, of war, because he is a soldier? Is Karl finally renouncing his loneliness and the violence of his Nazi education? Or is it that Karl, the romantic, cannot imagine happiness without suffering? Those who taste joy's grape will always be hung among melancholy's trophies, wrote Keats. I mull these possibilities but am forced to consider another: could it be that there is a very real obstacle that promises to break them apart?

A month later, on 9 September, Karl tells Louise they should break things off. He has been given leave to return to Germany for a short period. It's an opportunity to put some space between them. The early evening before his departure is one of passion and 'possession'. After they make love, in the stillness of the bed, sadness enters both of them. Neither wants to admit it.

As the sun sets behind the houses, they walk together along the Quai George V: 'The lonely streets were infinitely sad, destroyed houses and ruins, the witnesses of war. And then between the destruction and the ruins, the two of us, young and full of life asserting our rights.' Karl struggles with his overwhelming desire for Louisette, with how desire and love have come together. Nonetheless, he tells her they should put an end to it, 'for her sake'.

But why? Why end something so beautiful? Karl leaves for Marienburg and it is a month later – when he is back in Le Havre – that he writes again in his diary. He is consumed with desire. I see him lying in his quarters, mad with lust: 'I burn, I am hot and flaming, the night cannot take me into her arms.' The wind sings of 'lonely suffering'. He cannot find peace. He aestheticises his renunciation. Karl is thrown into a spiral of desire for Louise that he cannot shake.

A week later, in five entries that span the month of November 1941, Karl is ecstatic with misery. Louise might be a woman 'full of promise … grace and sweetness'. But he convinces himself that she will be happier without him: 'Louise, our love will never find fulfilment. Today, I know it!' He writes of 'burying his youth'. He opines that as soon as she gets pregnant with someone else, and has children, she will forget all about him, and be happy. He asks: 'Louise, do you even know if you love me? Maybe you just pitied my loneliness.'

He seeks pleasure in his suffering, in the foretold renunciation. He writes that love came into his heart 'with a torch' to announce: 'You have already suffered everything else, now suffer in love!' He promises to put an 'evergreen wreath' on the grave of their love. Louise is nothing but 'a bridge' to his 'faithful companion', loneliness. He calls out to solitude:

'Wrap me in your cloak of oblivion. The escaped man returns to you!' He contemplates the eternal, he contemplates death.

But Karl cannot shake another feeling: 'My love came to you and wanting to give and give, again and again … a lonely love that wanted togetherness, *Zweisamkeit*.'

Zweisamkeit: that evocative German word that suggests the loneliness two people can share. The intimacy that braves the world. Not loneliness (*Einsamkeit*), but 'twoliness'.

Love, War

Three months pass in which Karl does not write in his diary because he feels 'no desire' to put pen to paper. That desire has gone elsewhere. It has filled a period 'rich in mental struggles and suffering, but not without happiness. My happiness! What else could it be but my love and the knowledge that I am loved.'

In February 1942, Karl writes with astonishment about his discovery: he spent so many nights 'struggling' with whether love could make him happy. He searched endlessly until he grew tired and finally 'realised that love and happiness don't always go hand in hand' but that love will do its best to make him happy. He considers his obligation to Louise: 'When you gave yourself to me and I took you, it was a symbol.' He blames himself for 'destroying her life but you gave yourself to me not out of lust but out of great love. Oh, these cool evenings feeling the warmth, the delightful closeness, of your body. I will never forget them.'

The mysterious obstacle that has come between them is revealed in the next entry, from 27 November 1942. Nine months have passed since he last wrote. The time has been 'filled up with our love, Louise'. But Karl blames himself: for the look he sees in 'the sad eyes of Louise, her face getting thinner and thinner'. So much does he pity her that it causes him physical pain.

Karl lies in bed on his ship, struggling with his feelings, thinking about how many nights he and Louise went to the rue François Arago on dark evenings, just to look up at the windows of the house where her family lives, where Louise lived before they threw her out. Behind those shutters, 'we knew were Louise's sister and mother'. Walking home, he struggles because Louise's heart is 'full of sorrow'. He is struck by the 'injustice and suffering that has been inflicted on us because of our love'. Louise is an outcast because she loves a German soldier. This is at least one reason he was sure that their love would end with a 'renunciation'.

But Karl comforts himself, and her, because now 'we have each other. We merged into each other.' To assuage his guilt, he is determined to marry Louise, but he cannot get permission: 'All my efforts were in vain.' It is now that he makes another – and for this story, important – confession: 'I am ready to give up everything, even my future, just to creep off and live a quiet life with Louise.'

Is this what he will do? Make good on this promise? Having lost his family, his farm, his *Heimat*, is he not now free to follow the only person that had saved him from a crushing, even suicidal, loneliness? From those chilly heights of the superman? Will he choose her over Germany?

He soon learns that Louise's family has moved to a neighbourhood he's never been to before. He wanders alone, 'with the collar of my jacket unbuttoned', to the address he located. When he next sees her, he describes the new address. Louise 'listens eagerly to every word' and Karl cannot bear how sad it makes her. He is determined to 'take her back to her mother'. The family lives not far from a cemetery where one of his comrades will be buried. And so, the next Sunday, after the funeral, he rings the bell.

'With my heart beating, I opened the garden door … and asked for Madame B. – .' One of the two older women standing there 'must have been her' – someone he had never met before. He follows her into the house where he finds Louise's sister sitting, reading, on a divan. Recognising Karl in an instant, she jumps to her feet, and flings her arms around his neck, with questions about Louise. He tells the family that if they only wanted it, she would return home.

But we do not know whether Louise reconciles with her family. The diary only has two final entries. The first is almost six months later: dated 11 May 1943, Kristiansand, Norway. Karl has been dispatched far from France and Louise.

'Louise, it was our love that was always with me, that was my suffering and my happiness in all this time.' Karl describes how he left her on the train platform in Le Havre for 'the last time, smiling at me and bravely fighting back the tears' when he already 'felt something of the difficult path ahead'. He is keenly aware of his luck, 'how you don't know and don't appreciate what you have when you have it. Oh, how I longed for you! For your soft tenderness! Every day, every hour my thoughts were with you … with all the fibres of my heart I wished to see you again.'

His time in Norway, with the 17th Jagdflotilla navy fleet, is torturous. Unlike in Le Havre, where he was with a superior and comrades he knew and liked, here he refuses authority. He withdraws into himself. He loses all will to fight. He does not trust his superiors. He describes his commander, a vain man in his late twenties, 'pleasing himself' with 'big words like Total War'. Karl becomes 'obstinate', he stops following orders: 'I thought up everything possible to be reposted back to France,' including an application for a language certification. Finally, he finds an escape. He falls ill, and then falls ill again, in the winter fog and damp, with severe and recurrent sinus infections that confine him to his bed.

Karl's final entry is on Christmas Day 1943 – exactly three years since his first entry in the diary. He reflects on his time in Norway as 'bitter' and 'ugly', rainy, sunless, painted in dark colours – a misery that will heal only with time. 'I felt the greatest happiness being allowed to leave,' he writes. And leave he does: back to Germany, though, via Denmark – whose flat coast, from the ship, surfaces from the fog – and by train to the town of Flensburg, still unbombed, and then to Berlin.

Four days of leave in Berlin: the diary ends in the capital where I sit now, summarising in too few words everything that this young man has loved and suffered over three years in wartime. The life of the big city surrounds Karl. He finds a hotel room not far from where I used to live in the district of Mitte, near Nordbahnhof, or Stettiner Bahnhof as it was called then. He writes to Louise from the hotel room: Norway is behind me now, and we can finally hope to see each other again.

The days in Berlin pass 'so fast and yet so slowly'. 'In the loneliest of landscapes, one often does not feel as abandoned as among so many people in a metropolis.' Karl wanders through the city streets. They make him feel 'shipwrecked alone on an endless sea'.

After these four days, from the capital of Nazi Germany, he travels via Hamburg for eight weeks of training. In language? In espionage? We don't know. Hamburg was gutted by fire-bombing that summer. He hopes to see his brother there but cannot find him. A feeling of abandonment grows stronger in Karl. He reaches the training: 'New faces, new comrades.' These are the last words of the diary. The remaining pages are ripped out.

Bildungsroman

I cannot help but read a *Bildungsroman* into this story: a novel of a young person's sentimental education. A young romantic – impetuous, even ridiculous – looks for love. But he has been fed with an education that could easily tip into a Nazi ideology of the strong and the weak. Out of loneliness and disappointments, he could fall into the maw of the ideology and act out that cruel indifference on the battlefield.

But he is saved. By what? From dissipation, desperation, and suicidal thoughts, he arrives at love. To say that love saves Karl is not an exaggeration or a romantic projection. The cruelty and indifference in his writing disappear the moment he meets Louise. Does he not spend months grappling with his identity – as the German in love with a French woman? Does he not refuse to renounce their connection?

In Norway – where 40 per cent of the country's Jews were deported during the occupation, and which suffered devastating economic hardship under a collaborationist regime – Karl retreats from service. He questions the Total War propaganda. He despises authority. Isn't it partly love for another individual that motivates this rejection and his self-preservation?

We do not know yet whether it will motivate him to desert. But he has few other connections – no family, no *Heimat* – holding him down; he has only Louise. We don't know what brings Karl to France when he writes the letter in April 1944. Or what happens between then and August 1944 when he is arrested by Flora's great-grandfather. We don't know if he is killed at the hands of the Resistance – for whom Karl, after all, is the enemy. And there is another mystery: why are the pages ripped out precisely after he writes to Louise from Berlin, with the hope that they can finally see each other again? While the decoded document has already answered so much, it is the object – the remains of those pages – that continues to ask many questions.

Karl wrote early in his diary that he is:

> difficult to understand, too self-confident towards others, too much a gentleman. And yet, inside I am soft and sensitive. I love the beauty of nature. I love poetry and music. I like to remember those balmy summer nights, which caused strange feelings in me. To take my violin and play and play melodies that no one has ever heard or would understand.

Is Karl simply an enemy German? Even in the year 2021, there is a taboo about regarding a German soldier, in the service of the Nazi government, as a vulnerable, complex human being, as a bubbling teenager learning to enjoy life. I see the soft innards of a person salvaged from another path, of brutish indifference.

Kriegsverwendungsfähig

I call Flora excitedly, having received an envelope in the post. It is from the Federal Archives. The file is thick, like a doorstop. Why is it so substantial? Perhaps, after all, Karl was a spy. I tremble as I open it, searching through the folded A3 and A4 pages. His full name is Karl *Biedassek*. Nervously, I think: what if there's more than one Karl Biedassek? But as I shuffle through the papers, I confirm that his handwriting matches the diary. We have him!

There is one item I look for immediately. When I find the identity photograph of Karl, I am surprised. He seems gaunt and I can see the bones of his shoulders through his uniform. What do we get from a picture? Do we understand him better: this wisp of a man, our troubled lover?

I meet Flora in the Markthalle IX, an enormous food hall in Kreuzberg, me carrying the military file under one arm. We sit at a large table and go through it page by page, trying not to get it dirty with coffee and croissants. We have a photocopy of the enormous, annotated file folder, which in the archive contains the documents. The name Karl Biedassek is written in cursive along the edge; there's a catalogue number; the date of conscription (14 August 1940); and the date of decommission, which is left empty. At the top of the page is a plus sign (+) in crayon with a question mark next to it.

We flip through the pages contained within, scanning his health certificate and other call-up papers, stamped with eagles surmounting swastikas, to discover that Karl was born on 1 June 1922 in a place called Ziemianen, in East Prussia. That means he was only 18 years old when he started writing his diary, sitting alone in his quarters that first Christmas while his comrades celebrated below. He is as young as we expected from the tone of his writing.

His weight: 59kg or 130lb. His height: 165.5cm tall or 5ft 5in. A *schlank*, or thin, body form. Brown hair, green eyes. Excellent vision. Blood type: O. He has fillings only at the back and has had his wisdom teeth pulled. A large 'KV' annotates the medical report: *Kriegsverwendungsfähig*. Another unwieldy German composite noun, meaning 'able-for-war-usage'. I think of my grandfather's file and how he too was inventoried with so many abbreviations.

On Karl's conscription form, we learn the names of his parents, his address, that he is single. We discover he speaks English and French, and reads Latin. So, I am surprised to learn that at his high school, or *Oberschule*, he only attained the *Primareife*, or a diploma allowing study at a trade school but not a university. His profession is listed as *Landwirt* or farmer. His superiors indicate that, after the war, he wishes to farm 'in the colonies'. His religion is *evangelisch* or Lutheran. And his police report indicates he's been a good boy.

Military personnel tested their recruits: Karl gets low marks in mathematics, but predictably high ones in essay writing, literature, geography, and history. But the knowledge tested is ideological: he knows the name of the leader of the *Kriegsmarine*, he can name two cities in Sudetenland, and identify the birthplace of Adolf Hitler. Everything he needs to go to war! He has also taken a course on how to keep military secrets.

Then I come across a declaration. Karl affirms with a signature that he does not come from a 'non-Aryan background' and that none of his parents or grandparents at any time belonged to the Jewish religion. On 7 July, he again provides proof of his 'Aryan heritage', stamped with an eagle and a swastika.

Next comes the man's service record. Karl was not reluctant to go to war. We have three letters from the autumn of 1939, when he is only 17, in which he begs the navy to let him join as a voluntary recruit, each signed '*Heil Hitler*'. One is annotated by the military personnel (I imagine the official sighing at Karl's impatience): *wieder gerade*, or 'yet again'. Six months later, in March 1940, after writing a fourth time, Karl is asked to sign a declaration that he accepts that he will not be posted until the autumn. I can imagine his reaction then, on 25 July 1940, when he receives his marching orders earlier than expected. He has four days to report. Karl does so the same day.

Karl is sent to the *Hafenschutzflottille*, or harbour protection force, at Le Havre from 10 October 1940 to 11 January 1943. What kind of soldier was he? The file contains his 'report cards', or evaluations for his service. In Le Havre, he is praised by his superior as an 'impeccable soldier', 'sincere and decent of character'. He has 'healthy ambition'. He is 'absolutely reliable'. He might be a little gaunt but he is 'agile and tough'. 'Always enthusiastic and ready to work', he has excellent seaman's knowledge. He is 'popular with his comrades' and 'very clean, not just in hygiene but with his things'.

Karl is quickly promoted from being a private to a corporal, or *Obergefreiter*, in April 1942 and decorated with an award: a second-class *Kriegsverdienstkreuz*, or war service cross 'with swords'. This was given for exceptional service to those who had not yet seen battle. A year later he would be promoted to sergeant (*Fähnrich*). Karl was a model soldier.

But what happens when he is assigned to the 17th Jagdflotilla in Norway from March to September 1943? We know from his diary that his morale goes downhill. When he learns that he is required to leave France, Karl writes to his commander in Le Havre with an official request for language training that would allow him to remain in the country. Karl overstates his appeal. He claims he is an 'orphan', that he has two younger siblings to care for, who have no other relatives and require his support. The training would give him a necessary career. A translator is useful for German colonial interests.

The commanding officer is unimpressed. He underlines the word 'orphan'. He replies that Karl's only job is to remain in the navy, which leaves no time for language study, and – I sense here the tone is peevish – that apart from the two younger siblings, Karl also has omitted a married sister and an older brother. The commander did his research. He concludes that Karl's 'request is not in line with requirements of Total War in which the interests of the state take precedence over private wishes'. Karl will be sent to Norway.

But Karl still has not given up. He tries to pull as many strings as possible. He implores a former teacher in East Prussia to write to a friend, a *Gauleiter*, or Nazi district officer, in Schleswig-Holstein, to intervene on his behalf. It's a desperate attempt to stay with Louise. The answer comes back the same: impossible. The navy has even planned out the steps after Norway: from December 1943 to March 1944, he will be sent to a navigation school and dispatched to a U-boat. Categorically, Karl 'will not be redeployed to the French coast'.

In Norway, we see Karl's radical transformation from an obedient soldier to a superior's headache. Or, from another perspective, we have the bureaucratic residue of the love story. His evaluation from Norway on 1 October 1943 is indicative. His commanding officer writes of 'an initial disinterest' and then a 'string of major military failures'. Karl cannot be counted on without supervision, because of 'his arrogance and lack of responsibility'. He is 'easily misled when presented with fragmentary knowledge'. On 25 October 1943, Karl receives his first official punishment, to be inscribed permanently on his file. While working in the canteen, he is discovered to have had an illegal 'correspondence with a French woman' via the ship's cook. His comrades rat him out.

When the diary ends, we learn Karl left Norway, via Berlin and Hamburg, to the navigation school. The file now takes over the story and we learn this is submarine training at a small lake called Kulmsee, in today's Poland. Karl is not finished with his goal of returning to France. He writes to his superiors on 27 January 1944, begging to be 'sent to the front in France'. He must have been desperate to request front-line battle. This is dismissed out of hand in early February.

When Karl finishes his training on 7 March, he is evaluated as having done fairly well: 'faultless behaviour' with 'fairly good' performance. He is 'suitable as an officer' training on a submarine. But what happens next is confusing, to the reader of his file and certainly to the German military authorities. Something occurs, not noted specifically anywhere in his documents, between March and the end of May, which suspends Karl's promotion to lieutenant and makes him 'unfit for U-boat service'. As a result, he is reassigned to a former cargo ship, the *Athen*, turned to military purposes as the 2nd Sperrbrecher-Flottille, or a mine seeker.

The vessel would be used in the last days of the war as a floating concentration camp.

Is Karl's 'suspension' shorthand for him having disappeared? On 7 March, when he completes his course, his whereabouts are known. But on 16 April 1944, Karl writes Louise that letter – the one found in his diary – indicating he has just seen her. Karl has somehow found his way from Kulmsee back to France in the month following the completion of his course. And what happened between Karl and Louise between the April letter and his arrest in August? A mystery.

There is no indication in the file that he shows up to his next posting, on the *Athen*, which was planned for 28 May. Had he done so, he would have spent the next months on board in the service of the *Marineoberkommando Ost*, patrolling the Baltic. That boat did not go anywhere near France, where Karl was taken prisoner in August 1944. Karl's service record does not indicate any postings after the navigation school: the next lines are empty.

In the thick of the war, it takes some time for Karl's military file to catch up with his disappearance. Germany is losing the war. The Red Army is marching with success through Ukraine. In the confusion over Karl's suspension and demotion – both confirmed by an official letter on 6 June, or D-Day – Karl's disappearance may have initially gone unnoticed, or rather overlooked.

But not for long. The administrative matter of Karl's promotion, on hold for three months, resurfaces procedurally in August 1944. It puts our young man back on the radar for the authorities. A flurry of correspondence erupts between the *Marineoberkommando Ost* and the navy's Inspection Service. They discuss a 'suspended' soldier, not one who has 'deserted'. But the Inspection Service writes to Karl's navigation school to confirm his whereabouts between 8 and 26 March 1944. On 12 September, the *Marineoberkommando Ost* explains that Karl's assignment with the *Athen* was officially 'cancelled' on 15 May. But cancelled for what? There's no replacement posting. I can imagine no one wants to be responsible for losing the man. They play documentary ping-pong with letters. He will be 'suspended' until he is 'missing', and then only a 'deserter' if he is caught and tried.

The matter of Karl's whereabouts is finally directed to a higher authority, the 'settlement office' or *Abwicklungsamt*. But this takes time.

The communication is misdirected or misplaced: the inquiry sent in August is only stamped as having 'arrived' on 10 January 1945. The final flurry of correspondence storms between the *Abwicklungsamt*, the *Marineoberkommando*, and the Inspection Service in that month. The *Marineoberkommando* deflects, saying they have no information about Karl because his vessel is no longer in commission. But the Inspection Office presses the issue on 31 January, asking: where precisely then is Karl?

On 1 February 1945, the *Marineoberkommando* finally admits that they lost him. Karl's presence is 'unknown'. On 15 February 1945, the

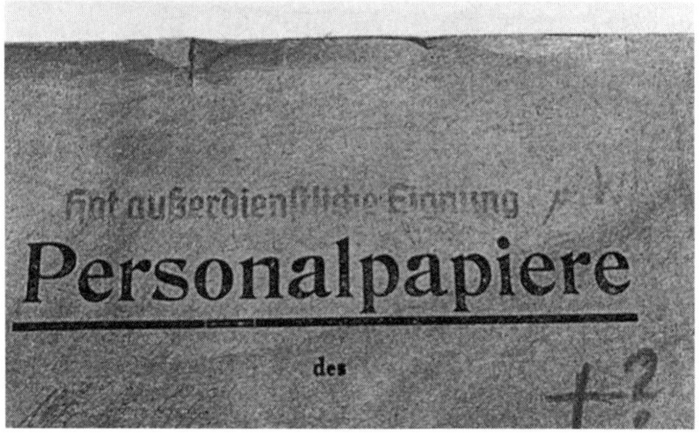

Inspection Bureau reports that Karl Biedassek is officially 'missing' and no further action can be taken at the time. No doubt they have bigger worries. Two weeks earlier, on 31 January, the Red Army rolled across the Oder River, bringing them to within 50 miles of Berlin.

Flora looks up at me. 'No one confirmed Karl was missing for ten months!'

'Or they thought he was dead. It was the endgame of war, after all. He was more likely to be dead than to have deserted.'

'Wasn't he dead? He was arrested in August.'

A look of epiphany then crosses her face, and she turns back to the very first page of the military dossier, on the table in our Berlin market. She points to that plus sign written there in crayon, with its question mark. 'It's not a plus. It's a cross!' she exclaims.

Of course: the symbol indicates whether a soldier has died.

'They didn't know whether he is dead.' She stares at me, hopefully. 'Perhaps we don't either?'

Discoveries

The focus of our inquiry has changed. I see in Flora's face how she reacts looking at the cross with the question mark next to it. We now know so much about Karl. So, was it Flora's great-grandfather who put an end to this story? To a love affair that had done its best to survive despite everything working against it? Was he the endpoint of the merging of these two lovers, the end of their *Zweisamkeit*? I know that Flora is not herself guilty. But I ask too how I would feel if her great-grandfather were a member of my family. We need to find out whether Karl survived his arrest.

It is at the metropolitan archives of the city of Bordeaux that I make a discovery. I find a series of photographs of German prisoners who were taken from Blaye to Bordeaux by the Resistance, or FFI (French Forces of the Interior), in August 1944. The photos were taken for a newspaper, *La Nouvelle République*. Blaye is a tiny town; there could not have been so many prisoners from there. Perhaps one of those in the back of this truck is our man.

I compare the photograph of the military file to the photograph of the prisoners found in Blaye. And I stop in my tracks. I look at the photograph from the file and see the same man in the back of the truck: the same square forehead, sunken eyes, straight line of his eyebrows, the slight arch above the eyes, angle of nose, thin lips, round protruding chin, large ears (softened in Bordeaux by the longer hair). Yes, this man is not as gaunt – five years have passed – but I am convinced we have our sailor. And his look! I see the 'fuck you' of someone resentful of the photographer, of having just lost his life and the woman he loves.

A truckload of prisoners from such a tiny town, brought all together in the month of Karl's arrest to the regional capital: I should not be surprised that he is on board.

I call Flora excitedly. We have proof that he made it at least as far as Bordeaux.

But Flora is not as categorical when I email her the images. She considers, 'Yes, quite possibly it's him.'

We look through other photos from *La Nouvelle République*, searching for Flora's great-grandfather. There is a group image of the Resistance soldiers. But he is not there.

I know that we will need more proof that Karl survived. Flora tells me her grandmother contacted the departmental archives of the Gironde region, to see if they have Karl on their lists of prisoners of war. They replied that they searched thoroughly four separate lists of prisoners, and he is not there. I grow worried, wondering if they put the POWs in camps and shot the deserters. But the second discovery comes from the German Red Cross, whose 'search service' in Munich responds to my inquiry about whether Karl was listed as a POW. The Red Cross helped many Germans find their lost soldiers after the war.

They reply that on 1 June 1948, Karl Biedassek came into their office and filled out a 'search card' looking for his siblings, two brothers and two sisters. Perhaps he had returned from being a POW in France. They don't know. His last known address was in the Saarland, occupied by the French forces. The Red Cross writes, wryly: 'Since he appeared in our office, it's unlikely that he was executed in France.' They attach copies of the search card, written in Karl's familiar script, except no longer in *Sütterlin*, but in one I can finally read.

It feels like a miracle. A cloud has lifted. Flora has no reason to let this story weigh on her any longer.

We now need to find Karl. Or find out what happened to him after the war. We scour the internet for individuals with the last name Biedassek. We send out dozens of letters with his picture and personal details. In them, I explain I teach at a German university in Berlin, that I am doing historical research on a figure of importance because he resisted the Nazis. It's a great story! You would be proud of him! But do I hear back from anyone? Not one. We turn to Facebook. We send emails. Finally, I get replies from Biedasseks who know nothing of Karl but tell me their own family stories from the war. It's all very fascinating but not what we are looking for.

Is it enough that survival is the end of the story? That we have solved the question mark hanging over the plus? Isn't the end of the trail this incredible relief that Flora and her family now feels?

'Or is it a disappointment?' I ask Flora when I next see her.

'What do you mean?'

'Was the story better when it had a tragic ending? Is the romance gone?'

Because I am sure that the story is no longer the varnished one that we first imagined. We could ascribe whatever we wanted to the diary when it was still an object. Once it became a document, our hunches became all the complications of a living, breathing human being.

Flora shrugs. 'I don't want to compare my situation too directly to Karl's. But unlike Karl and Louise, Simon and I can love each other freely. I think there is plenty of romance in that.'

Esprit d'escalier

I think we are at the end of the line with our research, but Flora texts me. She has found a phone number for a Karl Biedassek who lives in a tiny town in the mountains in the south of Germany. 'Should we call him?' she asks. '*Allons-y!* Let's!'

I reply that I have already sent this – one of the many – Biedasseks a letter and received no response. I had also found this phone number online but hadn't wanted to call it. It felt like an invasion: cold-calling people at their homes. But now I've had a glass or two of wine and Flora is there to join me on WhatsApp video as I pick up the receiver … why not? Let's just make the call.

'What should I say?' I ask, trembling. How do I ask him if he was in the Second World War? There are still so many taboos around the subject.

Flora says, 'Just call.'

I do. It's probably a different Karl. He would have to be 100 years old now. I expect there will be no dial tone. But, no, there is one and it rings three times, and my heart is pounding. And I can see Flora reacting too in the window of my phone, to the sounds on speakerphone, and then my heart leaps when a voice is heard on the other side.

'Biedassek,' a woman replies. Her voice is old but clear.

I explain in German all the things I had written in my query letter. And I ask, does that sound familiar?

The woman does not sound surprised to receive my call. I know from her tone she's received the letter already. 'It's such a long time since my husband died,' she says.

A shiver passes through me. I tell her that we found his diary. That it was written in France during the war. Does that ring a bell?

'There are things that I don't want to know about.' She has a very cool tone, replying firmly, to put an absolute end to our conversation.

I know at that moment that I have found Karl's wife. The man is no longer something almost fictional, a mystery in code, but the deceased husband of the woman on the phone. But I know also that she is not Louise. Where is she now? This woman speaks in perfect high German. And I also know that it is the end of the discussion. Anything more would be an invasion.

I quickly thank her for her time and hang up.

But then I feel I hung up too quickly. Like I've lost a chance. What could I have said? I think of that French saying: *esprit d'escalier.* I'm sure Karl knew the expression. The thoughts on the stairwell, the thing you should have said. But I just can't think of what magic phrase would have changed everything.

'Could I have said more?' I ask Flora. 'Could I have asked more? Maybe she doesn't want to learn about a love affair with another woman. I should have emphasised our research …'

'Most men have had another woman in their lives,' says Flora, flatly.

I want to call her back. Does she think the journal has accounts of atrocities? I understand why she might be afraid of the Nazi era. Can I tell her it's a story of public importance, of a man who resisted? But I already said so much in the letter. Perhaps she is sensitive to the deserter's stigma. I want to tell her that she is perhaps the only one who can fill in another fifty years of the narrative for us. But I also know that I cannot call again.

'She was adamant, Joseph. Germans have trouble with their past.'

I am so disappointed I want to cry. I am also a little angry because the person I spoke to is denying history. But is that not her right? A dilemma poses itself: Karl is a historical subject and I am allowed to tell his story. But he was also the husband of a woman who now very clearly expressed her wishes to me.

I do not know you, Frau B. But I do not want you to wake up one day embarrassed by your husband's love affair in a book. For this reason, I have changed our protagonist's name. Let's call him Karl. I do not know what happened after 1946 – only that he survived and that he married someone new – but it is your right to keep that information to yourself.

Nonetheless, I feel like we have just lost something.

Or maybe, we were the ones who found it.

A Recipe Book

'Have you ever talked to a historian, or a journalist, before?' I ask.

'A *Spiegel* journalist tried to interview me once. But when I told him I wouldn't talk about politics, he got up and left.'

'Well then, we will have to talk about something else, won't we,' I consider. 'So tell me, is there an ordinary object that tells your life?'

She pauses, and replies, 'Well, it would have to be a recipe book. A book of recipes. Except a good cook doesn't write down her recipes. So, I'm sorry I can't help you.'

'Instead of talking about politics, maybe we can talk about food? And as far as your belonging is concerned – your recipe book – maybe we can write one?'

A Very Interesting Story

A month earlier, Ana called me up on the phone. 'Joseph, there's someone you need to meet.'

Ana is a high-school friend and we found ourselves both living in Berlin. She explains that she has been volunteering with a local social service, cooking for elderly Berliners and visiting them in their homes. 'Come and help out next week at lunch. I'll explain everything then.' She gives me an address, a time, and hangs up.

A week later in Kreuzberg, I find myself in the social service's lunchroom, in what must once have been a basement flat, preparing for the elderly to arrive: peeling potatoes, cutting carrots, with water boiling for bouillon cubes. A people carrier pulls up outside and the old women – all in their late eighties or nineties – are cast down the ramp to the basement, chatting between themselves, delighted to see the young people, and finding their places at the table in a room that is now a fug of soup smells.

I stand at the door to the kitchen watching them until I am elbowed by an older organiser, very stressed, who has been barking orders while the young people – apparently inured to the organisation's hierarchy – obey. Many of them have faraway looks in their eyes and crosses hanging from their necks. A pile of leaflets on one table explains how to leave one's inheritance to the charity instead of one's family.

But no matter. The old ladies are cheery, teasing me out from my corner, greeting me with a 'Hello, young man,' which strikes me as funny as I am about 40. Then again, I'm less than half their age. So sure: 'young man' suits me just fine.

'You sit here,' Ana indicates, relieving me of my kitchen duties. I have old women to each side, each focused on me.

'From Canada!'

'Are you married?'

'Don't ask so many questions, Ingrid.'

'Well, is he?'

The soup is served, and the woman across from me sighs, passing her spoon through the broth, and I notice how her right arm is bound up in a tensor bandage. The ceiling light pools around her, illuminating her hair, short and grey, coiffed regally. She is like a wounded English royal. The Queen Mother recuperating after a horse-riding accident.

'Erna,' she introduces herself, and we chit-chat. I ask if she is a Berliner, and she replies, with a laugh, 'Only for a little less than eighty years!'

Erna tells me that where she grew up, on a large farm, is now Poland. Her family ran a tavern there. She drinks and recounts how they had servants, how she was destined to marry a large landowner. 'I was a princess!' she recalls, one hand to her temple. Erna speaks with a German that is crisp and upper class, old-fashioned. It's not a style of speaking you hear very often today. Is she putting on airs? Maybe, after all, she really is a princess!

The realities of country life in the New March region of East Brandenburg were not so glamorous; her mother decreed she must learn 'what work is' and help on the farm and in the kitchen, 'so that I would know later how to handle my own servants'. Erna passes her spoon through the soup again, it seems critically. 'Maybe I'll have a little more wine.'

She is not the only one filling up her glass, even though it's only 12.30 p.m. The ladies are laughing and joking, and Erna warns me, leaning over with a sneaky voice – 'Young man, you shouldn't pay too much attention to just me, or the others will be jealous.' Then she whispers, even lower, as if she has one up on them, 'Although, you know, I have a *very* interesting history.'

'Really?' I reply, wondering what intrigued Ana so much, as I lean in closer.

Erna grows hushed and serious. 'A *very* interesting history. I was' – dramatic pause – 'the wartime cook of the *Reichsminister* for Propaganda, Dr Goebbels.'

I proceed to knock over my glass.

This is how I met Joseph Goebbels' wartime cook, quite by accident.

A Secret Recipe

'Let me tell you a story,' she says, glancing at the other women, who are now long in the face, observing us glumly. We are in that lull between lunch and coffee. I ignore the glares of the charity organiser who would prefer I help in the kitchen. I don't need caffeine. I'm listening to Erna.

'Oh, what is the name of that street?' – Erna's left hand reaches for the arm of her neighbour as if the grip will transmit the information – 'the one that runs from near the Brandenburg Gate towards Potsdamer Platz?'

'Ebertstraße?' I propose.

'No, they've all changed names now.' She shakes her head, her eyes closed.

Ebertstraße was called Hermann-Göring-Straße under the Nazis. I drink more wine.

Then a light goes on and she pronounces – as if it's set in stone, reassured the memory has returned – 'Wilhelmstraße! *Die* Wilhelmstraße. That is where the Doctor had his Ministry.'

I can't count the number of times, when interviewing the older generation about their wartime experiences, that they return to a place or a belonging to find their memories. For the historian, recalling places and objects is strategic: you can invoke memories long buried by asking them 'Have you ever been *here*?' or a simple question such as, 'Tell me about your favourite dress?' They might not remember the street name – more often than not they don't – but the place still reappears before them – a palace, a building, a work office, a bedroom, a kitchen – as if it contains the memory itself. It is as if by just walking into that room that memory will become clear to them, just as it would by putting on that dress. I wonder too how that room – or the size of the dress – changes with the number of times a story has been told. The one Erna tells me now strikes me as one of her favourites.

It is the tale of two cooks: Erna and an ageing one at the Nazi Ministry of Propaganda on Wilhelmstraße. At the height of the bombing of Berlin during the Second World War, Joseph Goebbels attended to a matter of extreme delicacy and consulted both about the improvement of his salad dressing. It was not quite to his liking at the Ministry, and his young cook, Erna Mußack, who commanded the kitchen at his lakeside home north of Berlin, possessed the necessary intelligence. Goebbels instructed the older cook to contact her immediately for the secret recipe.

Erna went to Wilhelmstraße in central Berlin. Getting off on Unter den Linden – Berlin's symbol, the Brandenburg Gate, rising before her – she turned down the windy corner of Wilhelmstraße to Goebbels' Ministry. The complex was the headquarters of Goebbels' mass-media campaign of censorship and antisemitism: the war for the hearts and minds of Germans, to promote Hitler's cult of personality, and bring the *Volk* in line with his extremist world view. Most of the old Ministry was destroyed in the last weeks of the war. Only the Nazi extension at the back has survived.

I wonder if this is where she entered to meet the old cook. Is it here she keeps her recipe?

'What happened at the Ministry?' I ask.

'Ah,' she sighs, finishing her coffee. 'The cook at the Ministry was told by Dr Goebbels that he would like her to make the salad the way that Erna Mußack makes it.'

'What was this cook like?'

'She said I was much too young to teach her anything. I was only twenty-four at the time, and she in her forties.'

'You didn't get to tell her the recipe?'

'Oh no, I did. I told her you take vinegar and sugar and oil and salt and pepper; you do it as you can imagine it's done.'

'That's the recipe?'

'No, *natürlich nicht*. There's a trick, and it tastes much better that way. But why should I have just given that away? No cook gives things away for free.' She laughs, leaning back.

And so, the Minister would have to wait until he was home in the evenings for a salad that satisfied him. Not even one of Nazi Germany's most powerful men could get his way when it came to a stubborn cook.

I laugh too, but what I'm really thinking about is what else she can tell me about Goebbels, about matters more important than a salad dressing: about his political dealings, about his family life, about why he and his wife murdered their children. But the warning that 'no cook gives things away for free' strikes me as, well … inauspicious.

'Have you ever talked to a historian, or a journalist, before?' I ask, and, as we converse about her experience with the *Spiegel* journalist, I think about why we have collected so many stories of victims from this period, but so few from bystanders or perpetrators. Let the victim speak, don't give a platform for the aggressor. Many also feel contaminated by the perpetrator's presence. Is there not something awful about talking to someone who lived in the same house as the Goebbels family for years, and who has now grown old, lived a long life, and goes about daily tasks, it appears, unimpeded by this bad past?

I lean back and watch her, having listened to this little story about something seemingly as banal as salad dressing, and think that *not* to talk to her would be a disservice. I even think that – if I liked it – I would make Goebbels' dressing sometimes when I prepare a salad, even though I know a man like Joseph Goebbels liked it as well. I am not a superstitious person. I don't think for a moment it would poison me. I am willing to listen to his cook, now in her late nineties, even if she worked for a Nazi.

'May *I* ask the recipe?' I propose, with a wink.

'Ah, the recipe.' Her voice grows low, as if we have reached a crucial moment.

'Will you tell me the trick?'

'Come and visit,' she says, knowing she has me now. '*Maybe* I'll tell you then.'

The Pigeon

A few weeks pass, and Ana and I pay a visit to Frau Erna Jokisch, née Mußack, at her home on Delbrückstraße. She lives in Nazi-era housing on a street just outside the S-Bahn tracks in Neukölln, a blue-collar Berlin neighbourhood. Up the tidy stairs, Erna's apartment is cosy and full of pictures, with a ceramic furnace in the corner and mismatching furniture – including a formidable throne: a beige La-Z-Boy armchair with oversized headrest. Erna wears a lime green blouse, with broad lapels that would look good under a pea coat, and a dark wool skirt. Her right arm is still bound in its tensor bandage, and I think of how many years she spent stirring pots in kitchens.

Again, I notice something regal about her; she even has the sovereign's jowls. But I imagine the Queen Mum sent to the scullery and acquiring the hardness and ailments that come from manual labour. In her white pleather purse, the kind one expects to be bottomless, Erna carries a photograph with her everywhere. It is of the Goebbels children, and a photo I have not been able to find anywhere else. (And no, not even a Google image search turns it up.)

Erna tells me she took the picture herself; she has both the original and an enlargement and gives them to me to record with my camera. Now and again, she takes one or the other out, to show the curious, and she smiles gazing over the six children, in a row, dressed in white. The children look very thin. I keep examining their pencil-like legs and just how white the socks are that cover them. I wonder why Erna smiles looking at this picture, instead of weeping. I can't help but think of how Joseph and Magda Goebbels, in what must be modern history's most famous instance of infanticide, murdered their children, as Berlin fell to the Red Army.

'Do you mind being filmed?' I ask Erna, and she replies, no – quite the contrary – she is delighted, protesting only that she doesn't look quite like she once did. She points to a framed photograph on the wall, of herself at the age of about 25, from the time when she worked for the Goebbels family. I see those firm cheeks and features, like porcelain. 'Look how beautiful I am,' she says of the portrait. 'Look! I had no lipstick, everything was natural.'

Ana has brought pastries and a super-concentrated concoction of banana-cherry juice. Its sugar content will propel us through hours of conversation. Erna arranges them on a side table, next to the telephone, which rings. In a musing voice, the old cook says, '*Meine liebe* Charlotte, I have a young man visiting. And you know, when I have a young man here, I can't speak.' And then she laughs at me winking, before hanging up.

Then something odd happens.

Erna sits facing a picture window, where outside is a long balcony. We are facing south, and the light is not particularly bright this mid-April afternoon, so I wonder why Erna keeps looking up, it seems nervously or distractedly. It's almost as if someone is there, as if she is worried about being overheard. I put it down to a tic in a woman who is otherwise still whip-sharp. But then, all at once, I am taken off guard. What she is looking for catches her attention, and a current runs through her body, and her arm bolts up, outstretched, in what looks like a Nazi salute.

Both Ana and I pull back. Perplexed, I look behind me. And, staring back, through the window, is an enormous bird.

'Go back where you came from!' she cries.

The overfed pigeon – seeing or hearing her – follows her command. It opens its wings and falls right off the balcony.

Erna shakes her head, lowers her arm and resumes her position. She continues speaking as if nothing strange has occurred.

But a chill has come over me. Was it a fitting reincarnation, or a visitation? Perhaps a warning? I'm not sure; I am a logical person and don't believe in hocus pocus. But I wonder whether she thinks that – through the glass – someone is listening over our shoulders. I wonder who she imagines it is. I wonder how much she will tell me.

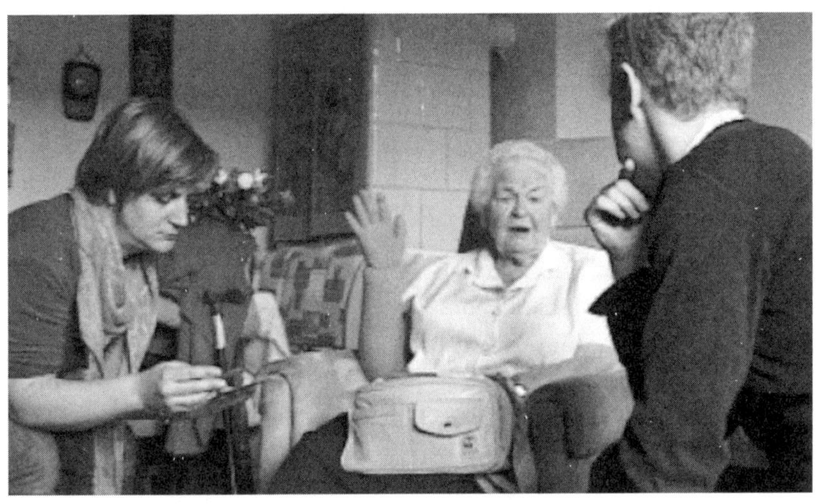

A Minister's Breakfast

Politics, I suspect, was very much a part of the daily choices of the Goebbels' life. But, as I begin to ask my political questions, I notice that Erna changes the topic. It's a problem, because I have prepared a detailed list regarding the Nazi leadership, the identity of dinner guests, their conversations, the household opinions about Hitler, Germany and the Final Solution, and even whether she ever thought of poisoning her boss. But Erna really will have none of it. She was in the kitchen the whole time: 'What did I know about politics? I didn't hear anything of what they said!'

Feigned ignorance – rehearsed, convenient – is familiar to Second World War historians working in oral history. Anyone who has heard, for example, filmmaker Leni Riefenstahl's remarkably sophistic testimonies is impressed by how skilfully she learned to dodge difficult questions. Like Riefenstahl, Erna tells me that she was never a member of the party (I later checked and confirmed this). But am I not confronted by the woman who was – if you think on an elemental level – most essential to Joseph Goebbels' well-being? Someone else could have fed him. But in the end, it happened to be the woman before me who kept him alive.

I already know there's a way around this.

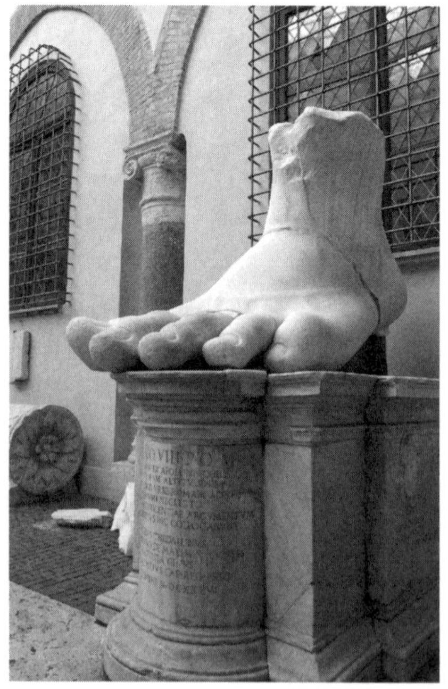

'What did he like to eat?' I ask.

Then she suddenly leans back, her arms open, as if to say, 'Now we are talking.' And I know that if I want to learn about the relationship between politics, Joseph Goebbels, and his family life, it is not going to happen by asking direct questions. It will happen, strangely, by talking instead about food. I think of the old classical adage: *ex pede Herculem*. You'll have to reconstruct the statue of Hercules just from the foot. Except in my case, it will be from the stomach.

The method of using an object to elicit stories about the past would be different than when looking at my grandfather's knife or Karl's diary. This is a variation on the theme. With the bayonet, I worked archaeologically, from etchings and symbols on a blade. The approach to the diary was similar, until it was decipherable as a document, illuminating differences between material history and written history. How would everyday recipes open up stories about the past differently, with the owner sitting right before me? Just as Erna's memories were unlocked by mentioning a particular place or street, I thought that recipes could also trigger memories. The knife had been a key and the recipes would be a strategy. As it turned out, some of what she told me about herself and the family did not require a discussion of cooking techniques. The strategy was needed when the conversation became too obviously political for her liking.

So: *quickly, quickly*, what can I ask about food that will explain the political fundamentalism of this family? To understand why he and his wife eventually killed their children on the eve of the Fall of Berlin? Could I really learn all this by asking her what he had for breakfast?

You have to start somewhere, don't you, so why not: 'What did he have for breakfast?'

Erna smiles and gets comfortable in her lounge-throne, preparing for what promises to be a long explanation on a favourite topic, and she tells me that, during the war, for breakfast, 'Dr Goebbels loved having a poached egg in a glass, cooked for three to four minutes, then butter on bread, or a bun, depending on what was there. And he drank tea. And he had every morning a tablet of glucose, a strengthening pill. He ate what was there, but he didn't have cheese and meat for breakfast. That was for dinner.' And she explains that when there were problems procuring butter, she would furnish from her own supply – her family was out in the countryside and could provide – 'Me personally, I got some extra when the Ministry didn't send butter. I really couldn't do breakfast without butter.'

And she gazes at me with a look that invites understanding and commiseration, as if the crux of the issue here is how terrible breakfast might be without butter. And I nod, meanwhile thinking, behind my eyes: I can imagine many things I'd prefer happen to Joseph Goebbels in 1943 rather than him not getting bread with butter in the mornings.

And what to do with the information she's imparted?

I sit back, holding my glass of oversweet juice, not sure what to do. For why should I care what he had for breakfast? I'm starting to sympathise with that *Spiegel* journalist. I try to imagine Joseph Goebbels sitting in his study, the breakfast on a tray, served next to a stack of important papers, or the fastidious diary he kept. Isn't there a reason why every other historian has focused on these important documents instead of the butter melting off his bread? After all, a poached egg, lonely in that glass, is just some banal fuel for a body. And his thoughts – intent on how the printed press, the radio, and the arts could disseminate hate through a society, and facilitate the destruction of millions of outsiders, or aid the propaganda war against the Allies – are arguably separate from his bodily needs. Is not his body some strange, coldly alien, and meaningless vehicle for his destructiveness? Why should I focus on the bodily needs of that club-footed minister – that leathery, hyenine physique (that I find very hard to imagine was attractive to women), down whose throat a half-cooked chicken embryo slithered each morning?

Or is there not something else, after all, worth knowing from a poached egg?

A Vacancy for a Cook

Erna Luise Selma Mußack was born on 10 February 1919 in Nieder-Lübbichow, Neumark (today's Lubiechów Dolny, Poland, a place of thick forests and ruddy baked-brick farmhouses). Erna's transition from the countryside to the capital is veiled in a little secrecy. She came to Berlin at the age of 17, in 1937, and stayed, although her mother was 'very much against it'. It was the year following the Olympics, and Berlin was celebrating its 700th anniversary, where she witnessed 'the celebrations of Adolf Hitler and the SS'.

To remain in Berlin, she needed to make money. She asked herself: 'What do you want to do? What have you learned?' And, by accident, she ended up working in a retirement home for elderly aristocratic women, where she became their cook, preparing meals daily for sixteen to twenty people. 'It was a lot of work, but the conditions were good,' Erna tells me.

When the home closed, she went to work for six years for the widow of a Berlin tax chief, one Frau Günther, who, although she was not blue-blooded herself, was connected to such noble circles, which gave Erna an entrée to the Berlin high life. Erna's job was that of a maiden companion, simply to provide company, and she accompanied the old lady wherever she went.

'How was the atmosphere in Berlin at the time?' I ask her.

'When I think about it now, I think it was good, but back then I didn't because I had to be home every night by ten! I didn't find that very good!'

'Why was that?' Ana asks.

'Something could have happened to me!' The old woman looks over me, and again she winks.

Erna and Frau Günther's life oscillated between the domestic and the debonair. They would sit together at breakfast, read the *Morgenpost*, and their mail, and then Erna would go choose vegetables at the market. People in the street knew who she was, and she would take a while stopping and chatting with them. The morning would pass, and by the time she was back from shopping, it was already noon, the table would be set, and they would sit for lunch.

Over the meal, the old lady would pipe up and say, 'We are going to Berlin!' And Erna would respond, 'But we are already in Berlin!' But for the old lady, Berlin did not mean the suburb of Schmargendorf; it meant dressing up and going into the centre, to Tauentzienstraße. The luxury department store Kaufhaus des Westens, or KaDeWe, had the Silver Terrace, where tables were all decked with white, with cloth napkins, where the staff wore black suits, and you could sit in the corner, and no one would bother you, unless you lifted a finger, when – in an instant – a waiter would appear, with a piece of cake or a glass of Sekt. Then, they would stroll across from KaDeWe, where there was a *Tageskino*, or 'daytime cinema', and the old lady would watch movies. Twice a month they would go to the theatre, but sometimes they saw three movie screenings in a day.

'I had something of a figure,' Erna laughs, 'and I was very exposed in society: and I met through the old woman artists, theatre people, film people.' She became acquainted with the Austrian film actress Hilde Krahl – 'We had lots of things in common, except … back then I was more attractive than she was, back then she was really ugly.'

Then suddenly, in 1943 – the war having already raged for almost four years – Erna no longer had work. Frau Günther's daughter's marriage had fallen apart after twenty years. Erna intimates, 'I was around for all of that, we'd be here two days if I had to explain it all.' The daughter demanded that the mother move in with her for company.

'So, I wanted to find a new job. I said … I am going to do something completely different. I am going to work in an office.' She declined an offer from an officer in the *Oberkommando* of the *Wehrmacht*, who was a little too fresh with her, and found herself instead at the *Arbeitsamt*, or job centre, where she followed the usual bureaucratic procedure of going to get her book stamped to receive an unemployment allowance.

'What? You are a cook? That won't do,' the bureaucrats at the job centre insisted, telling her she should be at work. Now, Erna speaks quickly, and relates what they said next: 'Dr Goebbels is looking for a cook and you must go to him.' The position might have been a replacement for the Goebbels' previous cook at their estate, Ella, who 'really got on one's nerves' because of her forgetfulness.

Erna shrugs, looking away from me. 'I didn't want to go, and they wouldn't stamp the book, and so I got one card from the *Arbeitsamt*, and then the second, and then the third, and it said: we have no other options for you.'

'I went to Frau Goebbels, Magda, in her private city apartment, in Berlin. I was asked into the yellow room, the chairs were really very small, tiny Japanese style divans, and why? Because it's posh, upper-class. That's how the world works' – and here she growls – '*Vornehm!*' The upper crust. 'In any case, I didn't want to sit on such a small chair.'

But sit she did.

'I was alone when Magda came into the room. I explained everything: the reasons I didn't want to take the job. And she replied: you are so sweet, please come to us in any case. Magda said that'.

This is how she says she was introduced into the employment of the household of Joseph and Magda Goebbels.

I have a knack, I think, as a historian, for knowing when I'm not getting the whole story. I don't take it personally. Witnesses, elderly or young, often inhabit the past as a fantasy world. Verifying Erna's story with documents was, thankfully, a series of eureka moments. Almost everything that she tells me matches – even minor details that could only possibly be known by someone with a minute and specialist familiarity with the historical record, or from having lived the moment itself. She accurately illustrates peculiar details of the layout of the Goebbels' home at Lanke, such as the interior of the cook's quarters that have been closed to the public. She knows the names of Goebbels' staff. She attests to the little-known presence of a French war prisoner on the grounds. Her descriptions of family life are corroborated by those of other historical witnesses. Her photograph of the children, in a private moment, that she says she took herself, I have found nowhere else, and gives additional weight to the veracity of her story. But her introduction to the Goebbels struck me as odd.

How is it that a young woman, connected to aristocratic Berlin society, to military generals, to the widows of high officials of finance, and then to the world of theatre and cinema – which was precisely the domain of the Propaganda Ministry – fell into a job at the Goebbels family home just by accident? Did she really get this job by going to the job centre? Or is this just another episode of rehearsed: 'I did not collaborate willingly'; 'I had no choice in the matter'?

But this is how she says she came to be working on the Goebbels villa, located in the woods about 20 miles north of Berlin.

The House at Lanke

Leaving the city in a saloon car, reflections of the metropolis rush by on the windows. Soon there is the encroaching stillness, the trees become dark shadows, and the growl of the engine sounds louder with the lost roar of traffic. Fog rolls in over the lakes and sand, and the lights of the car create a penumbra. Past a country rail crossing, one drives deeper into the woods, to a turn-off, the road plunging, then rising, to where the light pours down on to the threshold. Inside the villa on the lake, there was the family.

After a few years of living between the Berlin apartment, in the centre of the capital's rush, and the residence in Schwanenwerder – in the lakeside suburbia of the city's rich and famous – in October 1936 the Goebbels were given a relatively isolated and rural residence at Lanke on the Bogensee, a lake 25 miles north of Berlin.

Bogensee was more than a good deal for the Goebbels. Originally the *Stadtgut* was a birthday gift from the city and Goebbels had it at his disposal for life. The house's costs were billed to UFA (the German film company), so the place became a business expense. The move there was well timed, as Magda now found herself and the family far away from the doctor's romantic entanglements in the city.

Bogensee was described by the Nazi newspaper *Der Angriff* as a 'simple wooden cabin along a quiet lake near Berlin', fitting Goebbels' modest public image. In actuality, according to Goebbels' biographer Peter Longerich, it was a 'four-room timber house with various outbuildings, situated in the middle of a large forest plot on the Bogensee'. Over the years, it became more lavish: the space transformed in 1939 into a thirty-room house with a forty-room service building and garage, sixty telephones, and movie theatre. The interior decoration, one might say, was 'Frank Lloyd Wright meets fascist classicism', with an Old Mother Hubbard cottage entrance portal that was both woodsy and *völkisch*. Taken altogether, the space was either eclectic or a farrago depending on taste.

'It will be wonderful but is unfortunately too expensive' – or so wrote Goebbels in his diary on 18 March 1939. The refurbishment had a projected cost of 2.3 million Reichsmarks. The luxurious transformation of the wood cabin was epitomised by the hanging of a Gobelin tapestry worth 800,000 Reichsmarks on the wall. Erna's kitchen was located in the western wing of the main house; it had a door through a service room into a muted, minimal dining hall, with terrace letting out to the lawn.

The surrounding landscape was atmospheric, and Goebbels referred several times in his diaries to the fog, such as in November 1936: 'In the middle of the forest. The quiet develops a voice of its own. Back to Berlin in the fog.' And 'I work, read, write and am happy. All around me is woodland, faded leaves, fog, rain. An idyll in loneliness.' The family moved there on a more permanent basis after the bombing raids of the summer of 1943 on Hamburg. In Bogensee the children had parkland, farmland, animals to play with; they went to school by pony and cart.

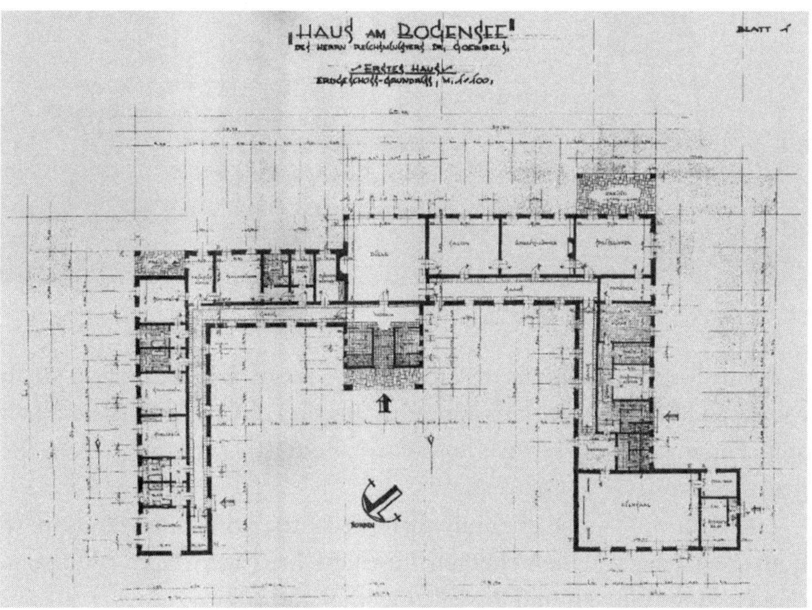

Erna has an insider's understanding of the complex's layout. 'It was a big house built in a horseshoe form,' she tells me, 'and over the kitchen was my apartment. Living room, bedroom and bath. And the other staff were in another house; I was the only one in the main house.' I have examined the plans for the house, and since visited its remains, walking around and peeking into the boarded-up windows. It is indeed built in this shape, and I saw how after the 1939 renovations – and this is a detail easily overlooked – that there is an upstairs apartment installed in the roof of only this part of the building. You can see it quite clearly from the outside.

According to the plans, it had a living room, bedroom, two small rooms, and bath, whose stairs appear to descend directly into the kitchen area. The forty-room service house was about 100 yards away from the main building.

Life with the Goebbels family furnished Erna with close exposure to both the parents and their children. I imagine Erna and Magda taking one of their long walks around the lake together and talking.

A few words are necessary here about the infamous couple: Joseph and Magda.

'How was Magda's character?' I ask.

And Erna describes the Minister's wife: 'I could talk to her,' but she was an indecisive person who 'didn't know what she wanted to eat or drink the next day; it was all up to me.' Indeed, Magda apparently couldn't cook to save her life, and once when Erna was ill, Magda's mother, Auguste, was required to intervene, recounting later, 'It wasn't easy at all.'

I wonder whether the closeness between Erna and Magda came from the fact that they had more in common than either might have liked to admit. Auguste worked as a cleaner but gave the Bülowstraße address of her wealthy employers as Magda's place of birth (her daughter was actually born in poorer Kreuzberg, on 11 November 1901, making her almost twenty years Erna's elder). Magda changed identities more than once in her life: she returned to Germany from education at a convent in Belgium with a French accent. Her politics changed with time: having an affair with a Zionist intellectual (who was later murdered) did not complicate becoming the 'first lady' of the Nazi Reich. She married strategically, which enabled transformations in her class status and wealth. Günther Quandt, whom she married in 1921, at the age of 19, was twice her age.

'She only married Quandt for money,' Erna tells me. 'I only heard a lot about it through the aristocracy; they were not of that class, they were lower. But financially, Quandt was very high up, because he had assets. But he was not noble. That explains why he wasn't so well thought of in our circles. Magda and her mother went to Paris to see if she could find a man, and they met Quandt there, but he was twenty years older than she was. And that's how it happened.'

The marriage did not last long. She had had a son, Harald, by him, but they divorced amicably in 1929. Two years later, in December 1931, she married Joseph Goebbels, having met him – according to the literature – at a party rally in the Sportspalast in Berlin (Erna holds instead to the rumour that Goebbels met Magda as Harald Quandt's private tutor).

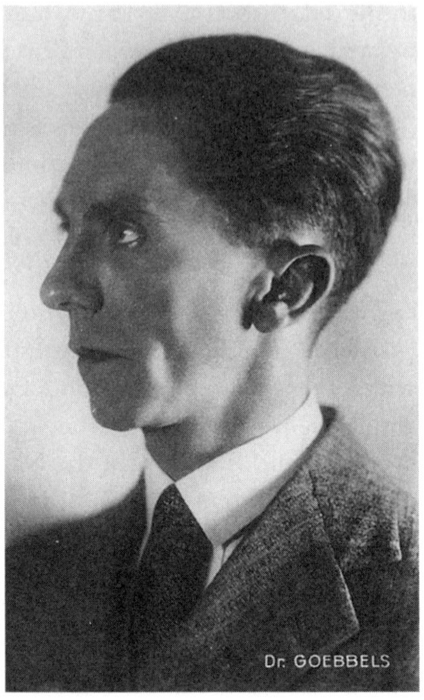

Just before the Goebbels' marriage, Adolf Hitler took a shine to Magda. Hitler caused Goebbels 'agonising jealousy', or so he wrote in his diary on 4 September 1931. Longerich speculates that in the end the three came to an arrangement. Although Goebbels would marry Magda, in practice she would become Hitler's social escort. Goebbels, meanwhile, was terribly in love with her, but not so much that it interfered with his political aspirations. He wrote, 'First comes the party, then Magda' (*Erst kommt die Partei, dann Magda*).

When you read histories of their private lives together, there are two dominant themes: infidelity and their children. Magda is often characterised in this story as the victim, although she too was not a picture of faithfulness. I ask Erna if there were problems in the relationship between Magda and Goebbels. 'Oh yes, there was lots of cheating. But that didn't interest me. We had a good relationship,' she adds, speaking of Magda and herself.

There are the things you almost always see in a Joseph Goebbels biography and one is a picture of the Czech actress Lída Baarová, usually in a showgirl dress, her shapely bare legs emerging from a jungle of pom-poms. She was, conveniently, one of Goebbels' neighbours at Schwanenwerder.

There is a quite famous story related to Lída Baarová, who had been dating the director Gustav Fröhlich. Erna tells me that Goebbels was slapped by the jealous man when he discovered Lída's infidelity. 'It could have turned out badly if Goebbels really wanted it to, [Fröhlich] could have landed in prison.'

The Baarová incident almost destroyed the Goebbels' marriage. Joseph Goebbels' dabbling in polyamory did not have the agreement of his wife, who sought a divorce. On 10 May 1936, Goebbels was writing in his diary that his marriage was '*zum kotzen*' (or 'vomit-worthy'), also because

of Magda's infidelities. By the summer of 1938, Hitler had to intervene to keep the couple together when Goebbels threatened to go to Japan as ambassador with Baarová in tow. Hitler, not wanting to lose his minister, organised a reconciliation with Magda, and Goebbels allowed 'both of us again to be brought under the will of the Führer'. After this point, in October, however, the marriage became one of convenience.

Magda, meanwhile, was having a 'passionate love affair' with – in a telenovela twist – one of her husband's most trusted advisors: Karl Hanke, Goebbels' adjutant since 1932, and later state secretary. He had been instrumental in practical matters in the past, having found the Bogensee house for Goebbels' family. During the Baarová affair, Magda turned to him for support, and he in turn compiled for her a list of her husband's affairs, so that she could revenge herself if necessary, even confronting Hitler himself about the matter. Hanke was shot by Czech partisans in the last days of the war after he briefly became the *Reichsführer* of the SS.

Erna suspects that one of the Goebbels daughters, born after the period of the Baarová affair – Hedwig (nicknamed Hedda), the blonde-haired second youngest, born on 5 May 1938 – was not Dr Goebbels'. 'I still say today that this daughter was not his. A senior SS officer often came to visit, and he would sit at an extra table with Magda, not with the kids. And when he was there, then Hedda was always called over. I thought he was the father.'

Apfeleierkuchen

'What were the kids like?'

'They were so lovely,' replies Erna.

'How many of them were there?'

'There were six.'

'And their names?'

Erna replies, an automatic patter, using nicknames. 'Helga, Hilde, Helmut, Holde, Hedda, Heide.'

'Do you still have the photograph of the children?'

'Yes, it's in my purse.' She starts looking for it.

'Do you always have it with you? As a memory?'

'People often ask me for it. I have to see where it is.' She rummages in her bag and finds one envelope, then another, which contains the enlargement. 'Here are the children. You can hold it.'

Then she finds the other photograph. 'Here is the original. I took it. I just had it enlarged.'

'Where did you take it?' I ask, holding the photographs in my hands.

'Outside … It was at the *Stadtgut*, at Bogensee. Waldhof am Bogensee.'

I can see the house in the corner of the photograph. 'What was the event?'

'The mother was in the hospital and they came back dressed like that.'

'And why was she in hospital?'

'Go there and ask her!' Erna laughs. Then she replies seriously, 'Because of her nerves. She had something frozen in her face that needed to be operated. It could only be done secretly.'

'A nerve sickness?'

'This nerve was frozen, and it needed to be operated. A professor came to the house and was there a few days.'

'And what was the difference between them?' I ask, pointing at the children.

'They were not all the same. But they weren't strong little personalities either.'

The Goebbels children all had names beginning with 'H', possibly in honour of Hitler. The children were always political beings, in a sense, in that they had a propaganda purpose, appearing frequently in party films. Quite by accident, even the first child of Magda – from the Quandt marriage – was an 'H': Harald (born on 1 November 1921). Harald was a 'German youth' who was blond, athletic, so different from Goebbels, who nonetheless signed his letters to him 'your father'. Erna recounts of her time at Lanke, 'Harald wasn't there any more. He was called up. He was a pilot, and was shot down, and became a prisoner-of-war of the British.' He was the only one of the children to survive the war; today, his heirs are billionaires with high stakes in the German auto industry, such as BMW.

Goebbels had a special fondness for the eldest, Helga (born 1 September 1932), and historians put this down to her father's narcissism. The question of physiognomy was important to Goebbels, and he wrote that she was similar to him in looks and just as intelligent. She proved a bond between Hitler and Goebbels and was popular with the Führer: '[Hitler] says if Helga was twenty years older and he was twenty years younger, she would be the wife for him,' wrote Goebbels on 2 February 1937. Hitler, in those early years, was often at home with the Goebbels family and was intimately involved in Helga's upbringing. Erna, when pointing to the Helga in the picture, tells me that 'she had to learn the piano. But she didn't want to. But she had to. She said, "why do I need to learn it? I will marry a farmer, and the cow can learn to play the piano."'

When Hildegard (Hilde) was born (on 13 April 1934), Goebbels was at first disappointed she was a girl, but then was full of 'joy and happiness'. Hitler went to Magda and saw the child even before Goebbels did, and the Minister noted that 'the Führer was again alone in getting it right. It's a girl.' Hilde was her grandmother Auguste's favourite child because she 'stood up for herself' and because of her sweet love of animals.

The third child was Helmut, born on 2 October 1935, and Goebbels was overjoyed to have a son, and also with his physiognomy ('And there was the small one, with a Goebbels face' – one wonders whether he was already afraid that the fathers might be other men). He wrote the next day he 'could break everything for joy. A boy! A boy! To bring home.' But Goebbels would later be disappointed because Helmut proved slow and had problems at school. His father is, in fact, more affectionate than some commentators suggest, even on occasions such as when he writes on 30 July 1938 – barbed – that his son is a 'thick-headed good for nothing, so sweet and nice'. And on 4 December 1944, Goebbels is delighted to report that, when Hitler subjects the 9-year-old to an exam about the war and its origins, his son 'passes with flying colours … especially for such a young boy'.

Holdine (Holde) was born on 19 February 1937. She was weak, suffering lung infections at first, and was later taunted by her siblings as '*doof und langweilig*' (silly, stupid, boring). Even her grandmother said she was 'the only dumb one in our family'. Hedwig (or Hedda) – the one Erna suspects was not Dr Goebbels' – was born on 5 May 1938, and Magda was the first to be decorated with the cross of German mothers, awarded to *kinderreiche Mütter* or multi-child mothers.

Heidrun (Heide) was born on 29 October 1940, Goebbels' own birthday – and Hitler showed up on 11 November. Heide has been called the 'reconciliation child' with the hope that she might heal the rift between the married pair. But she was known for being 'a real little beast' who loved to make her nanny angry. She would have been 3 and 4 years old when Erna worked in the kitchen.

'The smallest used to come to me and ask, "What are you making today?" and I would reply, "What do you want to eat?" and she would reply: "*Apfeleierkuchen*", or sweet apple fritters, and I'd say, "That doesn't work. I don't have enough eggs. And there are so many of you." Sometimes the older ones would go to the city, for some examination, or to the dentist, and I'd be left alone with the younger ones. And then she'd ask when the older ones were away: do we get the *Eierkuchen* today?'

This sweetness was not lost on the father. Longerich remarks that there are 'countless entries in his diary where [Joseph Goebbels] mentions romping around and horseplay with the "lovely", "sweet" children' but that these observations are 'remarkably stereotyped and superficial. Basically, he had little interest in their development and education. From time to time, though, he found himself obliged to give them a "thrashing" to beat the "stubbornness" out of them – as Goebbels saw it, a tried and tested educational method.' Family happiness comes to mean only part of 'his personal success story'. Indeed, Goebbels never writes so much about his children as when they are in the presence of Hitler (his greater focus of attention – such as on 4 December 1944) and often they appear as sidenotes to his reports on the progress of the war or work at the Ministry. But, on the other hand, there are also many remarks about how truly fulfilled and happy the man feels when he spends time alone with them. And late at night, they would watch films with their father.

I ask Erna if they were severe as parents.

Erna replies, 'No, he just didn't have a lot of time. He was often in his office. He had so many secretaries, adjutants, etc., he had little time … No, he was never strict. He was kind and sweet with the children. He acted like an educated person. He was born in the Rhineland and educated in a *Kloster* [abbey or parochial school]. But he was no holy man; he was no longer in the church. He was strictly brought up. [But the children] weren't at all.'

The one thing that Goebbels was strict about was religion. As a student, he tipped between German nationalism, idealism, and even communism. Like Magda, Joseph Goebbels came from a Catholic family, but they rejected their faith. Erna describes how he imposed his position on religion to those who worked for him at his house in Lanke: 'His people were not supposed to have anything to do with the church. Also his staff. There was a situation with one of his *Wachdienst* [round-the-clock security] men … They were a couple, about thirty years old, and were so happy they were going to have a child, and the lady had a little girl, but she was not supposed to be baptised. Everything that was faith was out.'

'That was supposed instead to be Nazi ideology?' I reply.

'Yes, the wife of this man really wanted her to be baptised and was so unhappy … I often spoke to him. And so, he explained to Goebbels: "My wife is so unhappy." And he replied: "Send your wife best wishes from me." Imagine: he's here the whole week on *Dienst* [duty], why should it matter what he does back in Berlin with his wife?'

Did the man manage to get his child baptised anyhow, against Goebbels' wishes? I wonder. Already I am starting to understand the extent to which the personal and the political were never separate in the Minister's mind.

Erna recounts yet another episode involving the household ban on religion. She tells me, 'The first year I was there, the children wanted an *Adventskranz*. You know what that is?'

I nod. The children wanted an advent wreath.

'So, they asked the gardener, a French war prisoner, if he could make them an *Adventskranz*. The kids came and were so excited. After we had lunch, I said, "Let's go into the forest" … I went with the big ones into the woods.' There, they secretly installed their Christian symbol. Interestingly, even Magda was involved in this activity which would displease the

Doctor. Then again, she had insisted they marry in a church, and had an interest in other religions, especially Buddhism.

'They tied it up at the top [of a tree]. And Magda said to me: "What can you not do?"' Erna then reflects that being capable, 'being able to do things', has been the one thing that has helped her most in life.

But I am interested: if Goebbels had strong ideas about religion, did he talk to them about politics as well? After all, he required opinions about the war from his 9-year-old son.

'No, he didn't have time for that, those few minutes when he was alone with the children,' she replies.

'Did people speak about politics in the home?'

'There was not even a Hitler salute [she raises her hand again]. Just *Guten Tag*, or *Guten Morgen*.'

'And did the children talk about politics?'

She dismisses me. 'Politics was not at all on the programme. They did not even get it at school.'

No, it's not at all on the programme. Or is it? The children attended mass rallies enthusiastically, after all. Then again, as historians suggest about these visits, they didn't 'understand everything' that was said at them.

I observe Erna in her armchair and my head starts to hurt a little. I'm feeling like I've had too much banana-cherry juice. So, it is good that I already have manoeuvres to get politics back 'on the programme'.

I turn the conversation away from the political discussions – the ones the children apparently did not have with their father – to pose my question strategically: how did she manage to cook so well for the family in a time of shortages?

Erna's eyes sparkle, as if she has a trick up her sleeve. 'Now, let me tell you …'

(False) Whipped Cream

There are some things that recipes alone can tell you. The close intertwining of politics and food gets us a little closer to the Goebbels' fanaticism, and the subsequent tragedy that would befall the family. This fanaticism was seen to some extent with the question of rationing. I begin to tease out the subject when I ask Erna about her budget and how she cooked for large numbers of people in a Germany where, as the Red Army approached, there were food shortages.

'Frau Goebbels didn't have any ideas about the kitchen,' she replies. 'So, I always had to organise and do the ordering. I would order meat on Fridays … No one believes me, everyone thinks we had our own budget because he was the Propaganda Minister. But he lived as he preached. And that was the crazy thing. How he was as a Nazi is a story of its own. But we used our own ration cards and the children had their butter for the quarter, and each had a little butter ration, and when someone took too much for their bread, there was no butter left for them. Each quarter when I received the deliveries, they would each get their portion, each had their own portion of sausage. Everything was measured.'

The children's nanny, Käthe Hübner, later remarked how one could tell the difference between the character of the children by how they managed their butter ration: some would save it, while the others would eat it right away.

'But as Minister of Propaganda surely he could have got more than that!'

'They didn't,' Erna insists. 'Me personally, I got some extra.' And here she is referring again to her own supplies.

Goebbels had been used to leading an expensive lifestyle, and Magda had had one also with Quandt. In the 1930s, Magda would buy expensive presents for the domestic help, 70–80 marks a present, and give them 400 marks in cash. The extravagant refurbishment of Lanke foresaw items for the kitchen as sophisticated as walk-in coolers, a refrigerated countertop for pastry (I'm sure Erna would have been thrilled), or even a special cooling room for beer, except these were nixed because the company could not deliver them on time without pushing back important military contracts. At the beginning of the war, Magda may have used public transport and cooked with ration cards. But the biographer Hans-Otto Meissner says that six months later she returned to her spending habits. Early in the war – in 1940, when Germany had had its string of victories – Germans did not feel any pinch in supplies of food and materials; in fact, they drained them from the whole Continent. Goebbels bought a Mercedes, 'a magnificent car' that he couldn't even drive because it was 'only suitable for peacetime' and the family was 'shielded from the worst of the everyday hardships that war entails … the war did not touch [Magda] directly to any great extent'. Air-raid provisions were luxurious, as were amenities in the house, including a stocked wine cellar. Meanwhile, Meissner mentions elaborate kitchen arrangements when Hitler was around (to cater for his famous vegetarianism) and that although 'during the war, Magda's table was simply set, she did not have the slightest idea what it was like to be dizzy from persistent hunger … she lived under an indestructible bell jar'.

For many, there was the assumption that the Goebbels family did not suffer the war like ordinary Germans. But with Germany's changing fortunes in the war, so did conditions in the household change. By the time Erna had arrived – even before then, from what she heard from her predecessor with whom she overlapped for fourteen days in 1943 – the Goebbels tried to live like other Germans. During this period, Magda planned to work at a Telefunken plant. As Magda's mother, who lived at Lanke, reports, the household provisions were remarkably meagre; they were 'not allowed to get even an extra gram of butter'. The butler collected rationing cards from guests. And when the Adlon Hotel made a present of a smoked ham to the family, 'which Magda placed without commentary on the dinner table, the "Doctor" came, stopped short, made big eyes, and was … hopping mad: "that's absolutely out of the question; we do not want, and we are not allowed, to live better than our ordinary national brethren. The ham will be brought back immediately!"' I have only found one mention of extravagance late in the war, and that was near the end, on 10 January 1945, when Magda put in an order for tailor-made shoes and expensive hats. I wonder if, at this point, she was aware that no amount of rationing would save her Nazi Germany.

Perhaps the best example of the new austerity is how the children ate. 'They were obliged to eat what was given to them,' Erna tells me. 'What came to the table they had to eat. There were dishes that Frau Goebbels didn't like to eat. And then she would get something extra. But it would be put on a separate table, not the one where the kids were eating.'

'And did they ever get a treat?'

'Well, the kids didn't know what it meant to have a piece of cake on Sunday. They had such a spartan upbringing you wouldn't believe it. I talked with my predecessor about it – and my God, a little piece of *Blechkuchen* [tray-baked cake] with a little fruit over it or *Streusel* [crumble] would make them so happy like kings. Then there was a situation when a kid had a birthday – I don't remember which child – and each child was allowed to invite one other child. They were already enough, the six of them, and then you had six more. Twelve!'

'One would think a minister could have a big party?'

'No, no, he didn't do a thing in these situations. So, the table was set, and the chambermaid was there, but not the butler who was only there when Goebbels was there (he was only for him). So, I made some cakes and hot chocolate (*Trinkschokolade*), and I made false whipped cream. The real stuff wasn't available.'

I'm curious. 'And how does one make false whipped cream?'

'I remember how to make it but I don't remember the exact quantities. You take skimmed milk and flour, and you cook it together. And when it is cooled you beat it and beat it and beat it again. And it looks like real cream. Because air comes into it. My poor kitchen maid; we didn't have electric gadgets back then, so she had to go upstairs into my room, into my bathroom, and in the flowing cold water, beat and beat. And then with sugar, it tasted – if you weren't too used to real cream, mind you – like whipped cream. And then when the bowl of whipped cream appeared, the children rejoiced and kissed us, and when Goebbels came for the weekend from Berlin, they told him: "*Pappa, pappa*, we had whipped cream." And he replied, "No, no, there is no whipped cream." "*Jawohl*, but we had whipped cream anyway." And he fought with them, "There is none!" and said, "There will never be whipped cream in this house!"'

Fricassee

Erna tells me three amusing stories from Bogensee. At first glance they might have little to do with politics – or do they? One is about dirty salad, the second is about being sneaky with the soup, and the final one is about cooking with a rabbit from the estate.

'I had a kitchen maid, a picture-perfect pretty girl who did everything I told her to do. There's this expression: *Da fehlte eine Tasse und die andere hatte auch noch einen Sprung*. "There was a cup missing, and the other one had a crack." It's what you say about someone who is not entirely there. But', and Erna smiles, 'she was picture-perfect.'

'When I asked her, Otti – is the roast in the oven? She would have to go and look and make sure it was still there. But she did do everything. But you had to tell her. And then we were making the salad, and I told her to make it, and she did, but she didn't wash the salad. I didn't notice. In such a kitchen, you can't keep your eyes on absolutely everything. I made the dressing and was mixing the salad in the bowl, and the butler took a few bowls to the Minister. Then I prepared the next batch of salad, making more with the dressing, and then one leaf fell out, and I picked it up and ate it, and I said: "Oh my god. Otti, why didn't you wash the salad?" And she replied: "You said only to get it ready!" And so, they ate it with the sand; nobody said anything.'

'Were there things he didn't eat? That he was allergic to?'

'No, he ate everything I gave him.' And then she goes on to tell me about dinners prepared in the kitchen.

But we are interrupted again by the enormous pigeon, which – rising from her seat – she salutes, before sitting down again. Ana and I glance at each other; by now we are getting used to the apparition.

'On Fridays, the meat was ordered, and I also got some brew bones for the soup. One day there was pudding, and then the next there was soup.' But she never served soup and dessert on the same day. 'I boiled the bones all week … and one day I made *Gebrannte Grießsuppe* [semolina soup]. You roast the semolina, then you add the brew, and cook it, and then you make a soup; it's a soup to drink.

'So, it was Friday, 10 a.m., and my phone rings, the Ministry is there, and says, the Chief [Goebbels] is coming out today, but with a large group: the officials, the secretaries, adjutants, etc., and he will arrive around noon. I'd spent all week boiling bones, and I ask myself: what can I possibly get out of these bones? I take them out, look inside, and see what I've got to work with. Then I had from my sister, personally, a little bowl of goose fat. And so, I added both to his [Dr Goebbels] and to her [Magda's] cup a little of it. Not for everyone … I mixed it up so the fat didn't swim on top.'

'Did the others notice?'

'That was the joke of it. They got something good and the others got the dishwater. Then I think, is there going to be a problem with this? And the kitchen door opens. And the butler is holding the cup up. And I think: now there's a problem. And he stands before me and says: please I'd like another soup for the Minister. You have to imagine, he got another soup while the others had dishwater. And he thought that the others also liked the soup.'

There is yet another cooking story. When Erna cooked fricassee for the Goebbels family, they did not know all of the ingredients. One of the things that gave this cook much joy was tricking her employer on minor matters. I can see the pleasure she takes in telling these stories many years later.

'How do you cook a good fricassee?' I ask.

I'm now reminded of the violence of the kitchen, and of meat, that most people simply take in stride. Skinning a rabbit is not that difficult provided you make the incisions in the correct places. Tie the animal up so it is hanging by a rope, head down. Then, after having cut around each leg, above the leg joint, continue the incision to the back, cutting through the tail bone. Then with strong arms pull the hide right down off the body. It should slip off easily. Erna points out where the best meat is found. 'The stomach is a rag, but the back is everything with a rabbit. And the legs. But the stomach is not that useful.'

'First, the meat needs to be cooked with soup greens.' Here you can fill a pot three-quarters full with water with salt and then add the chopped meat. Soup greens can be bought in prepared bundles at any Berlin farmer's market: celery root, leeks, carrots and green onions tied together. Erna advises that you 'take them out when they are cooked' so they are not overdone, 'Then I make *Mehlschwitze*, do you know what that is? No.' She shakes her head at my ignorance. This turns out to be a roux sauce: 'You put butter in a small pot, let it melt, a little bit of cream, a half spoon of flour, then lightly stir it, then add the brew slowly to it, stirring so it too doesn't become clumpy. You know what clumps are?' Yes, I nod, I know what clumps are. 'And then you spice it. The brew is cooked already with salt, so perhaps there's already enough there. But next comes a little lemon, a tiny little bit of sugar, you have to be careful there, and then it needs the egg yolk. Get rid of the egg white, you can use it with many things, but here we don't need it. And then stir properly. And then sauce comes from that, and it should taste good if you do it properly.' Then add the meat and the cooked vegetables to the brew, and you have a good rabbit fricassee stew to serve with rice.

But the fricassee was not to everyone's liking. Erna tells me a story about Goebbels' private chauffeur, Alfred Rach, who had a violent reaction to certain foods. An SS-Hauptsturmführer, Rach regularly drove the Minister to Lanke from Berlin and was present in the bunker for the murder of the children; he later escaped.

'This driver, Rach, I have to tell you, often came to me in the kitchen. There was a dining room for the staff. They also got something to eat, even if I didn't have the supplies. He came to me once and said: "There are people who will raise a memorial to you when you die, but you already have your memorial because you have managed somehow to feed us".

'One day, we were chatting over food and this driver wouldn't eat game. I eat game, though, I like it. A few weeks pass, and I manage to get my hands on a few rabbits … And I made the fricassee. It's dark meat, but when it's cooked correctly, it becomes white. So, I made fricassee just with that meat.'

Erna's recipe quickly led to a dispute after dinner between Magda and her mother. 'The mother of Frau Goebbels was there – as she often was, she lived on the other side of the lake – and the butler comes in and says that the two of them had fought. The mother insisted it was fricassee of veal, and Magda said it was fricassee of chicken.'

Both women visit Erna separately in the kitchen to find out who was correct. To the mother, Erna says it was veal, to which Auguste replies: 'I was right.' To Magda, she says it was chicken. 'I was also right!' And then the driver, Rach, asks her: What was it?' Erna repeats: 'It was veal.'

A few weeks pass, however, and Rach finds himself again in Erna's kitchen. 'He was only around when the Minister was and he asked: Do you have veal again? Fricassee? That was a beautiful dish. I told him: Do you have any idea what you ate? I said it was rabbit and he ran to the toilet to vomit. For weeks, he was still vomiting until he had nothing left in his stomach, that driver from the Ministry.'

I listen and wonder what I can soak from a story about cooking rabbit. That servants ate the same food as the family? Chicken and veal were unavailable in wartime even in a family as high-ranking as the Goebbels? Or, rather, that Erna lied to her employers and enjoyed lying. Both this story, and that about the senior cook at the Ministry in Berlin, might broadly fall into generalisations about Berliners: the dominating characteristic of underhanded *Schnauze*, or 'sass'. We fall into a stereotype, only to dismiss another: that of Germans simply as subservient rule followers. Erna was nothing but. But her disobedience was limited and misdirected: political resistance probably never crossed her mind.

There is one story I do not find as innocent as the others.

Duck and Vegetable Stew

How far did Erna see from the kitchen during all these events? Did she see as far as Stalingrad, the battle that raged in the winter of 1942–43? Perhaps she was aware of Goebbels' Total War speech in the Sportspalast on 18 February 1943 (his response to the carnage further east)? Or followed closely the Nazis' war fortunes: the Normandy invasions that began the next year, on 6 June 1944? Or the assassination attempt on Hitler of 20 July 1944 that badly bruised the Goebbels' morale?

But the cook would not talk to me about any of these events. She had been more concerned by Magda's serious deterioration of health. She was in hospital with heart ailments. This was followed by facial paralysis – trigeminal neuralgia. Hitler had been aware of this problem in September 1943 and was concerned an operation would disfigure her.

The operation occurred nonetheless in Breslau – where Karl Hanke was posted – in July 1944. It was successful. At this time, Goebbels met Hanke in Breslau (and wrote in his diary on 8 July: 'Hanke is extraordinarily amiable to me. I am glad that this visit will put our old conflict at rest') and in December, Hanke visited the Goebbels. Auguste, the mother of Magda, meanwhile, moved to Lanke and would sit with her daughter, day and night. She thought Magda was not physically aggrieved but going through a mental breakdown.

And yet, despite the way that the family had isolated themselves in the forests north of Berlin, there was a connection between what was happening in Erna's kitchen and the battlefields of Europe.

Erna tells me about the times when they received something extra from the Ministry (a piece of meat) or from Goebbels' friend in Denmark (who sent regularly crates of smoked eggs). But there was one event that stood out.

'I once got, from soldiers who were somewhere in Ukraine, twenty ducks. I was on my feet the whole day just trying to get ducks out of the house.'

'What happened to the ducks?' I ask.

'Listen, we were just overjoyed to have something in the house. With the small ducks, I made a small stew, a duck and vegetable stew, from the small vegetable garden: this is what Goebbels liked to eat more than anything else. Not what's boiled or fried but what came from the garden.'

Duck and vegetable stew: I stare at the old lady and I am making different connections. Her mind gravitated to the vegetable garden. But mine further east. Had she not made the connection, and asked where those ducks had come from? From which farm? In the east, the region that historian Timothy Snyder calls the 'Bloodlands', where the repeated advance and retreat of the Soviet and Nazi armies had brutalised a landscape and its people? Ukrainians were starved as German managers took over their farms. Who raised those ducks? Were they taken from a farmhouse whose occupants had been led away? Could she imagine the way these ducks were collected, and then taken away in a box, only to be opened again in Berlin, in the heart of the Nazi machine, in the kitchen of its leading minister?

Hitler's Last Visit

On 1 December 1944, Hitler visits Lanke and is 'welcomed as a member of the family'. They spend an afternoon 'chatting and remembering', musing over artistic subjects such as 'degenerate' art and music. Hitler is impressed by the tranquillity of the house, how removed it seems from the war, and takes a perhaps unsavoury interest in the older girls, 'especially Helga and Hilde, who have already become little ladies'. The closing in of the war front brought him into the Goebbels fold once again. Hitler was in bad shape – a groaning, cracked man.

Erna tells me of the time directly after Hitler's visit: 'I worked there from 1943 to 1945. And then between Christmas 1944 and New Year's 1945, I had a nervous breakdown. My heart couldn't take it any more. I then went to my doctor – he was the doctor of the old lady [for whom I'd worked in Berlin] – and he asked: What is happening? You must get out of there, he said. I tried each month to resign, but it wasn't possible, and Magda would throw out my dismissals.'

'It was a good job, though?'

And now Erna throws up her arms, 'But I didn't want to work for the Nazis. I was not even in the party. I was also not with the Nazis, I wasn't in any *Bund* [association], not anything, but Goebbels said, one New Year's, "Tell me Fräulein Mußack why don't you want to join the party?" I replied, "Herr Minister, I am full and totally in my work, and there busy, and in that way try to be a good German." And a little taken aback, he replied, "Maybe you are a better one than any other one of us." I was at the doctor, and he said, "Give me the private number of Magda and I will call her." And I went back by cab, and as I came out of the taxi, I was asked immediately to come to *Mutti* (we called them *Mutti* and *Papa* because of the kids). "*Sagen Sie mir*, tell me, why didn't you say anything, that you are doing so badly! We could have employed an assistant cook!" said Magda. And she said: "I have to let you go for a quarter of a year, says the doctor, but you must promise me to come back at the end of your time away." I could promise a lot of course, and then on 17 January 1945, I left for my parents.'

It was at this time, too, that the Goebbels family also left Lanke, to Schwanenwerder, as the front neared. Lanke was empty. And then, in mid-April, the family entered the bunker where Joseph and Magda Goebbels would kill their children.

Hot Chocolate

I ask Erna, 'When did you hear what had happened to the Goebbels children?'

She says, blankly, '*Ja*. They were killed. They cooked hot chocolate for the children and the parents, and they put cyanide inside. An adjutant – a stupid boy, who was married very young at twenty-three – he poisoned himself with them.'

I blink. Hot chocolate. The only time the children were allowed a luxury by their parents, it accompanied their deaths. What the children ate and drank, after all, helps explain why Joseph and Magda Goebbels murdered them. The everyday details of food, even their desserts, speak to how uncompromising politics infused every aspect of their lives. Ideology was demonstratively lived and not simply discussed.

'Was it a shock for you that it happened?'

She does not answer my question and instead says, 'I was away by then. But I heard it from a messenger, and he explained to me how it happened, because he was there, and this Herr Ochs, I said: Your name will go down in history.' Josef Ochs was an SS- and police officer.

Can we imagine what it was like to be driven to Hitler's bunker, or *Führerbunker*, after having spent the war lakeside and isolated from its horrors? The children would have arrived to the stench of buried bodies, under the rubble of the bombed city, full of starving and desperate people. They would have walked towards a conical tower, through which stairs descended under the grounds of Hitler's offices, the New Chancellery.

The bunker was the most fortified place in the Reich, built in two phases by the firm Hochtief, in 1936, and then in 1944, when thicker walls were needed to withstand the advancements in bomb technology. Joseph Goebbels, and Hitler, occupied the better-fortified section, while Magda and the children slept in the less-fortified section, not far from the canteen; the couple did not share a bedroom. The bunker had many domestic conveniences: kitchens, bedrooms, baths, ventilation systems, machine rooms. But it also served as Hitler's war rooms on the edge of defeat: offices with staff furiously typing, tables blanketed by maps, Goebbels retreating into a world of superstition, consulting astrology cards, Hitler in withdrawal from opioids and cocaine, becoming increasingly unpredictable, raging. The macabre spectacle was watched over by the SS guards. I imagine the children playing between the legs of the terrified secretaries, wondering what will come next – then diverted by Hitler's dog giving birth. I imagine the series of memories associated with each room of this sprawling underground complex.

Magda describes the spartan conditions of the bunker, in a letter of 28 April 1945, to her son Harald: 'Independently, they take care of themselves in these more than primitive conditions. Whether they are sleeping on the floor, or washing themselves, or getting something to eat – never a word of complaint or tears.' This account is false, and Helga is terrified, begging to leave, saying she does not want to die.

On 19 April 1945, Goebbels gives his last radio address, and then on 21 April 1945, the Red Army crosses the city limits into Berlin. Many people offer to save the children: Quandt, Speer, Hitler. Even at the eleventh hour, when Hitler's driver, Erich Kempa, tries to get the family out of the bunker in an armed car, the parents refuse. Goebbels' postscript to

Hitler's testament read that he was 'acting for the best as far as the future of the German people is concerned, for in the difficult times that are approaching models to live up to will be more important than men' and that his decision to commit suicide was being also made for the children because they 'are too young to be able to express themselves, but if they were old enough would entirely agree with this decision'. Magda's earlier letter to her son Harald, from 28 April, explained: 'The world, that will come after Hitler and National Socialism, is not worth living in, and for that reason, I have brought the children here with me.' There is also some discussion as to whether she was willing to sacrifice her children because she believed in Buddhist ideas of reincarnation.

Hitler, after his forty-hour marriage, committed double-suicide with his bride Eva Braun. Rochus Misch, a telephone operator in the bunker, testified that it was the next day, on 1 May 1945, that he observed an 'orderly arrived carrying a tray with six cups and a jug of chocolate. Later somebody said it was laced with sleeping pills. I saw her [Magda] hug some and stroke others as they drank it.' This description clarifies the testimony of Erna who believed the poison was in the hot chocolate – and, again, I can't help but think what a delicacy the hot chocolate must have appeared to these children after so much food rationing. The hot chocolate was no random choice. Magda's mother recounts in her memoir how her daughter said before she died that hot chocolate 'will be our last ever drink'.

Dr Stumpfegger later administered the cyanide pills, forcing them into the children's mouths. Heide was heard rhyming on the operator's name: '*Misch Misch, du bist ein Fisch* [Misch Misch, you are a fish]' before they all disappeared. Then later, upstairs in the courtyard – 'That way you won't have to carry us,' said Goebbels – Magda herself swallowed a cyanide capsule, and Goebbels shot himself. The six children were then found in white nightgowns, dead in bed, ribbons still in their hair.

The bodies of the parents had been taken to the surface to be incinerated. The Nazi leadership had seen how Mussolini's body had been hung up like a pig in the main square of Milan and would have wanted to avoid similar treatment. But the SS officers doing the job did not have enough time to finish. The half-burned remains of the couple, alongside those of the children in their nightclothes, were then filmed in the bunker's garden by the Red Army.

Cream and Eggs

As the children waited in the bunker, Erna was in the east fleeing the approaching Red Army.

'My father was in the *Volkssturm*; he wasn't around any more,' she tells me. 'And on 3 April we fled from the house. And then we were stuck on the road until May, and on 21 May came back home. But what did we find there? The house was emptied, looted. The day when we fled, I had left a tall earthenware pot full of cream, and on the kitchen table a bowl of fresh eggs, that I just left there, because we just needed to get out so quickly.

'We were afraid. The Russians sat there naked, so to speak, looking for young virgins of all stripes. It was a horrible time. I lost everything. I lost my homeland, my fiancé in war three days before the wedding, but the one thing I kept was that no one managed to take my body.'

Her fiancé? This is the first time I have heard about him. I wonder how much she represses this memory of him. Perhaps it is less painful for her to recount her time with the Goebbels.

'We arrived, on our trek, finally to the Americans, who said that we were allowed to turn back to where we came from. I had a little brother, who was sixteen years younger, he was only ten years old, and my mother obviously wanted to take the kid back home, and I couldn't do it alone, so I followed. So, we went back, but what we saw and lived on the way back – the horribleness of it, how many dead soldiers we saw. All these things I just can't get out of my head today.'

I ask her, 'Didn't it happen that some women took on one Russian soldier as a lover to protect her from the others?'

Erna replies, 'Yes, many found a long-term lover, and that was something I was able to avoid. We were sent back from the Americans to the Russians, and I remember there was a Russian this big [she indicates: big] sitting on a seat, at a table, on the side of the road, and we had to pass by him. And then we came to a very big square – we were not alone in the trek – where there was a hall where we were supposed to spend the night, and there was a fire there, and everyone went there to cook, and I also wanted to go too, but my mother said, no you stay by the wagon, because I have seen how the Russians are acting here, and they want something, they are looking for something.

'And I will never forget that night, because a young woman, who was seventeen years old – oh how her mother later screamed – went off, and she was completely fucked over – worked over – by the Russians, that she was left half-dead, thrown half-dead on to the wagon afterwards. It was crazy. That night, I sat on a wagon, with an old coat from my father, and a scarf over my face, and made myself look a little nasty, and then the Russians came with their lantern and asked: 'Hey you, how old?' I said seventy. My mother said: You can say eighty, you look it. [Before] we went down into the wagon, with my brother – I don't think he realised what was he was doing – nonetheless, he slept with one hand over my face, but somehow he knew to protect me. And then two young women came to sleep next to us. And when the Russians came, the women got up and tried to run off. And I then went up on top of the wagon. And I must say, I must have had a guardian angel, I think she was my grandmother, that night. I had the feeling that night up on top of the wagon that I had this great protective ring around me, because I could see the men coming and going, but they left me alone. That was what saved me.

'And then there was a young woman with a baby carriage, and the child died, and then she went to a hillside, and just threw the carriage off there. We are talking about things that you wouldn't be able normally to do with a clear head, but we were hypnotised. My mother had some old things she sold to the Russians, but they left us without any money; they also stole from us. It was a terrible time.'

Ana and I stare at her blankly: a woman of nearly 100 has revisited with us her escape from a mass rape. She sits before us in her armchair, but I can see from her eyes that she is back there: it is as vivid as if it is yesterday, on top of that wagon at night.

But then, once more, we are distracted. Erna looks troubled, blinks, and then motions towards the window, half-standing, and raising her arm.

Cyanide Soup

Millions of Germans suffered: they were bombed, 12 million lost their homes, as many as 100,000 German women were raped in Berlin alone. Any one of these individuals naturally experiences their own suffering, and those of their loved ones, more intensely than that of even a million others they do not know. Nonetheless, these tragedies must be differentiated from victims who were killed in greater numbers by a state policy of racial extermination. Approximately 6 million Jews were killed by the decision-makers of Goebbels' circle, and others, while Erna was stirring pots in her kitchen.

Erna's everyday position in the kitchen was not isolated from these crimes. The story of her ducks from Ukraine strikes me, still, as a more explanatory lesson about why the Holocaust happened than lists of the deceased or pictures of charred bodies. This story, like others by Erna, gets closer to the essential question of why everyday Germans accepted or turned a blind eye to the killing of so many people. Just as Erna saw the ducks and not Ukraine – she could hardly pronounce the word 'Ukraine' – many people today cannot place Bosnia or Rwanda or Syria on a map. The space that many occupied in their work and private life during the war was often only affected by the ordinary – by breakfast, or children, or meetings – even as the horror happened outside their doors. The intimate view explains inaction. One can otherwise come away from the dramatic images of mass murder during the Second World War that impart the horror without understanding how any of it actually happened.

Erna's role was many levels removed from such crimes of her employers. But after a few hours in Erna's kitchen, I am confronted with the everydayness of their world as well. The stories most people know about the Nazi leadership come from Hollywood films, not kitchen-sink naturalism. Even beyond the political drama, one still looks for dramatics in private life – the licentious affairs – because the music that accompanies the Third Reich is almost always Wagnerian, and not the sounds of a quiet wood outside of Berlin, isolated from harm, even as millions died elsewhere. They had such a protected home life precisely because of their station in the hierarchy. Working for the Goebbels did not strike Erna as odd or extraordinary in the least; she was occupied with the basic needs of these living, eating, shitting humans. Erna never saw past the kitchen. Magda did not see beyond the clinic. Nor the children, for that matter, past the lake at Bogensee.

I went into my conversations with Erna thinking she was hiding something: that she was in denial. Why else wouldn't she talk about politics? But Erna, and the children, were not political figures to themselves. This seems like a banal observation, but it is the crux of something important.

Nor did her employers strike Erna as fanatics, unlike Anja Klabunde, a German journalist who published a biography of Magda Goebbels and wrote: 'I decided to pursue the story because Magda Goebbels' life seemed in a sense to reflect the tragedy and blindness of Germany in the first half of our century … how could such an intelligent and cultivated woman fall prey to such fanaticism?'

A fanatic is given to excessive, unreflecting zeal, and violent behaviour. What happened in the bunker, when the parents killed their children, is the very definition of fanaticism. But is it difficult to reconcile this choice with the family life Erna observed, with its cultivation? The Goebbels were people who had their dinner parties, stayed up late with their kids, who went for long walks. But fanaticism does not only lurk, cinematographically, in communes of deranged cults. Its worst consequences may emerge in moments of stress, but fanaticism is also a banal, everyday state – just as Hannah Arendt observed. The Goebbels saw their infanticide as *konsequent* – rigorous, consistent, resolute – an expression of their ideology. They were *konsequent* right down to the choice of hot chocolate.

The Goebbels family's relationship to food – the recipes of that virtual belonging Erna says tells her life – illustrates the connection between their ideology and the everyday. The rigorous rationing and denial of luxury, when there was a choice to live better, helps us comprehend the sudden shift from the isolation of Lanke to the killings in the bunker. The children's final drink was a symbol of this consistency, in the sense that only death could justify such a luxury. Not once did Erna express any surprise at what happened. I am left with a paradox: few people would kill their children even under such circumstances. But at the same time, if we clinicise and insist that fanatics are outliers, we indulge in a safety measure that helps one feel immune to the *Alltag* frequency of hatred, and the zeal of those willing to act on it.

What did Erna do, in the end, with her everyday position at the service of a powerful figure in the Nazi leadership? Such questions have been asked thousands of times in Holocaust literature: why did someone who 'could do anything', do nothing? Why did she, like other Germans, not overthrow the tyrants? Why did the cook not poison her boss? She was in an ideal position, in her kitchen, to bring down the most important men in the Nazi hierarchy with a little cyanide to flavour the dishwater soup. But such questions never bothered Erna's world. She was concerned about the availability of meat and how to pass it off as something else. She was disobedient and garrulous, but her world ended, like so many Berliners', at her kitchen door. Like so many then – and now – she lived in a bell jar of very ordinary concerns.

Innocent Recipes

I keep thinking I should follow up with Erna once more. But I feel blocked, that I do not want to see her again. While I found her sympathetic on an individual level, and do not see her as a serious collaborator, I cannot disentangle her stories from this terrible family, their politics, and their role in the Shoah. It wears me down, it makes me feel sick inside, and it makes me hate being in Germany, a country where I normally like living. I even start to wonder about the innocence of everyday objects, of her recipes. I cannot get Erna out of my head.

Perhaps as a kind of exorcism, I begin to write her recipes, as I promised her, down in a book. I love to cook and when I'm in a bad mood I can work out my feelings kneading dough. I buy a bound notebook, with a neutral black cover, and list ingredients and methods. I find I have a menu for the whole day: *Frühstück* (one egg, poached, served in a glass, with buttered bread, and black tea), a glucose pill as a late-morning pick-me-up, then *Mittagstisch* (rabbit fricassee), *Kaffee und Kuchen* (tray-baked cake with false whipped cream, which is as bad as it sounds), *Abendessen* (washed salad, semolina soup, and duck stew). I even drink hot chocolate, but not before I go to bed. It gives me nightmares.

I find myself changing the recipes slightly and trying to rewrite them, to 'de-Nazify' them. Baked beans alongside the egg. Some mango curry to the duck or cumin in the fricassee, all in an effort to dispel my feeling that it's really a *Nazi* fricassee. If I cook these things for other people, I don't tell them where I got the recipe. But isn't this superstitious? To give guilt to ingredients, to food? I sometimes wonder whether I unnecessarily contaminate my daily life in Berlin with the Nazi past. Very few of today's Germans were even present during those years, after all. But Nazism seems something sticky, like I've got it all over my fingers.

Would the recipe book be of any use to a historian? What can you tell from the recipes themselves? Can you tell a story through them? Does rabbit speak of famine? Does the absence of butter explain the war? My object is hardly archaeological. It's a transcription and not a relic. And without Erna, the object is no longer a strategy.

The object should be printed on old paper. It should be something that Erna would have owned herself. So, I go to a second-hand shop in Berlin and pick up a vintage cookbook: Charlotte Löfflerin's *Newest Cookbook for Households of all Classes*. A brown volume, with a stained binding from too much time on kitchen counters, its pages stick together, especially in the dessert section. I'm told by the bookseller that it is a bible of Teutonic cookery: the frontispiece indicates that 229,000 copies of just this 1920 edition have been printed. The first version appeared around the time of the French Revolution. It feels like I have a universal history in my hands: instructions for daily life, enacted in millions of kitchens over generations. It is similar to many of the books that I saw in the hallway leading to Erna's kitchen.

Is that Charlotte herself on the cover leaning over a stove, overdressed in her busty frock and pansied sleeves? Probably not. Charlotte is a pseudonym. Löfflerin sounds a lot like 'Löffelchen', or 'little spoon'. I use Charlotte when I am confused by the recipes I jotted down in my notebook from my conversations with Erna.

Does it matter where I got the recipes? From Erna or Charlotte? Does it matter where they are written down? Or that Erna recited her recipes to me by heart and I got to ask her questions? That she didn't need to consult Charlotte Löfflerin, a fictional character, who tells us herself that 'a cookbook doesn't make the cook'?

Why then did I buy *Newest Cookbook for Households of all Classes*? Because when Erna goes so will her recipes. All we will have left is Charlotte. And if I serve her recipes to you, following only Charlotte, you might not think much more about it than that it's a very traditional Prussian meal. But if I cook the same meal for you according to Erna's instructions, you might feel rather differently about it, knowing she served it to the leaders of the Nazi party.

One day Ana tells me that Erna has moved out of her apartment and into a care home just down the street. She gives me the number and I take a deep breath and force myself to call. A brusque nurse replies and tells me not to call again. Frau Jokisch will no longer be taking visitors outside of family; she is too unwell to speak. I am almost relieved not to interview her again. But I am also troubled by her declining state and think that I work too slowly for my subject matter.

Then one morning, I read in the newspaper, at my favourite local café, an article about the house at Lanke. Its 'historical burden' has meant that the property – for sale – has failed to sell. The house, unlived in for years, is fighting against crumbling plaster, rot and weeds. It is a huge financial liability for the Berlin Senate who, as in Goebbels' time, own the house. The SPD state representative Sven Heinemann intones that 'Bogensee only has a future without the Goebbels' estate'. Conclusion: the villa will be detonated. Yet another place of Nazi history – of Nazi perpetrators – is slated to disappear, in the service of the future.

A Trick

Not once in his diaries does Joseph Goebbels mention the quality of his meals. The only testimony I have of him having enjoyed a meal is now standing before me.

'Maybe you would tell me?' I ask. 'What was in the Doctor's salad?'

'The salad is salad [just leaves]. You could add tomatoes, radishes, but salad stays salad.'

'And how did Dr Goebbels want it?'

'Just leaves, and the dressing, so it tastes a little different than what he was getting elsewhere.'

But now I'm getting towards the secret. I ask, 'And what was in the dressing?'

Erna has already told me that a 'cook doesn't give things away for free', so perhaps I am going to get away with a small theft?

But she laughs, 'Don't forget that the salad needs to be washed! Then you take oil. You could today use lemon but back then we didn't have it, you can use very normal vinegar, or apple vinegar, but it's not important. Back then you only had very ordinary vinegar. And then you add a little salt, sugar, a little pepper. Then, in a small bowl, take a little [she indicates] onion, and wash it and then grate it, then really mix it, so it's everywhere, and then make the salad. Everyone used to use their hands to mix it, instead of cutlery. But this onion cannot be made a half-hour before, because if you let it stand more than a half-hour it will become bitter. There are things this old lady can still teach you.'

'That's it?' I wonder, trying not to sound too disappointed. 'An ordinary recipe?'

But it's precisely that – its ordinariness – which is the point.

She pauses, then asks me, 'And you want to write a book?'

Not exactly about the salad dressing, I want to say. But I reply, 'Yes, I'm interested in people's memories.'

'Will I also be in the newspaper?'

'Who knows? I hope it's something people want to read. It's important to record these things.'

She replies, 'I always say: ask me today, because tomorrow maybe I won't be there, and who then will know? There are few left who remember. And those that are alive often having nothing left in their heads.'

'You are still very sharp,' I comment.

Erna laughs. 'Yes, a little is still there. Not a lot, but something remains. But now I must say goodbye.'

We follow her out of the hallway, exchange farewells, then follow the stairwell down along the landings with their wooden door frames until we come out of the plain, dark stucco building on Delbrückstraße, into the street full of trees.

Somehow, I know I won't be going back. As I walk away from the door, with the recipe written down in my pocket, I ask myself whether she gave something else away without knowing it.

A String Instrument

Erich Hartmann (left) with colleagues, April 1965

Flowers

It is December 2018, a cold but sunny day: dark coats and bright scarves, black bikes shuffling through the old leaves. Frau Annemarie Bastiaan waits for me at a bus stop on Kurfürstendamm, an elegant avenue in West Berlin. I am holding the flowers she suggested I get Herr Erich Hartmann. Amaryllis, because they bloom for a long time.

Hartmann is the last witness. No one else is alive who played in the Berlin Philharmonic during the Nazi period. The meeting comes thanks to a friend in today's orchestra. 'If you are writing about the war, you should talk to him about his instrument,' she suggests. An email to the intendant of the orchestra brings me to the woman I now see at the kerb; she visits Herr Hartmann regularly at his care home.

Frau Bastiaan addresses me with the formal pronoun *Sie* instead of the informal *du*. At the top of the double-decker, in the much-desired seats right above the driver, we make well-mannered conversation. We share the awkwardness of two people who don't know each other going to a third location. But a masterful view of the street passes beneath us. The fancy shopping boulevard, with its Christmas decorations, gives way to unbombed villas along parks in the western suburbs. Through the branches of the skeletal woods, I see the gleam of a lake. The light is angular and precise.

Frau Bastiaan tells me that her husband, Johannes, or 'Hans', was a concertmaster of the Berlin Philharmonic during the Nazi period. He joined the orchestra shortly after the regime took power and remained for forty-two years. They married in the 1990s, she much his junior. Herr Bastiaan was the penultimate survivor of the Nazi's orchestra, dying in 2012. Now, only Herr Hartmann is left at the age of 98.

We arrive in the well-manicured spaces of the care home. It's a low, modernist affair, with well-meaning, comfy touches that don't quite match the institutional needs: holiday ornaments pinned to the antiseptic, no-stick walls. The watchful nurses at the curved entrance desk are so used to Frau Bastiaan's visits that they give a smiling hello without raising their eyes. We follow a confusing set of stairwells and hallways, past closed doors marked with the names of Herr-this and Frau-that, up to the second floor.

'He gets a lot of visitors,' says Frau Bastiaan.

I say, 'I hope I get as many when I'm old.'

She replies archly, 'That doesn't just come on its own.'

She knocks on Herr Hartmann's door and opens it immediately. He is standing in the middle of the room, his walker in two hands, at an angle to us. Having got up to meet us, he's made it only a short distance, smiling with bright eyes. He outstretches his stiff hand from his walker and says: 'All the way from Canada! I don't think I've ever had a guest from so far away.'

Frau Bastiaan shakes her head, referring to my West Berlin neighbourhood, 'Erich, he lives in Kreuzberg!'

Three Bows

If Herr Hartmann were a bird, he might be a crane, examining you curiously: tall, very thin, a long oval face and nose, and small eyes that peek angularly. These eyes, interested and unclouded, are easy to engage. Herr Hartmann wears a pressed shirt.

I look around, at the case of antique books with leather bindings; the bed with its knitted quilt and hand grips; oil paintings of flowers; a large photo of the orchestra playing in the unbombed Old Philharmonic Hall; a gold-plated Beethoven vinyl; a photo from Hartmann's retirement in 1985 after forty-one years (he is being congratulated by the principal conductor, Herbert von Karajan); a framed photograph of Wilhelm Furtwängler peering down. From the window, we peek into a dying garden.

I look around for Hartmann's double bass. The object closest to a musician's story is his instrument – part of his body, an extra limb – and I want to tell its story. But below the television is only a small electronic keyboard, unplugged, with keys that are too small. Then I notice three old bows from his instrument that hang from a wall. They have a synecdochic relationship to the missing *Kontrabass*, too large to keep here.

I ask why he has three of them.

Herr Hartmann replies, 'They are all a little different. They need to be restrung with horsehair.'

I admit they all look the same to me, and ask, 'When was the last time you played the double bass?'

'Such a long time ago! When I could still drive. Twenty years ago. That was the last time.'

He tells me that he played a Dvořák quartet. Or perhaps Schubert. He can't remember.

'You must miss it.'

'Naturally. Also, the piano. Here I can practise a little. But it's hard to plug in. And it's such a small instrument.'

Frau Bastiaan makes him comfortable at the table and puts out the almond cookies she made among the glasses and books. She has a capable manner, practised at dealing with old people, and she speaks loudly. I try to do the same. Herr Hartmann is so pleasant in his replies that he gives the illusion that getting old is OK. As we sit near the window, I'm again astonished by how quickly it gets dark at this hour in December. Frau Bastiaan gives us our starting point when she says: 'Your father was a piano maker in Leipzig …'

Youth

Erich Hartmann grew up around instruments.

'My father had his own shop,' he explains. 'A large one that sold pianos, harmoniums.' The workshop was below street level – 'The basement is still there!' Erich and his sister would help their father with the repairs. The firm engaged a piano tuner who was blind: 'He was the best, with the best ear.'

I listen as this 98-year-old describes the delicate atmosphere of early mornings in his father's workshop. The boy would go down to the basement – 'around 7 or 7.30 a.m. before the customers came at 9 or 9.30 a.m.' – and took the opportunity to play the instruments. 'I was very young. It was lovely.' He was also an accomplished pianist – no wonder, growing up with a traditional Saxon approach to music education, learning more than one instrument, and even composing. 'You shouldn't just play music, you should know it!' went the dictum.

'How old were you when you started playing the double bass?' I ask.

'Fifteen or sixteen years old. I went with my father to the music conservatory, and they explained how they needed certain instruments. Bassoon, double bass. "We don't need flautists or violinists. So, think about what you want to play." It was a difficult choice. I thought about it for a long time. But I knew I wanted a string instrument, and I was tall!'

'Did you know you wanted to be an orchestra musician?'

'I heard the Berlin Philharmonic in the Altes Gewandhaus in Leipzig. It was the first time I saw Furtwängler and his orchestra. It was so superb for me. But I could never have imagined that one day I would be there with them, in the thick of it.'

Berliner Philharmoniker with Furtwängler during the war years

As a young man, however, he would find himself sooner on the Eastern Front of Hitler's war, at precisely the moment that Germany's fortunes turned towards defeat, after a period that he spent fighting in France and Poland. The Battle of Stalingrad raged between August 1942 and February 1943. Meanwhile, the Soviet battles against the Germans south of Moscow were known, due to the many casualties, as the 'Rzhev meat grinder' (named for the town on the Volga). Around 30 million people died in battles to the east.

Hartmann tells me, 'I was in Russia. It was snowing and there were no winter clothes for the soldiers. Hitler said the clothes would come and the soldiers should just stay there and the war should go on! That's what Hitler said. I was attacked in a bombing raid that hit six or seven people, me too.'

Hartmann survived by the skin of his teeth. Badly wounded, he was sent – his right arm shattered – to Warsaw. 'They said, we have no place for you.' So, he was sent onward to the south-west of Germany near the city of Ulm.

Frau Bastiaan remarks, 'I notice your hand is cold. Let's close the window?' She stands up and Erich Hartmann describes the months he spent in a well-supplied Catholic recovery home in a cloister.

'They almost took your arm off. Why don't you show him?' Frau Bastiaan says, pulling up the old man's sleeve.

Startled, I draw back. Half of Erich's right forearm has been sliced away, right to the bone.

His skin – taut, freckled with age – is like on an ancient, bevelled tree trunk. Over time, the tree has compensated for the gash with a weathered knot. I see how the skin buckles around the scar before growing smooth again towards the elbow. I watch this distortion for just a moment, before the sleeve is pulled down.

Physical evidence from the Russian Front on one of its last living bodies. I am brought closer to the war than in a long time. The testimony is visual, even sensual in its violence, something a document has trouble articulating. The incontrovertible proof is part of this smiling man. It is as if 1943 is just outside the window. Herr Hartmann reaches with his other arm and tries more of the almond cookies.

'It must have made playing your bass difficult,' says Frau Bastiaan.

'I couldn't play with the right hand,' he replies, 'but I could hold the bow in it. It took me nine months to recover. They took good care of me; the doctor knew my profession. Soon I could walk a little.'

The clinic was a respite from the bloodiest battles of the war. The patients went on an excursion to the enormous cathedral in Ulm – 'It was beautiful. We really loved it' – and Hartmann played a small organ in the room of a nun. She encouraged him to improve, and also to visit.

Once recovered, he went to his parents in Leipzig, and was exempt from service because he could no longer operate a gun.

'In Leipzig, my teacher told me there was a position free in the Berlin Philharmonic and that I should go and audition. I told him there's no sense in doing that because I'm not far enough along in my studies. "That's not important," he replied. "From every performance you will learn something." And he was right.'

Hartmann decided to go at the spur of the moment and describes the anticipation in the family as he prepared to travel to Berlin. The capital still appeared relatively safe, due to a lull in bombing from 1942 into most of 1943, when naval battles in the Atlantic took priority. It was only in November 1943 that British bombers redirected their air power to the city, precisely when Hartmann made his way to the metropolis.

'I didn't know Berlin at all. Then, my sister wanted to come along too. My mother also wanted to go with us. So, the three of us, with the double bass, all went. It was 1943.' I imagine them all packed into a train compartment with the very large instrument.

'And what happened at the audition?'

'I went and apologised that I had not brought an accompanist with me. And they said, that's not important. We have everything here. So, I went upstairs and there was someone from the orchestra there to accompany me. Furtwängler wasn't present but the whole orchestra listened to me. After I played, I expected them to say it was good, or it was bad, or to come back later. But they said absolutely nothing.'

'Nothing?'

'They only gave me a sheet of paper with the next rehearsals and performances I needed to participate in.'

'Boom!'

The Double Bass

Erich Hartmann, engaged from 1 November 1943, was thrown into performances without a moment to breathe. Additional pressure came from the one-year contract: after an obligatory trial year – like today – the orchestra would vote whether to keep him. He needed to convince two-thirds. But he was unlikely to do so with his current double bass.

Hartmann explains to me that, while he played a good solo instrument, with a clear sound, it was not appropriate for orchestra playing. He presumed it would be difficult to find another *Kontrabass* but his new colleagues said, 'Of course you can, you just need to make an effort!' Berlin, of course, was full of instrument makers. With a fistful of addresses, Hartmann began his hunt.

'At the first place I went, it worked out! I told them I wanted a beautiful, old double bass. They said, "You're lucky; one has just come in." *Ja ja*, but what will it cost? And they replied, "Nothing at first since you have been engaged by the orchestra. Take it with you. You just need to be careful you don't damage it." I replied that I was careful. So, I took it and showed it to my colleagues. And they said: immediately, *this one*. They liked it: everything was there, it was a splendid instrument. Everything was good about it except I had no idea what it cost! And they said: "Don't worry about it. We'll pay for it and then you can pay us back monthly." And I thought: that's not a bad idea. And so, I went for it.'

'How long did you play this instrument?'

'Until I retired.'

'And how young were you in November 1943?'

'I know the answer,' replies Frau Bastiaan. 'Should I say? Twenty-three years old.'

'So young!'

'My husband was thirty-four at the time,' she says.

'With your husband, I always had a good relationship,' says Hartmann. 'We understood each other immediately. I will never forget him.'

I imagine Hartmann, in his new city, with his new instrument, his new job, going to rehearsal. A young man starting his professional life at the height of a war.

A Nazi Orchestra

The orchestra that Erich Hartmann joined in 1943 had, for ten years, been under the direct control of the Nazi government. This came about in the autumn of 1933 – officialised in January 1934 – when the Philharmonic, on the edge of bankruptcy, was saved financially by the regime's takeover. Trading independence for fiscal security, it bent to Nazi cultural policy

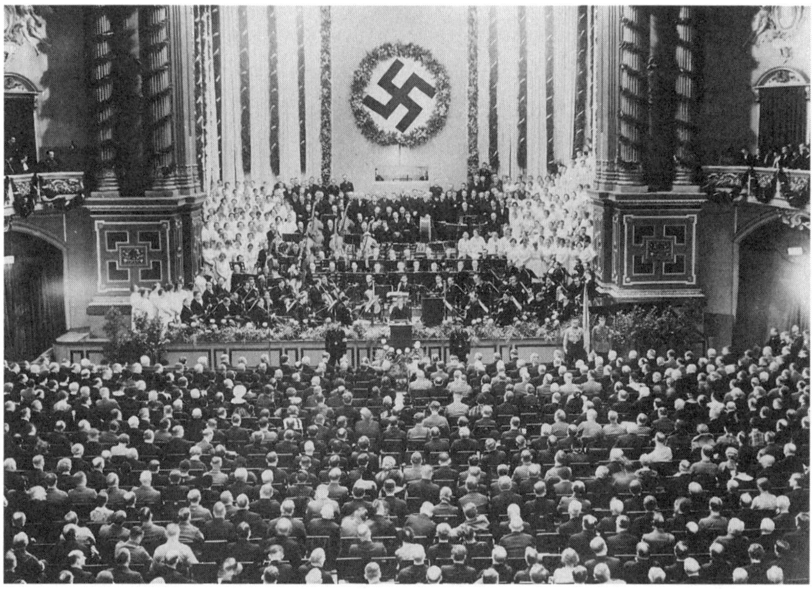

Opening of the Reichskulturkammer, 15 November 1933

and its members became employees of Joseph Goebbels' Ministry for Propaganda. In fact, this crown jewel of the German cultural scene would become an essential part of the state's propaganda arsenal. After the war, many would claim that the orchestra had 'never been a Nazi Orchestra', because only 18 per cent of its hundred-odd members belonged to the party (compared to 44 per cent at the Vienna Philharmonic). This argument ignores the orchestra's ownership, mission, and privilege.

Nazi cultural policy was guided by the *Reichskulturkammer*, or office for the coordination of arts. Richard Strauss was appointed the first president of its Reich Music Chamber, founded in the Alte Philharmonie – making it not only a venue for Philharmonic concerts but also a site for propaganda events. The Nazis' approach was 'self-administration under state supervision'. In other words, the musicians themselves were to do the dirty work.

The Berlin Philharmonic excelled for the Nazi state. A prized presence at official events, the orchestra played for Hitler's birthdays every year from 1937. Before the war, it played Beethoven's *Pastorale* and Bruckner's 7th symphonies at the 1936 and 1938 Nuremberg party rallies respectively, celebrating the remilitarisation of the Rhineland and the annexation of

Austria. Hitler Youth concerts were on the programme, as were performances in Hitler's Chancellery and Goebbels' Propaganda Ministry. To reach the national community, or *Volksgemeinschaft*, it played affordable concerts as part of the state's leisure programme, *Kraft durch Freude*. These were enormous public events, draped in swastikas, vicious slogans, and other propaganda. Between October 1944 and April 1945, the orchestra also played eighteen concerts for the arms industry. One might argue the orchestra had no choice but to play for such purposes, but this does not change that they did. Hitler, with his love for orchestral music, and Wagner in particular, would force his unwilling men to attend classical music events, even though they had to be shaken awake.

The Philharmonic plays in the AEG Factory, Berlin, February 1942

In return, the musicians were given elite privileges. The state lavished the ensemble with money: one need only peek at Furtwängler's astronomical salary of 184,000 Reichsmarks in 1940 (750,000 euros in today's coin), individual members' forgiving expense accounts, and the quality of the instruments they played.

Hitler complained that the Vienna Philharmonic had such fine old instruments, so why didn't the Berlin Philharmonic? There was no lack of availability. Thousands were being plundered by the Nazis all over occupied Europe from Jews and other enemies; one special unit, *Sonderstab Musik*, was created specifically to raid such treasures. The Propaganda Ministry set out on a procurement programme to provide the Philharmonic musicians with their fine instruments. Some were legally bought during the war. But the Nazis also used middlemen or agents, employed by a Nazi intendant, Heinz Drewes, who had been a conductor himself and became Goebbels' music advisor. In many cases, the agents' records are missing, obscuring the trail to the conditions in which an instrument was acquired. Documents from the Nazis themselves shed some light: one Propaganda Ministry memo, to give an example, traces an instrument to a Jew, who likely fled Austria for Italy. Once the instruments were brought to the German capital, musicians were given the extravagant choice of which one they wished to play.

Confiscated violins being examined, Łódź Ghetto, 1942

The greatest gift, however, was the exceptional status that saved many of these musicians' lives: *Unabkömmlichstellung* (*Uk-Stellung*), or 'non-conscription' status. Considered essential to the war effort – since they performed a propaganda purpose – the orchestra members escaped the universal draft.

When the war began, there was understandable jealousy directed towards them, writes Hartmann in his 1996 memoir, which he presents to me on my visit. He describes how odd people thought it was to see a man of his age wandering around the streets of Berlin in the final days of the war: shouldn't he be in uniform? No, the orchestra was considered part of the Total War effort: able-bodied musicians were foot soldiers carrying instruments instead of guns. The Berlin Philharmonic, along with the Bayreuth Festival, which Hitler attended religiously, were the only cultural employees of the state to retain these privileges after September 1944, when all other theatres and symphonies closed and their members mobilised.

The Philharmonic too was complicit in the sanitising of musical taste and the extrusion of Jewish and avant-garde artists, by not playing their music. Again, one might excuse an orchestra that had little choice in its programming under an authoritarian regime, but such a position ignores deeds and results. The dissonant sounds of Schoenberg's twelve tones and other experiments of the 1920s were seen as much more than a metaphoric assault on the harmony of the racial community. The identity of the composers was also paramount. Works by Felix Mendelssohn, who was of Jewish descent, were a too obvious, and moving, example of Jewish contributions to German culture. They were quickly condemned after Furtwängler programmed a concert for his 125th anniversary in 1934. Wolfgang Stresemann, who later became the intendant of the orchestra, wondered whether an image of Mendelssohn left hanging in the old Philharmonic Hall 'averted his gaze at the sight of Hitler'.

I ask Herr Hartmann what would happen if he played Mendelssohn or Mahler in these times, if someone heard a melody coming from an open window?

'You'd have to leave the country, to America … We played so much Wagner and Beethoven … also no Russians. In the war, they banned Tchaikovsky … the programme got thinner and thinner.'

'Wasn't it boring for the musicians?' I had read that during the war the orchestra played Beethoven's 9th symphony three times in a single month.

'No, it wasn't. It would have been much better, obviously, if we could have played everything. After the war, it was especially appreciated that we could.'

'Was there a piece after the war that you said: Thank god, I can play this again?'

'For me, it was Mendelssohn, his violin concerto. And his famous symphony. And, of course, also the Russians, which were banned during the war. The Nutcracker Suite ... It's so comic that everything was forbidden. The composers had nothing to do with any of it! All this happened so long after they lived!'

Stravinsky and Furtwängler, c. *1923*

'Yes, but what was considered bad was that it was "Jewish music",' adds Frau Bastiaan. 'It occurs to me that you were born in 1920. In 1933, you were thirteen years old. So, it means that you did not play Mendelssohn as part of your studies?'

'No.'

'It was different for my husband. He was nine years older and joined the orchestra in 1934. He learned all that repertoire at the music conservatory.'

Herr Hartmann sighs. 'I was the youngest.'

Johannes Bastiaan's experience of the orchestra was indeed different; he saw the rise to power of the Nazis. Again, I feel the tug of losing the subjects of research: how much I would have liked to interview him! Although he was born in Nuremberg and grew up in Berlin, Hans Bastiaan came from a Dutch musical family on his father's side. To remain in the orchestra, he was forced to give up this citizenship. In the momentous political year of 1932–33, he played in the Berlin Radio Symphony, and in the next season joined the Philharmonic, to become a permanent member in October 1934. Over the next twelve months – just after he was given the opportunity to join the great orchestra – the Jewish musicians of the same institution would lose their jobs.

Playing for Furtwängler

'But tell Joseph about the first time you went into the Old Philharmonic Hall to the rehearsal. And when you played with the orchestra for the first time. How was it? He really wants to know!'

'It was not easy for me,' he says, of standing with his double bass before the great conductor. 'There were pieces I had never played before and I had to play well with the others. But I got along so well with them!'

There was a reason for this. Herr Hartmann had a talent, which allowed him to get around the problem of new repertoire, so he could play it presentably for Germany's best orchestra.

'I could play from sight. That's what saved me … smoothly without rehearsing,' he tells me. For this reason, the State Opera's orchestra also wanted him, except that Hartmann refused the offer and stayed with the Philharmonic.

His first months must have been dramatic. Music did not die in Berlin during the war; in fact, it flourished. In November and December 1943, as a new member of Germany's most celebrated cultural institution, he was directed by Wilhelm Furtwängler, whose programmes that autumn included Bruckner's 6th and Brahms' 4th symphonies, and the Schumann cello concerto played by Pierre Fournier. Wilhelm Kempff appeared in the New Year as a soloist, with Chopin's 2nd piano concerto. On 26 January 1944, the orchestra played Strauss' *Don Juan* and *Ein Heldenleben* (*A Hero's Life*) for the composer's eightieth birthday. But these big-name concerts were punctuated by the horrors of war, as intense air bombing returned to the capital. What would have been one of Hartmann's first concerts on 28 November 1943, under maestro Karl Böhm (who had been an ardent supporter of annexation of Austria into Nazi Germany, the Anschluß), was cancelled because of an air attack. The Philharmonic offices were bombed the following week.

Furtwängler, with Göring, Hitler, and Goebbels in the front row, 1935

Richard Strauss, Heinz Drewes, and Joseph Goebbels in 1938 (left to right)

'Did you play for Goebbels in the Ministry?' I ask. Goebbels called the Berlin Philharmonic *his* orchestra and Hitler was also present for concerts.

'I don't remember doing so. But he was often at our concerts. Speer too – he was definitely the smartest one of them,' he replies, speaking of Hitler's chief architect.

I ask him how it was to play with Wilhelm Furtwängler, the orchestra's controversial conductor, and perhaps the most celebrated of the twentieth century. He was appointed to conduct the Philharmonic in 1922 and remained in the post until January 1945 when he fled to Switzerland, before returning after the war. He had ample opportunity to leave Germany after the Nazis came to power, such as in 1935 when offered the helm of the New York Philharmonic. But he remained and had a close relationship with Joseph Goebbels, with whom he would go on long walks.

On one hand, Furtwängler is known for defending Jewish musicians in the orchestra and for being suspended for premiering the opera-based symphony *Mathis der Maler* by Paul Hindemith – a composer Hitler abhorred. The conductor defended Hindemith and artistic freedom in a newspaper article and was suspended from his post on 4 December 1934. He crawled back to Goebbels in regret, however, on 28 February 1935. Thomas Mann would note in his diary: 'Furtwängler was made to submit so he could be redeemed in grace.' Hindemith's music, meanwhile, was banned in 1936 and the composer left for Switzerland two years later. The extent of Furtwängler's complicity with the Nazi regime would remain a subject of fierce debate.

'Furtwängler was very strict,' Hartmann tells me. 'He could observe each musician, individually. He knew exactly if someone played properly and well with the others. Karajan could do that too. Most think: "Oh, he can't even see me." But we had experiences in rehearsals when [Furtwängler] could even tell if someone was reading the newspaper … He was tall, so he could see well. He'd say, "You there, you need to make more of an effort". Karajan didn't say that, he'd let the administrators tell you. Furtwängler would tell you directly. It was better that way.'

'Was it different playing with him than other conductors?'

'It was a feeling you had. Here is a great conductor. He wasn't just tall in stature but also spiritually'.

I listen to Herr Hartmann, as he eats more cookies, and ponder how easy it is to confuse the man with the music. Is the metaphor lost on him: nearly 100 men, dressed the same, facing the same direction, following, in unison, the direction of their spiritual leader? Wasn't this optimal precision – here producing glorious music – also desired by the generals? For a moment, I see the musicians holding – instead of violas, oboes, and horns – machine guns trained on a public who, due to the stage lights, they cannot see.

Nazis and Jews

'And what were your relationships like with the other musicians?' I ask. 'When you joined, you were the only former soldier in the orchestra. Others didn't have this experience. How did they react?'

'I might have been the youngest man in the orchestra but, since I had fought in the war, the others said: "He knows everything."'

Hartmann describes that, while many of the other musicians were a little afraid of him, he was popular with the Nazis precisely because he had been a combatant – a war hero. One Nazi member even helped him find a place to live. Hartmann is forgiving of them in his memoir: 'I wouldn't today want to judge them too harshly, those who still had some human feeling, despite the political sentiments they had at the time.'

The Philharmonic was a volatile political environment, difficult to navigate. Hartmann tells me that most musicians were against the regime, but among the 18 per cent who were party members there was a hardcore group of Nazis, who kept everyone else in check. Among the double basses, Arno Burkhardt was a member of the party, but he was not as radical as, say, violinists Werner Buchholz and Reinhard Wolf, cellist Wolfram Kleber, and trumpeter Anton Schuldes.

'One wore his SA uniform in rehearsal!' Hartmann tells me, referring to the violinist Hans Woywoth.

In 1937, a majority of the Philharmonic elected a small group of Nazis to represent the entire community and in 1938 the whole orchestra participated in an oath to the Führer. The 1939 service contract made their relationship to the Nazi state quite clear, committing the musicians to the 'National Socialist world view' and 'the unwritten laws of German culture'. The document was not drafted by the government but by the musicians themselves. As the Propaganda Ministry expected, the orchestra self-administered its allegiance to the Nazi state.

'Were these party members dangerous?'

'Yes, they were dangerous. If you said too much, they could report you.'

'Was there pressure to join the party?' I ask, knowing it was not a requirement.

'Yes, certainly. There was pressure, also from the management. Many did it. But many did not. Many of those who did were harmless people.'

'Why didn't you?'

'They didn't trust me because I had been a soldier. I would have declined in any case. But they didn't try anything with me. They thought: he can also be dangerous. They didn't know me. And I didn't know them.'

'Were there any minority groups in the orchestra? Roma, homosexuals, disabled people?'

'We had a disabled musician. I don't know why he was disabled. It did not affect his playing. He did everything, even the tours.' And Herr Hartmann says of homosexuality in the orchestra, 'I didn't know anything about that.'

'And what of those with Jewish connections in the orchestra? Bruno Stenzel was half-Jewish. Did people know that?' I refer to the second violinist who had been allowed to remain in the orchestra even though he was of 'mixed blood'.

'I don't think anyone knew except the management.'

Frau Bastiaan remarks, 'He must have been under huge amounts of pressure.'

Szymon Goldberg and Gilbert Back during a concert tour, 1931

'Herr [Ernst] Fischer, the clarinettist, had a Jewish wife. It wasn't easy for him. It was horrendous what they did. They burned books. They burned scores.'

Many Jewish soloists had stopped playing on German stages in 1933. At this time, many of the most important Jewish composers and conductors also left the country: Kurt Weill, Otto Klemperer, Arnold Schoenberg, Bruno Walter. Furtwängler was known for criticising Jewish musicians and composers; no Jew had joined the orchestra since the 1929–30 season. But the conductor was also known for protecting them. As long as the Philharmonic was state run, its Jewish musicians were not directly affected by the 7 April 1933 law purging Jews from public cultural institutions. Furtwängler, despite his antipathies, withstood a public campaign against his Jewish musicians in the press. But when the orchestra came into public hands, the Jewish musicians were more exposed.

Approximately 10 per cent of the orchestra's musicians were directly threatened by the state's race laws. During Furtwängler's brief absence resulting from the Hindemith debacle, the Philharmonic's four Jewish musicians lost their jobs. The two who were classified as 'mixed race', and the four with Jewish wives, stayed on, but in precarious conditions, harassed by the Gestapo. The Jewish spouses were not allowed to attend performances.

In 1935, signs at the Philharmonic's entrance stated that Jews were forbidden, and Jewish patrons had their subscriptions cancelled. By the 1935–36 season, there were no more Jewish members of the orchestra. They had all left, mostly to America. One, Szymon Goldberg, whose family would be interned in Dutch Indonesia, never performed in Germany again; he died in 1993. I wonder what he thought of his colleagues who stayed and continued to play?

Alte Philharmonie

Of the spaces in which his double bass sounded, the one that stayed most in Herr Hartmann's memory was the Alte Philharmonie, or Old Philharmonic Hall, on Bernburger Straße in Berlin. It's hard to imagine that the Alte Philharmonie used to be a roller-skating rink. With its oval shape and arched ceilings, it was from 1888 the seat of what would become Europe's best orchestra.

I like to think of the rink itself turned into the orchestra rows, the bleachers into loges, the whole space tarted up with pillars and decoration. The neoclassical *Gründerzeit* refurbishment was of questionable taste and unpopular with the Bauhaus-enthused crowd of the 1920s; the hall would better suit the Nazis. The wooden seats were famously uncomfortable and, from many of them, you could not even see the very high stage. There was talk about demolition (they would have to wait only until 1944). To truly enjoy its most famous quality, you had to close your eyes. Pablo Casals, Fritz Kreisler, Sergej Rachmaninoff, and a 22-year-old Vladimir Horowitz all played here before the Nazis came to power.

'It wasn't long that you played in the Alte Philharmonie.'

'Only a quarter year!'

'Why, then, does it stick so deep in your memory?'

'The wonderful acoustics.'

He tells me that while today's Philharmonic Hall has 'great acoustics', the Alte Philharmonie was better, comparable to Hartmann's favourite venue in the world: New York City's Carnegie Hall. Even when it was a rink, visitors had noticed the great sound. I imagine that of rollers scraping the floor. I imagine a fabulous roller-disco! The Alte Philharmonie was actually used for formal and costume balls, along with political rallies of the left and right.

Frau Bastiaan says the hall must stay in Hartmann's memory because it was the location of his first experience with 'this famous orchestra and famous conductor'. It's where he stood with his instrument in the back row for the first time, perhaps next to a party member, looking up to Furtwängler.

Great music was made in this 2,500-capacity space and the adjacent Beethovensaal, which was built for chamber music. But on 30 January 1944, the eleventh anniversary of Hitler's coming to power, the Alte Philharmonie was bombed.

Alte Philharmonie in 1939 with Wilhelm Furtwängler on the podium

Destruction

Hartmann, extraordinarily, was there, among the members of the orchestra chosen each night for air-raid duty. This was a rotation of musicians who slept in the building, bringing their own pillows, and who donned uniforms, gas masks, and helmets in case of attack. I can't help but wonder what a few members of, say, the string section could do against an Allied bombardment.

Animated, he tells me, 'Six people were always there to make sure everything was ok. None of them is alive any more. Just me. That night came the intense attack from English or American planes … the firefighters were there. They said, we can't put this out. It's not just fire. There were phosphorus bombs that can only be put out with sand. What could we do?

'It was difficult to go into the hall: the roof could break down on us. We only were able to save rows of chairs. I wonder what happened to all of them! Maybe people took them or they were used as firewood. We had no firewood. Very few of those chairs still exist.'

He continues, 'They said, don't go in! Before we had gone in and out, until the point we couldn't go back in, because the entire roof came down.'

I imagine this scene of mayhem and the enormous, superheated, chandeliers crashing to the ground. The musicians then focused on the Beethovensaal, and the instruments kept in the building's basement.

'When the Alte Philharmonie burned, where was your double bass?' asks Frau Bastiaan.

I imagine Hartmann emerging from the burning building with his instrument, but that was not the case. He says, 'It was safe. It wasn't there … it was in a storage stall under an S-Bahn line … And the soloists always had the small instruments with them at home: violins, cellos. Many were very valuable.'

Even seventy-five years later, he is visibly saddened: 'I can't tell you how quickly the word got around in Berlin that the Philharmonie had been flattened. One conductor, Hermann Abendroth, came the moment he heard about it. He was so horrified. We all were but couldn't do very much. It was war. You could only say: we hope it ends soon. Yes, *that's* happened. But you don't lose this atmosphere. One always has it inside oneself. I'm happy to have known these halls, to have practised there.'

After the war, the Alte Philharmonie remained in ruins. On 18 September 1952, the skeleton – including part of the façade – was detonated, leaving 140,000 sq. ft of rubble, which was slowly hauled off to a giant man-made hill of debris, Teufelsberg, or Devil's Mountain. The new Philharmonie, designed by Hans Scharoun – an expressive and organic icon of post-war architecture – opened in 1963, alongside the Berlin Wall next to the Tiergarten.

We do not need to imagine Herr Hartmann standing where the Alte Philharmonie once was. Frau Bastiaan tells me there is a touching scene in the 2007 documentary film *Das Reichsorchester* when he visits the space. He found, on Bernburger Straße, a cleared lot between two 1990s buildings, several boulders huddled around a drain, and a plaque on the ground.

I say, 'You went to the location of the Alte Philharmonie. When you see this space, how do you feel?'

He replies, 'I thought, this place has changed so much that I can't even imagine that a Philharmonie was once here. There should be a proper memorial, at eye level: "Here stood the old Philharmonie" ... I think about how the building was. And how different it is now.' He continues, growing gloomy, 'Kids at school see old Berlin on photos and everything is so superb and, after the war, everything was so destroyed.'

'They can hardly believe it,' Frau Bastiaan adds.

With the loss of the hall, the Philharmonic became itinerant between Berlin's remaining performance venues. The Beethovensaal was too small for the orchestra, so they relied on other locations such as the Theater des Westens, the Titania Palast, and the State Opera House. Hartmann tells me, 'Most of the concerts we did in the afternoons because the bombs rarely came during the daytime. The people came then. There were air-raid sirens.'

Even a daytime concert could be interrupted by bombs. The orchestra would go into the bunker, wait, come back, and then keep playing. Hartmann describes one concert in the Admiralspalast when they were playing Beethoven and the lights went out, and they simply kept playing in the dark.

The bombing did not only affect the musicians' workplace but also their homes. Erich Hartmann also lost his apartment due to the bombing raids. He explains, 'I used to live in the Kirchbachstraße, four floors up, and I met a woman there, and she said during an air-raid siren that she

PHILHARMONIE

wouldn't go down. Nothing will happen. But anyway, we went into the bunker, and when we came up this little street was completely destroyed. Everything was gone, including my house. If I had been upstairs … let's not think about it. It was a lucky break.'

'Looking back at this time, is it like a dream?'

'It's shocking. When one thinks back on it, to think what kind of mistake one would have made not to go downstairs. It was always better to be in security. Some didn't do it. They died. Many people died. Not only were their belongings destroyed but there were so many corpses.'

As he recounts, I am keenly aware that he is able – even at the age of 98 – to relive everything as if it were yesterday. Even though the ruins of the building have long been dragged away, the tragedy remains distinct, as if he were still standing in that hall, as it filled with smoke, watching the roof on fire. Sensations – like heat – sear the memory.

Tours

'Each instrument had its box,' Hartmann tells me. 'The double bass went well inside. It didn't rock around. It was tightly bound. All the other instruments also had other boxes, the cellos or the harps, the timpani … They were always sent in advance that way for tours.'

In the absence of a hall – without a fixed address – and with the dangers of the bombings, the Philharmonic increasingly relied on tours. Hartmann describes the orchestra as a 'figurehead for German culture for the propaganda offensive'. Not only would this monument of German culture tour German factories. It would, remarkably, cross war-torn Europe. In September 1940, the musicians toured the bombed-out shell of Rotterdam. Later, as an ambassador, it neutralised the image of dictatorship, violence, and racial murder, while garnering excellent reviews in the foreign press. According to violist Werner Buchholz, tours allowed the musicians to 'conquer countries', albeit more peacefully than *Wehrmacht* soldiers.

The tours brought the Philharmonic to Prague in March 1944, Norway in late March and April (Hartmann did not participate), and then Spain, Portugal, and France from April to June. Dispatched like soldiers, by military trains, the musicians were told to remain among one another to eat and drink and were discouraged from consorting with locals. In both the

Nazi press and post-war denazification trials (a process which questioned suspects in formal tribunals), the touring Philharmonic was suspected as being a cover for Gestapo agents involved in espionage.

Hartmann writes in his memoir that Spain appeared as a 'land of milk and honey' to the orchestra musicians. They had a great success touring many cities, playing a predictable repertoire of Wagner, Beethoven, and Brahms, under the direction of Hans Knappertsbusch, who gave them much free time as he did not require rehearsals. In Barcelona, the crowds enthusiastically threw wreathes on stage. A propaganda film, *Philharmoniker*, directed by Paul Verhoeven, recorded the tour and premiered in Berlin on 5 December 1944.

One of the advantages of being in a country not at war was the availability of products impossible to find at home. The Philharmonic musicians became smugglers. They packed their train home with olive oil, canned goods, and textiles. A valuable bag of coffee could keep a Berlin family fed since it could be exchanged for all sorts of merchandise at home. As Herr Bastiaan said in an interview, 'We never thought about whether we were playing in a friendly country or not … we only tried to buy coffee.' At the Spanish border, this proved a problem: would they be controlled? The *Konzertmeister*,

Gerhard Taschner, had a brilliant idea to get them past the guards without a proper inspection.

'Do you know Taschner?' Hartmann asks me. 'The *Konzertmeister*? He played so well for the customs guards in Spain that they let us go! ... Those guards said, "Everything is ok, you can go." Taschner was an amazing man.'

Reception after a concert in Paris: principal cellist Arthur Troester (third from left) and concertmaster Gerhard Taschner (right) with a German general and other guests

Hartmann shared his compartment with an enormous percussionist, who sat on his colleague's hat, and whose dripping olive oil destroyed another's luggage. But this was the least of the travelling musicians' troubles. In France, the rails were bombarded by Allied planes. The passengers scattered out from the carriages, terrified, as the bombs fell. Once the terror passed overhead, the orchestra was ordered north, to Paris, where they played on 9 June 1944. The concert was amid the drama of the Allied invasions of France, only days after D-Day.

Arriving at Anhalter Bahnhof in Berlin, many orchestra musicians stored their smuggled goods in the Philharmonic's locker under the S-Bahn line, normally used for instruments. The musicians came back the next day and found it had been broken into and their loot nicked. Hartmann chuckles that the double bass was too unwieldy to be stolen.

Hitler was already afraid that his great conductor, Furtwängler, would succumb in a bombing, and arranged for him to be evacuated. The orchestra, too, did not remain long in the capital, and spent August and part of September out of danger in a spa town. They stayed in a luxurious hotel with a sauna and herbal treatments.

'The whole orchestra was offloaded in Baden-Baden because in Berlin it was so dangerous. They didn't want more victims in the orchestra. Three had already died. So, we went to Baden-Baden. I have a memory of it: there was no real war. We were eight weeks there. It was only a time before we returned because our public in Berlin wanted to hear us.'

Arriving back in mid-September, Furtwängler conducted a series of 'excellent concerts' from late October to early December in the Staatsoper and Admiralspalast – predictably including more Brahms (3rd symphony, violin concerto) and Schubert (the *Unfinished Symphony*).

'You also played for factories, for *Kraft durch Freude* ...' I say.

'That too. They listened very carefully even though many of those factory workers had never heard a concert. For them, it was something special. The Berlin Philharmonic was very famous but they had not heard how good we were ... Even though they might not have had a special feeling for music, they still appreciated it.'

'I haven't understood why the orchestra kept playing in the last weeks of the war. In the middle of April. Right up until the end.'

'We played as long as possible. Why? The people wanted to hear us.'

Indeed, they came in great numbers, looking for comfort. The Philharmonic played in venues such as a *Wehrmacht* war hospital of injured men, located in the Olympic Village, on 7 April 1945, weeks before the capitulation. But there was also a propaganda mission: the orchestra that played until the very end was, of course, a symbol.

We discuss how afraid people were as the Russians approached. Altogether, six Philharmonic members were casualties of war, including three suicides. Hartmann tells me, 'Herr [Bernhard] Alt committed suicide with the whole family [two daughters and his wife] in Silesia. He was afraid. I knew him well. He wrote a piece for four double basses. I was so upset. He did it because he feared for his life. Such a war will not repeat itself, I don't think.'

The concert programmes contained dramatic music to fit the times, such as the immolation scene from Wagner's *Götterdämmerung* played amid the Battle for Berlin on 12 April, during which members of the Hitler Youth distributed cyanide pills to the audience as an encouragement to suicide. The repertoire fit Hitler's notion that his fate and Germany's would end together. The last concerts, ordered by Albert Speer, were on 15 and 16 April. The Philharmonic percussionist, Gerassimos Avgerinos, questioned the programming in his diary – 'Unintentional?' – because the last piece was Strauss' *Tod und Verklärung* (*Death and Transfiguration*). A few days later, the remaining part of the Alte Philharmonie complex, the Beethovensaal, was in flames.

Stunde Null

Hartmann describes in his memoir how the musicians were used to a hyper-organised work life. Shielded from many of the excesses of war, the orchestra scattered during the Battle of Berlin and its members were thrown into panic. Hartmann in our interview 'can't find the words' for the lawlessness and violence that accompanied the battle, speaking not only of shelling and bombings, but also the Red Army rapes, the Nazi atrocities, and the stink of the city. Hartmann narrowly escaped being taken as a POW by the Red Army, by jumping over the S-Bahn tracks with a friend.

Given a permit to move around the city, he presents a wild image: Hartmann walking through the ruins of Berlin with his double bass pushed in a baby carriage. He observes the city in disarray: people pumping for water, without enough food. He describes a grand piano hanging from a pillar on a ruined building.

The Philharmonic reunites for its first meeting on 13 May 1945. They need to establish who survived, who can conduct them, and the fate of scores and instruments. Many of the latter were lost but some second instruments had survived in the basement of the ruined Philharmonie. That said, many were also stolen, as the Red Army sent objects of value back to the Soviet Union. Hartmann tells me that if I go to the musical instrument museum in Berlin, I will even find some rescued instruments: 'Thank goodness not everything was lost. But the Russians took many with them. They could have taken harps and timpani and double basses, but they only took what was light to carry.'

'Perhaps also the chairs!' says Frau Bastiaan.

'And slowly, slowly, we are getting them back from the Russians. Also scores,' he tells me.

Russian thefts at the end of the war, in the shadow of the Holocaust, are largely overlooked. But I can't help but think instead about the parallel question of stolen property taken from Jews by the Nazis. Jewish losses have, for good reason, historically been the main subject of conversation regarding restitution in Germany. In fact, they have consumed the national consciousness. I recall how the German state, for example, is a signatory to the 1998 Washington Conference Principles and 2009 Terezin Declaration on Holocaust-Era Assets, which include non-binding agreements regarding Nazi-confiscated and looted art. Its members have obliged themselves to support and actively conduct provenance research and make this available publicly.

Hartmann continues to speak, telling me that, to everyone's surprise, they had orchestra sets of scores: the music that had been forbidden. 'We had a colleague who had the banned music hidden … They said it had all been annihilated [*vernichtet*]. Our [Friedrich] Quante, the trombonist, he said, *ich vernichte nicht* [I won't destroy]. I will save it all instead. He could have been sentenced to death. He did everything secretly. After the war, we suddenly had all these scores when we thought they were gone … We have a lot to thank him for.' Quante, incidentally, was a party member but did not face denazification.

The Philharmonic's first concert after the war was on 26 May, less than a month after their previous appearance. The programme included banned pieces such as Mendelssohn's *A Midsummer Night's Dream* and Tchaikovsky's Symphony No. 4. It was conducted by Leo Borchard.

'When Furtwängler had to be – or should have been – denazified, we didn't have a conductor,' Hartmann tells me. 'Before Celibidache, we had Borchard. He was a good director. You know the story with the auto … '

Borchard was chosen precisely because he had been blacklisted by the Nazis and this provided the orchestra with the expected image of distance from the Nazi regime. Borchard, however, died in an accident, shot by American border control for not stopping his car on 23 August 1945. The Philharmonic was faced with an emergency. Sergiu Celibidache, a Romanian conductor, was hired in December 1945, but the players found him difficult: he was a slavedriver in rehearsals, he conducted by heart (unfashionable), and made war on the bass section because he didn't like low notes.

A few years later, Bruno Walter and Otto Klemperer returned to conduct. The orchestra enjoyed working with the former but came into conflict with the latter of the Jewish maestros. Hartmann explains in his memoir how Klemperer resented conducting an orchestra that had been so privileged during the Nazi period.

Meanwhile, the Philharmonic found themselves well fed by the Americans. Having been a propaganda machine for the Nazis, the orchestra turned into a symbol of hope for the Berliners. Continued involvement, however, was uncertain for the Nazi members who were under investigation.

The orchestra already in May 1945 did not include five of its former musicians. Hartmann said, 'We cleansed ourselves,' but this redemptive declaration occupies the realm of myth, as nowhere is it documented that these dismissals were forced by the orchestra itself. Between 1945 and 1946, of the eighteen Nazi party members who survived the war, seven of them were permanently forced out in an uncoordinated and haphazard process resulting from the Allied denazification procedures. Three more were allowed to return after a suspension and the rest were absolved. Those extruded found work in other orchestras outside the

American sector of Berlin, where the orchestra was based. My research in the German Federal Archive unearthed that both Hartmann and Bastiaan were interviewed by the Allies, but neither investigation was pursued.

Hartmann was sorry to see friends go, some of whom 'did no one any wrong. They were great artists and true colleagues.' He writes, 'Unfortunately some were thrown out who were only party members, even though they had the goodwill of the orchestra.'

I say, 'I've read orchestra members testified to support party members during denazification trials.'

'My Hans,' says Frau Bastiaan of her husband, 'did it for Hans Gieseler.'

'He was first violin. He was completely harmless. I wasn't close friends, but we understood each other … Not all the ones in the party were dangerous,' says Herr Hartmann. Many had joined the party very young or simply for careerist reasons, apparently, such as Gieseler.

I ask about Herr Woywoth, and Herr Kleber, the cellist.

'I always wondered why he [Woywoth] wore that SA uniform. He was kicked out. And Kleber ended up in the Deutsche Oper.'

Frau Bastiaan adds, 'And Dietrich Gerhardt [a Philharmonic violist] said that was also a punishment!'

'Herr Kleber came back to play in the orchestra, to fill in as a guest sometimes after the war – ' I mention.

'People didn't care,' replies Herr Hartmann. 'It was all OK.' Woywoth, meanwhile, found a job in Düsseldorf with the opera orchestra.

'And Furtwängler also needed to withdraw – '

'He needed to be denazified. Some say he was a Nazi. But he never had anything to do with politics. He only did his job, his music, that was what was most important to him.'

Hartmann goes on to describe, 'Goebbels was our boss. I didn't meet him personally but he was always around … Furtwängler, however, was only there to direct. He stood high up there on the podium and the public was quite far below. One can hardly see who sits down there. When there was applause, he always held the baton by the right hand, so that he couldn't make the Hitler salute. He did this on purpose. Many people don't know that.'

'I've read that you do not think of the Berlin Philharmonic as a Nazi orchestra. What does that mean?'

'It was not one, as one can imagine it. It was not the case.'

'Weren't people in the Philharmonic in the Nazi period political? Did people talk about politics?'

'No, we didn't at all. We had to play.'

'And when you think back on those times, what do you think we should learn from the Second World War?'

'Not to burn music, not to burn scores.'

Frau Bastiaan intervenes. 'We also need to remember what happened to the Jews.'

'Yes, that was horrific,' he says.

We are interrupted because a nurse comes in, abruptly, with pills for his patient, wanting to make up the bed. He is brusque and remarks that the visitors are still here. 'Ah, that man!' Hartmann says once the nurse is gone. 'I know I shouldn't say anything ill of people. I really shouldn't. But – but he's just so uncouth.' And I see this old man struggle to say something negative.

Hartmann insists on rising to see me off. 'I hope that you were well served today!'

Just as when we arrived, he wants to be hospitable and come to the door but doesn't make it very far.

'Thank you so much, Herr Hartmann.'

'Thank you for coming from Canada!'

'Actually, he just came from Kreuzberg,' Frau Bastiaan reminds him.

He replies, '*Jetzt!*' Only now!

On the bus on the way home, I tell the wife of the concertmaster that I find questionable Herr Hartmann's assertion that people didn't speak about politics in the Philharmonic. Frau Bastiaan looks at me in disagreement, from the adjoining seat, and says that these men were politically detached. 'They were so busy that they didn't really wake up to what was going on. As employees of the state, they were freed from war duty, but every meeting was mandatory. They were in service. It was like being under a bell jar, or so my husband said.'

In an interview, Herr Bastiaan said that, politically, the musicians were like 'children'. Busy children. The musicians, in any given year before the war, would perform 200 times and rehearse twice that number, leading to many instances of burnout. Work was a distraction and, in the war's quotidian, most people only lived their immediate experience. Goebbels' cook couldn't see beyond the kitchen. Herr Hartmann – who struck me as the mildest mannered of men – could not see beyond the stage. It was so high that you hardly saw the audience. Up there, he hardly saw beyond the notes. After all, he said the lesson of war was to save the score.

The Instrument

Let us take Herr Hartmann's story from the instrument's perspective: the journey and survival of his double bass. We can follow the instrument's purchase during the war, its performances during blackouts, its survival under the bombs, transport on orchestra tours through occupied Europe, and how it was spared when the Russians marched into Berlin. Since it is such a large instrument, and difficult to move, the challenge of survival was even greater. It was lucky, just as Herr Hartmann had been so many times. He was spared despite his wounds on the Eastern Front, during the bombing of his apartment, or when travelling through occupied Europe and observing the end days of the war. Ultimately, he was saved because of his non-conscription status at the Philharmonic. The man and the instrument are joined in their survival; the instrument magnifies his story.

Yet, this object history is only half-told. As it stands, the instrument remains an observer, a bit player in the corner of the orchestra pit, a belonging following its master from place to place. For a musical instrument really to tell the story of the Philharmonic during the war, it must be implicated in its acts.

The story of these musicians' collaboration with the Nazi regime comes together precisely with object history when one considers the provenance of their instruments. Some of them could well have been stolen from victims of the regime; this would link the individual musician to an apparatus of state theft.

Hartmann told me that he had obtained his double bass in 1943 from a shop in Berlin. He also told me that it was an old instrument, and I immediately thought that any instrument acquired during the war ran a high risk of having been a confiscation. I was determined to find out more about the double bass's provenance and that of instruments played by his colleagues. Although I knew that Herr Hartmann did not get his instrument from Goebbels' procurement programme, perhaps it was nonetheless on a list of stolen instruments. Did the Nazi-procured instruments remain in the hands of musicians after the war? What had happened to them since? If they had been confiscated, were they back with their original owners?

Not allowed to visit the double bassist myself, due to restrictions in the care home because of the coronavirus pandemic, I tasked Frau Bastiaan with finding out the details of his instrument. She struck me as a good anti-fascist and was speaking to Herr Hartmann weekly. She came back to me with the information that the double bass had been bought in Berlin from an instrument maker and shop called Pilar. It was founded in 1909 and has been four generations in the same family. It still exists today in Berlin-Schöneberg. A current double bassist in the Philharmonic later tells me that there are three instruments that Hartmann owned, and the one he bought at Pilar was most likely made by Kaakstein (an unfortunate name, sounding like 'shit-stone').

Having now additional information about the instrument, I could turn to the professionals. I get in touch with Jason Price, founder of Tarisio, the world's leading auction house of old string instruments in London and New York, and now Berlin. He maintains a database of stolen instruments but does not find Herr Hartmann's on it. He tells me that this 'chapter of musical history is notoriously opaque. There is an especially large documentary gap with the German wartime dealers. But there's someone you should meet who has an open book of all the unanswered questions.' He puts me in touch with Carla Shapreau, a lawyer and academic at the University of California in Berkeley, who specialises in the provenance of instruments confiscated by the Nazis.

Shapreau elaborates: 'A great many musical instruments were obtained during the Nazi era through confiscation by the Third Reich, while others were acquired through purchase. Some of these purchases may have been legitimate, but others appear tainted and provenance gaps raise serious questions about where these instruments came from. In some cases, proof of these transfers survive in scattered archival records in several nations and languages, such as confiscation records, victim claim files, and post-war Allied records reflecting discoveries of looted musical objects evacuated during the war to salt mines, monasteries, and other caches.'

I had already read just how difficult it would be to establish whether a specific instrument had been stolen by the Nazis. As Nazis scooped up collections, they used middlemen, or dealers, whose records are usually unavailable, thrown out intentionally or as soon as the taxman lost interest.

Shapreau remarks that, 'Historical dealer records serve an important and often essential role in both authenticity and reconstructing the history of ownership. In some cases, these records are accessible in public archives or with descendants of wartime dealers who welcome research. But in other instances, these records are unaccounted for or are privately owned and inaccessible. Prominent contemporary dealers have acquired some key historical dealer records for legitimate business purposes but ready access for study may be limited.'

Charting an instrument's past is as if through an unkempt labyrinth, in many places overgrown. I learn that even today it is industry standard to provide a 'certificate of authenticity' for an instrument being sold but to redact names of prior owners, which can obscure its provenance. Even confirming one has identified the right instrument is tricky as often there are no historical pictures of a stolen instrument, and current owners will not allow an inspection. Even if one identifies such an instrument, different jurisdictions in this multinational story make restitution problematic, yielding varying results. There are so many obstacles and one cannot say that all instruments coming from Goebbels' programme, for example, were necessarily stolen or subject to a forced sale under duress. As for Herr Hartmann's instrument? I have no indication that it was a confiscation; it remains an unanswered question.

I turn to other instruments in the orchestra. It's in Misha Aster's book on the Philharmonic under the Nazis that I stumble across a brief mention of the orchestra's musicians who, in 1942, were recipients of instruments from Joseph Goebbels' procurement programme. We know of a Pietro Guarneri violin that went to Erich Röhn, a school of Guarneri cello for Tibor de Machula, and the promise of a Stradivari for Gerhard Taschner. And, to my great surprise, I discover that, in 1942, a valuable Guadagnini violin was given to a name that is already familiar to us: startlingly, Frau Bastiaan's husband, Hans. The handover of the instrument is documented in a Philharmonic programme from the 1942–43 season.

Tamino

A musical reference, the plot of Mozart's *Magic Flute*, comes to mind. Prince Tamino intends to vanquish Sarastro, the high priest, but discovers he is a fount of knowledge. He arrives at the truth through indirection. I began my research with the idea of telling the story of the Philharmonic during the war from the perspective of an instrument. How is it that I was looking for Herr Hartmann's bass when the story was another instrument belonging to the husband of the woman who introduced me to him? The object, and the right path, was always there, but just to the side. It's easy to mistake the protagonist.

I have no proof yet that Herr Bastiaan's violin was stolen. But I do know that it was part of the Nazi wartime mission to acquire instruments that was linked to theft and atrocity. I learned, too, that he played his violin until retirement. The Guadagnini must be incredibly valuable today. Such an instrument normally auctions at more than a million dollars. It's worth the same as a high-end apartment. I'm full of questions: how did he live with the unease of not knowing the instrument's origin? Or did he? Did he think not knowing was better? Did he feel he was benefiting from someone else's loss? I am determined to find out where this instrument is now. To do this would take some caution and skill.

It's Monday and I'm stressed out because I am getting ready to go over to Frau Bastiaan's for coffee on Wednesday. I don't know how to confront her. She wants to show me pictures of her husband and Herr Hartmann. I am going to be sitting there with her over a cup of coffee and cake – specialities she's bought for a pleasant afternoon – and I'm going to turn on my tape recorder and speculate: your husband got his violin from Joseph Goebbels. How do you feel about owning such an instrument? Are you going to sell it? No, that would be too aggressive: I don't want to be shown the door. I need to be tactful. All I want is the truth: 'I know some of the story of your husband's violin. It must be difficult to inherit an instrument that came from this programme.' No matter, I will do my job. The chapter is about how instruments tell the story of the war. And you have one that does precisely that. If she kicks me out, so be it. At least I will have tried to find out the truth.

I gather my documents. She lives just a few streets from me, it turns out, also in Berlin-Kreuzberg, in what looks like a Dutch modernist block of flats overlooking the dappled changing autumn trees. The interior of the house is full of old books and furniture and, again, a bust of Furtwängler. I sit across from her over the expected coffee and cake – it's all so very pleasant, also the conversation about family and music – and I am trying to make sense of how to broach a difficult subject.

But as it turns out, she brings it up herself.

She tells me, 'I never saw the instrument. After my husband retired, it was given to another musician in the orchestra because it was only on loan. My husband was always so happy with how the violin played, and when he thought of its origin, he thought only of where the Guadagnini was made, in Italy. But he didn't ask the question: who played it before me? Even during the filming of the documentary, *Das Reichsorchester*, when the director briefly asks about the provenance of the violin, it was as if the heavens opened for him. It never occurred to him that it might have been confiscated from a Jew. That it took until 2006 for him to recognise this speaks for itself.'

Not only is Frau Bastiaan not a participant witness, but she is not a witness at all. That the object was on loan makes all the difference. I am so relieved, because I like her so much! I am also ashamed because I underestimated her. A great weight lifts and I go home finally to watch the film. In a fleeting clip, Herr Bastiaan says: 'It never occurred to me that the violin could have been from a Jew or someone else … I was just glad that there were violins owned by the state, and that one could be lent to me.'

Frau Bastiaan tells me that her husband passed on the violin to the new concertmaster of the Philharmonic, Professor Kolja Blacher, the grandson of the composer Boris Blacher who was part-Jewish. The latter was born to a Russian community in Manchuria, ended up in Berlin in the 1920s studying music, and was then labelled degenerate by the Nazis. He had a very successful, and influential, post-war career. His son Kolja did not stay long with the orchestra, so the violin must have passed into other hands. Whose? I am going to start asking around musician friends to find out.

But I quickly understand that instrumentalists will be put on guard if a historian is asking too many questions that might eventually result in the confiscation of their 1.5 million euro Guadagnini.

But the news that the instrument is on loan brings the investigation to an entirely new level. Before, I thought an individual member of the orchestra was playing an instrument of dodgy provenance. Now, I understand that the instrument is likely owned by an institution. This leads me to the astonishing suspicion that the Berlin Philharmonic has been passing on through its ranks an instrument stolen by the Nazi regime. My hunch would prove incorrect, but the truth would turn out to be much more problematic.

Violins plundered by the Nazis

Looking for a Violin

I put together a team of people who will help me find the violin. The British cellist Natalie Clein puts me in touch with colleagues. Everyone I speak to sees the justice of the search, even if it means that some, perhaps unsuspecting, instrumentalist will find out that they have been playing a violin possessed by the Nazi regime.

I follow two lines of enquiry. The first is the individual musician: who has played the violin up until now? I need to find out to whom they passed on the instrument so I can get to today's player. The second route is institutional. Who could own it: the Philharmonic itself, a museum, a private or public foundation, a government? Is this institution aware of the instrument's murky origins? Can it justify why the violin is still in circulation? Is it profiting from it? I search for where these two routes intersect and think that is where I will find my conclusion.

Frau Bastiaan has already told me that there was a tradition in the Philharmonic to pass on instruments after retirement to one's replacement. Perhaps that is why the violin was passed on from her husband to the soloist Kolja Blacher. He studied violin at Juilliard and was first concertmaster of the Berlin Philharmonic in the 1990s under conductor Claudio Abbado, before launching a distinguished solo career.

Professor Blacher replies immediately to my email and is ready to help. He was given the violin in 1979, he tells me, not by the Philharmonic, but by the Preußischer Kulturbesitz, or Prussian Cultural Heritage Foundation, a federal government body that oversees Berlin's state museums. Before German unification, the foundation offered instruments to promising musicians. This happened well before he became concertmaster, he corrects me. He now plays a Stradivarius. I imagine Kolja Blacher, as a teenager, receiving the expensive Guadagnini and taking it with him to New York, where so many Jewish instrumentalists deprived of their citizenship and property went during the Nazi period.

'Did you know the history of the instrument?' I ask him.

'I had no idea until a few years ago. I would not have accepted this violin had I known its history. It was incredible to me.'

'What was the violin like?'

'It was made by Giovanni Battista Guadagnini, while he was in Parma, not Milan. It is rather dark brown colour – unusual for a Guadagnini, which are usually reddish – and narrow. I played it until 1985 when I passed it on. I remember that, after I gave it away, I went to see a performance of the Trio Fontenay. From far away, I recognised the violin because it was so unusually narrow. I talked to Michael Mücke, from the trio, later and it was the same violin! He played it for a long time and now plays with the DSO, the Germany Symphony Orchestra.'

I follow the next links in the chain. As it happens, I know the former head of the Prussian Cultural Heritage Foundation and write him a message, and at the same time, I contact a very approachable Mücke and the archivist of the Berlin Philharmonic. The latter tells me that the instrument is not, to her knowledge, in their possession. She does find me, however, the programme indicating when the violin was bestowed on Herr Bastiaan in 1942.

PHILHARMONISCHE NACHRICHTEN

Dem Konzertmeister des Berliner Philharmonischen Orchesters, Hans Bastiaan, wurde als Anerkennung für seine künstlerische Tätigkeit vom Reichsministerium für Volksaufklärung und Propaganda eine wertvolle Geige zur Verfügung gestellt. Sie wurde im Jahre 1761 von Giovanni Battista Guadagnini erbaut. Hans Bastiaan gab mit dem Pianisten Gerhard Puchelt unlängst einige Abende in Br lau und Berlin, an denen er Werke von Bach, Beethoven, Schubert, Paganini, Höller u. a. spielte.

The news item confirms the 'valuable violin' came from the Reich Ministry of Propaganda, and that it was made in 1761 by Giovanni Battista Guadagnini. It was given to 'the concertmaster of the Berlin Philharmonic Orchestra, Hans Bastiaan … in recognition of his artistic activities'. Before me is an essential document as it proves the violin came from the Ministry. I feel like I am starting to connect the dots.

The friend at the Prussian Cultural Heritage Foundation tells me that, after German Unification, ownership of instruments was reorganised. He puts me in touch with the head of one of the foundation's museums, the

Musical Instrument Museum in Berlin, which lends instruments to young musicians, and occupies part of the Hans Scharoun architectural complex where the new Philharmonie is located. The director of the museum replies quickly, telling me that they don't have the violin I'm looking for. Instead, they suggest an organisation in Hamburg called the Deutsche Stiftung Musikleben, the German Foundation for Musical Life, which administers a lending programme to provide young people with invaluable, career-changing instruments they would otherwise never be able to afford. Apparently, according to the museum, this foundation has two Guadagnini violins from Parma. Could one be from 1761? I write to them, worried they won't write back, as I question the provenance of their valuable collection.

They write back almost immediately. They have it.

The Owner

The 1761 Guadagnini is lent out, as part of a national competition, by the German Foundation for Musical Life to highly talented young people, who can keep it only for a limited time, until they reach the age of 30 at most. They also tell me that the violin is not owned by them, but – adding a whole new level of intricacy to the story – by the German state.

After Mücke, the Guadagnini was played by the most famous German violinist of her generation, Isabelle Faust. After her, it was passed on to Tanja Becker-Bender, Korbinian Altenberger, and Alexander Gilman. Since 2013, it has been played by the Romanian-born violinist Ioana Cristina Goicea.

I have arrived at both the current player and the institutional owner: the German government is lending out property acquired by the Third Reich, which it inherited. Furnished with the name of the head of the music section of the federal government, I write another missive. I am moving further from the everyday history of the instrument into high politics. My journey is up, up, up administratively.

I expected the heavy door of the Ministry to be locked. But there is no Kafkaesque obstructionism. It only takes a day to get a reply. I am amazed by how helpful everyone is. After all, I am writing to tell them: I am going to publish a history of the circulation of instruments with dodgy provenance, something that has long remained hidden from the general public.

Herr Martin Eifler, head of the music department at the Federal Commission for Culture and the Media, answers all my questions. Yes, the German federal government owns the instrument from Goebbels' procurement programme. And not just one – and the next piece of information takes me some time to absorb – but seven! A hoard of Nazi-acquired string instruments is a veritable open secret.

He tells me that the Reich, which originally possessed about forty such instruments, concluded loan agreements with individual artists. After the war – the instruments having been lent rather than given away – the Federal Republic asked for them back. A search for the forty instruments was begun by the Federal Ministry of the Interior between 1951 and 1953, relying on interviews of those who had received them, and asking them to remember other names. Only seven instruments were retrieved, their keepers willing to return them to the government. The others are still circulating. One of the seven returned string instruments belonged to Herr Bastiaan.

In a letter of 8 December 1952 to the Ministry of the Interior, Johannes Bastiaan writes his thanks for being allowed to keep the instrument on loan, promising that he will keep good care of it and that he 'possesses no documents from before [regarding the provenance of] the instrument'. The Ministry informs me that Herr Bastiaan – bravely I think – was the only person who spoke publicly about the history of his instrument. I begin to wonder about the other thirty-three or so instruments from the programme that were never found, or not returned, or whose owners refused to reply, as Herr Bastiaan did. I imagine how many of them could fetch millions on the international market.

The seven known instruments, the Ministry informs me, are a 1731 Camillo Camilli violin, an undated Guarneri cello, a 1734 Nicolo Gagliano violin, a 1698 Matteo Goffriller violin, a 1736 Pietro Guarneri violin, and a seventeenth-century Giovanni Maria del Busetto viola. Guarneri cellos are quite rare and so I think this one might well have belonged to the Philharmonic cellist Tibor de Machula. The Guarneri violin, Eifler tells me, was played by Erich Röhn.

The division of Germany would play a role in determining these instruments' future use. In communist East Germany, the regime promoted young instrumentalists by loaning them beautiful and old string instruments. With unification in 1990, the new Germany decided not to abandon the idea. Rather, the seven instruments owned by the

Federal Republic of Germany were at first added to this young artists' programme, to be administered by the German Music Council and the Federal Ministry of the Interior.

The question of restitution, however, weighed on the minds of the authorities. They were obviously aware of the 'provenance gaps [that] raise serious questions about where these instruments came from', as Carla Shapreau articulated the general problem to me earlier. In 1993, the government searched through the Federal Archives to find previous owners but could not. They found no evidence of illegal sales but these – as we know from other sources and given the wartime context – could have been forced. Agents, again, could have acted as middlemen for stolen property. As the government wrote to me: 'We do not yet have any information on how they were acquired by the dealers of the time, and this remains a matter of conjecture.'

With the origin of the instruments uncertain, but with the knowledge that they had come from a Ministry known for stripping victims of the Third Reich of their property, the current government did not subject the instruments to long-term loans. Instead – allowing the possibility for them to be restituted at any time – the instruments went on short-term loan and to the idealistic programme I had learned about earlier, run by the Deutsche Stiftung Musikleben, established in 1993. It now administers more than 200 instruments from a collection called the Deutscher Musikinstrumenten Fonds. Six of the Nazi-era instruments are now loaned to young people – the seventh is the Goffriller violin which was damaged and is in the Musical Instrument Museum in Berlin. All remain owned by the German state; in fact, they belong now to German society.

New Players

Could a valuable eighteenth-century instrument, which any musician would give their legs to possess, suddenly become unplayable, because it is associated with the Nazis and considered 'contaminated'? One short period of history, in the many centuries of history that was part of the instrument's performance practice, could suddenly cast it as a 'Nazi' violin, so it is no longer simply a fine assembly of wood, resin, and strings that makes beautiful music. I think about my grandfather's knife, a fusion of metals, thrown in a horrendous light, because of the swastika. Does the Nazi past change the essence of the violin – indelibly transform it into a 'Nazi instrument' – or do our associations with that past, or a stigma, have this effect?

A missing piece in our story is those musicians who have most recently played the violin, under the post-unification loan programme. I write the list of these recipients, wanting to understand how much of the violin's history they know and whether it affects their relationship with the instrument.

I wonder whether these musicians will want to speak to me. But I quickly get replies, some within hours. Some want to talk on the phone, others want me to email questions. It's only a matter of days before I come to the most recent chapters of the violin's biography.

Ioana Cristina Goicea moved to Germany from Romania as a student, and now lives and teaches in Austria. She has a career of playing on world stages and winning first prizes in international violin competitions. In short, she's a crackerjack. It's no surprise, then, at only 27 years old, she was appointed a professor at Vienna's University of Music and Performing Arts. I speak to her first on the phone.

Goicea has played the Guadagnini since 2013 and very soon – after a decade – she will reach the end of her loan and have to give it up.

'Is it a good violin?' I ask her.

'It's not just a good violin. It's one of the best,' she tells me. 'I love this violin so much. It's very powerful and at the same time tender. The sound has so many possibilities, I keep finding colours also when playing it in chamber music. Especially the G and the E string [the lowermost and uppermost registers]. I think the darkness of the G string is the best thing about it. It gives the violin this deepness. Then again, all the strings are good.'

At this point, she suggests we switch to WhatsApp video so she can show me the violin. It's a remarkable moment for me because I have never seen it before. The violin has a deep, caramel colour. There is something ancient but also vibrant, warm, and alive about it. I'm riveted. I've reached the end of a road.

'Look at how incredibly beautiful it is,' she says. 'I love the dark colour. And on the back, there is a line in the wood, a knot. But it's the front that is really beautiful. And there are cracks that have been repaired. It's small, the neck is not too thick, it really suits my body. The violin fits me. It's something that I felt the moment I got it.'

After all this enthusiasm, I am pained by the task of telling her that, although we don't know whether the violin was stolen, we do know that it was acquired from the Propaganda Ministry at a time when the Nazis were confiscating valuable instruments all over occupied Europe.

She considers, then takes the information in stride. 'I would have taken the violin even had I known its history. It's not the fault of the instrument. And an instrument like this needs to be played. It is something to do with the wood, about maintaining its resonance. Otherwise, like an old tree, it would get stiff. And there is something about these old instruments that is different from modern instruments: the depth of sound that comes from its history, from its age. No, you have to play it. It's not the instrument's fault.'

I speak also to Korbinian Altenberger, who is now the concertmaster of the Bavarian Radio Symphony and a professor at a German music university in Würzburg. He is a thoughtful man, built like a kite, who played the Guadagnini a decade before Ioana Cristina Goicea, from the age of 19, from 2001 to 2008.

I ask him what he knows about the violin and he tells me he is only aware of who played it immediately before him and that it is Italian and from the eighteenth century. He tells me a specialist once told him the instrument might be older than 1761. Altenberger loved playing the instrument: for its sound, its peculiar dark colour. We begin talking about the violin's particularities and he tells me he thinks there is a cigarette burn in the lower-left corner. He muses, perhaps someone took it to a bar? If the violin had a personality, he tells me, it would be a gentle person; there is nothing shrill about it.

Like with Goicea, I now have the task of revealing to him the Nazi-period story behind an instrument that he has described to me as a 'short-term marriage' for the formative years of his twenties. I understand – from lecturing at a music university – just how close musicians become to their instruments. They are with them more hours a day than their partners or family. The object works on the musician, just as the musician works on the object, in a kind of synthesis – a relationship. What does it mean to discover a secret of someone to whom you've been married for almost a decade? To feel inscribed into the performance history of a violin such as this Guadagnini?

In what feels like a 'reveal', I show him – sharing my screen on Zoom – the extract from the 1942 *Spielzeit* that announces the gift from the Ministry of Propaganda to Herr Bastiaan. Altenberger reads it and I ask, worrying how he will react, how he now feels about the violin.

He is obviously stunned and, eyes blinking, explains that he recognises the suffering behind the story, but – like Ioana Cristina Goicea – that this history doesn't change his relationship to the instrument.

'The violin doesn't choose its part,' Altenberger tells me. The violin is independent of these histories and it was a gift to him to play such a beautiful instrument. 'Such a violin changes the way you play,' he says.

But there is another aspect to Korbinian's story, something that he was shy to tell at first, and that I had to tease out of him. Both sides of his family were victims of the Nazis. He tells me that his paternal Czech family fell afoul of the Nazi authorities, and his father spent approximately four years of his childhood in a German concentration camp, while his mother's family is Jewish and was hidden during the war.

Korbinian is not the only one. Alexander Gilman played the violin between 2008 and 2013 and is now based in London, where he teaches at the Royal Academy of Music. He is descended on both sides from Jewish Ukrainians from Odessa, who suffered at the hands of the advancing German troops. He explains, 'We are not an Orthodox family but we have strong Jewish roots, and we suffered a lot like other Jewish families. Everyone on my grandfather's side was killed. Everybody: brothers, sisters. It was always a big subject and part of my identity.' Orphaned, his grandfather joined the Soviet forces at a young age, and later raised children in the Caucasus. Gilman's family left Georgia in 1980 and scattered to Israel, the USA, and to Germany, where Alexander was born.

He tells me, 'If I had known in 2008 that it had been proven that this violin was part of the tragic history that my family went through, of course it would have been emotional and difficult for me to play it.' He also says: 'I wish I were still playing this violin. I am really happy it is in the possession of the Stiftung Musikleben and they are doing a very important job. If we don't find out to whom it belongs, what better alternative is there to giving it to young people to play? We will not destroy the instrument or throw it into the ocean. As a musician, I cannot see an alternative to it being played.' Gilman gave up a Stradivarius for this Guadagnini, which he thought was even better: 'I am beyond grateful that I could play it so long.'

I listen to Altenberger and Gilman and feel that it would be difficult to find biographies of players more suited to the biography of the instrument. I know that Alexander and Korbinian miss the violin. I like to imagine that the violin wonders where they are now too.

Provenance

Erich Hartmann, 1984

Frau Bastiaan writes to say that Herr Hartmann died at the age of 100 on 6 July 2020. He was an indirect victim of the coronavirus pandemic because of the strict rules that restricted visitors. Despite frequent phone calls, he lost the will to live, hardly ate or drank. But she and another intimate were allowed to sit with him for the final days. On the day of his death, while they listened to his 1967 double bass quartet, he took his last breath and death came softly.

I am saddened to hear this news. But it's also a victory to have lived so long and through such terrible times. As Hartmann told me, he had so often been lucky.

I struggle to return to the work at hand. But inevitably I am left wondering who can tell me the location of the man's object, his double bass?

I have since followed two of Hartmann's three instruments to a former student in Hamburg, who writes that the final one – the one I am looking for – is indeed in Munich somewhere, but he doesn't know where. Hartmann's instrument has its pre-1943 story to tell. But if I were to find the bass, would it be able to answer questions about this past? No, just as the instruments that we know were part of a troubled Nazi scheme cannot tell us to whom they belonged.

In January 2021, the Franz Hofmann and Sophie Hagemann Foundation made the news for refusing to compensate the Jewish heirs of a 1706 Guarneri violin – seized by the Gestapo and then auctioned – despite the recommendation of the German government's Advisory Committee on the Restitution of Cultural Property. The instruments discussed in this chapter – to draw a stark contrast – are in the hands of the German government itself, which has tried on more than one occasion to discover their former owners and keeps its door open to researchers.

The instruments are, meanwhile, being usefully loaned to gifted young people. Indeed – as many of the players told me – it would be a tragedy for an instrument to go unused. The vibrations keep the wood flexible; they prevent worm rot. Unlike paintings or sculptures, they cannot become museum objects and left to deteriorate, to be unplayed for the first time in their long history. Alexander Gilman explained that the Stradivarius he played in 2006 had spent many years in a bank's safe: 'I played it for two years and every day it got better. But at the very beginning, I thought: "This cannot be a Strad." They need to be played, not just for the health of the instrument. The fact is that these masterpieces have been produced to make music and us musicians have that responsibility.'

And yet, there is still something unresolved and unsettling about these '*Reichsinstrumenten*'. I wonder whether the coincidence that the Guadagnini found its way into the hands of so many descendants of Nazi oppression counterbalances the unease of its murky wartime origins. Tanja Becker-Bender, who played the violin between 1996 and 2002, is now a music professor in Hamburg while also performing internationally. She told me, after I showed her the 1942 *Spielzeit* programme and she first learned about the instrument's procurement under the Reich:

> To know this comes as a shock. But why didn't I ask the question myself? I was young, I saw the opportunity to play a valuable old instrument. But, in Germany, aren't we all obliged to ask: what happened during this time? I think it is right to do so now. To recalibrate. But then comes the question: what does it mean for a young and entitled German musician to be given such an opportunity without knowing on whose fate it is built? Even the possibility that there is a terrible story behind all this,

> that someone had to forcibly give up his instrument – that alone can be devastating for a musician ... What is astonishing for me is to learn that it was this Herr [Bastiaan] who played the same violin. I saw the *Reichsorchester* film about a year ago. It stirred up a lot of thoughts in me, about how apolitical so many musicians can be, how innocent these men [Hartmann and Bastiaan] seemed, and what enthusiasm they had for their work, even when Jews were chased from their orchestra and others continued to play. I don't have answers; they wouldn't be worthy of the subject. The questions are simply there.

Her disquiet leads to a debate. The post-1993 recipients of the violin whom I interviewed did not have the faintest idea of their instrument's Nazi-era history before I spoke to them. There is the argument – articulated by Kolja Blacher – that had he known this history, he wouldn't have wanted to play it as a young prize-winner, no matter how beautiful the tone. But I also understand those voices which say that 'it's not the instrument's fault' and 'it didn't choose its part'.

Comparing Ioana Cristina Goicea playing the Adagio of the Brahms Violin Sonata in D minor to Altenberger's performance of Shostakovich's Violin Concerto No. 1, one hears the instrument's gentle, individual tone. The Guadagnini has an identity or – as many of the musicians told me – a 'personality'. It has too a 'cultural biography', like someone who has been through fortune and hardship. For a moment, I think: perhaps the violin doesn't belong to anyone but instead passes through keepers. In that perspective, one emphasises the autonomy of the instrument from ownership or trade. In the same breath, I think – *oh shit* – does not my argument dismiss injustice, to think of the violin not as a thing but as a person?

The Nazi stigma, associated with horrific state crimes, is a can of worms for any public institution. One need only think about the public relations nightmares faced by museums housing artworks 'contaminated' by dubious provenance. But I know that if I were a young musician I would want to know the instrument's history and to choose whether I become part of its performance history, even if the instrument itself is indifferent to that same past. Because the object will not tell us, on its own, to whom it belonged before it was acquired by the Nazis. The object is mute before the troubled history that it, paradoxically, instantiates, and – as Becker-Bender told me – the instrument's tone, clear and radiant, carries no hint of past violence.

There is an opportunity to bring the musicians into the process that is called *Vergangenheitsbewältigung* in Germany, or 'struggling through the past', as they continue to write a better chapter for these instruments. And indeed, the government's Department for Music communicated to me in late March 2021 that 'we never concealed the origin of former Reich ownership of the instruments, but their history was also very rarely inquired about'. The Stiftung Musikleben – possibly as a result of our discussions – has now decided to create a data sheet for each of the instruments, containing the essential information about each's history, to be given in future to the musicians. Even more public visibility of these instruments' murky provenance, however, could open up paths to justice. As the Terezin Declaration states, 'restitution cannot be accomplished without knowledge of potentially looted art and cultural property'.

An American soldier guards looted goods in 1945 in a church in Ellingen, Germany

Indeed, the important work that needs to happen now is on possible restitution. Perhaps, after all, Herr Bastiaan's violin was a legal sale. Yet, any instrument acquired by the Nazi Ministry of Propaganda during the war – a period of mass looting – has an enormous question mark hanging over it. Perhaps someone reading this book will remember that their family once owned a 1761 Guadagnini violin – with a line on its back and something like a cigarette burn on its front – or an older instrument that fits the same description. Perhaps one of the other instruments I have listed is recognisable. Perhaps the hunter of violins stolen by Nazis, Carla Shapreau in Berkeley, has already found a forced sale among some salvaged receipts of a wartime agent. Perhaps someone living in Argentina or Israel or Canada does not know that a violin worth more than a million euros is theirs. A family who lost it at the hands of the Nazis would be the rightful lender of an instrument to a promising young person, perhaps even to the same young woman who plays it now.

Alte Philharmonie, Again

I find my way to the site of the Old Philharmonic Hall. The district has installed a new memorial plaque there, three weeks after Herr Hartmann's death. It comes too late for him; it would have made him so happy.

I stand in the empty yard between the new buildings, where there once was so much rubble, and put music on my headphones: Furtwängler's November 1943 recording of Beethoven's 7th symphony, recorded here, in the old hall by Radio Berlin, using the best technology of the time.

The downside for the sound engineer of using such sensitive recording instruments, placed directly in front of the orchestra in the hall, is they also pick up all the peripheral audience noise, like chatter or coughing. But for the historian, these imperfections are chilling, a document of a shared public moment under fire. I compare the dates of Furtwängler's recordings to those of major bombing raids and the destruction of the Philharmonie and try to imagine the state of the audience. Who was listening? How long did they have to live? What did it mean to them to listen to this music with the war outside?

The music immediately transfigures today's urbanscape, which is quite indifferent to it. Furtwängler's many wartime recordings have a knack for forward movement. They seem to drive straight into oblivion. The second movement, or 'Death March', of Beethoven's 7th is particularly poignant. It was first played in Vienna in 1813 for the war wounded of the Napoleonic wars, celebrating their sacrifice and patriotism. There's a reason it is a favourite soundtrack for YouTubers posting and retouching videos of Second World War damage. Beautiful performances were produced under a terrible government and the emotive soundtrack adds an inescapable filter to all discussions about the Philharmonic and the war. I cannot imagine having the same reaction to the work of any other servants of the Third Reich: those in the tax administration or public works, for example. But this music ... what a tremendous conductor! What an amazing orchestra!

I begin to be susceptible to the arguments that this was not a 'Nazi orchestra', which is what Erich Hartmann contends, and is repeated in Misha Aster's book. I want Furtwängler to be exonerated, the man who, according to Hartmann, tried to 'protect Jewish musicians' and who was 'completely apolitical'. In his memoir, Hartmann says 'we have to thank him for staying in Germany during the Nazi period'. I want these talented musicians, who produced extraordinary music, not to be contaminated by the crimes of the Third Reich.

But when I take off my headphones, I find myself in an unsightly empty lot, with the only sound being the siren of a passing ambulance. I recognise the halo effect of the music and think of the concertmaster of the Philharmonic playing his violin to divert the customs guards at the Spanish border. This music is a distraction, standing in the way of the damage that was done here. The Philharmonic was precisely, for this reason, the ideal fig leaf for Nazi atrocities. I understand better why it was granted such importance and the musicians afforded so many state privileges. They were its elite foot soldiers, living in unheard-of luxury as most of Europe burned.

Because the Berlin Philharmonic is self-governing today, as a private limited company, contemporary critics anachronistically emphasise the politics of the individual musicians to determine whether it was a 'Nazi orchestra'. They emphasise that 'only' four Jews were forced to leave or that half-Jews were allowed to stay or that 'only' 18 per cent were Nazi members or that the orchestra purged itself of Nazis after the defeat. But it was not the individual musicians, with their various political beliefs – or, rather, their apparent lack of political engagement – which defined the orchestra under the Third Reich. The Berlin Philharmonic was a Nazi orchestra precisely because it was directly operated by the Nazi Ministry for Propaganda for which these musicians were servants performing a valued function.

No one operating a public institution under the Nazis could have been apolitical, nor were its civil servants. The orchestra was central to a cultural policy that, in Goebbels' words, intended to bring about a 'spiritual mobilisation', in concert with other art forms such as the controlled domains of film, theatre, visual arts, or literature: 'The spiritual awakening of our own time will emerge from this will to culture.' It also achieved a foreign policy aim, to present an acceptable and cultured face for a brutal regime. Nazi arts policy, meanwhile, destroyed the lives of many banished or murdered artists. It stole their property, their instruments, and it vandalised their artistic creations. After Richard Strauss, as is often said, no great composers came out of this period. The Philharmonic was the crown jewel of this cultural mission.

Should the musicians have left Germany? As historian Richard Evans points out, hardly a writer of merit remained in Germany by the end of 1933. Visual artists followed. But writers and painters can write and paint almost anywhere; the same cannot be said of artists who are dependent on film studios or theatres. This accounts for why so many in these fields stayed, although musicians were certainly more transportable than native-speaker actors whose craft was often impossible on foreign stages. Furtwängler, again, turned down a job at the New York Philharmonic to remain in his *Heimat*; there was a choice.

Was the orchestra fully denazified after 1945? Not in the eyes of the international public. On the first tour to America in 1955, the Philharmonic was subject to vigorous demonstrations, and met by signs reading 'No Harmony with Nazis'. Already in 1952, the former Nazi party intendant, Gerhard von Westermann, had returned to his position. Hartmann, in his memoires, celebrates when Karajan takes over as maestro

Herbert von Karajan, 1941

in 1954, inaugurating a 'new era'. But Karajan, of course, had joined the Nazi party *twice* to advance his career. I understand Otto Klemperer's discomfort when he guest-conducted the orchestra after the war.

The moral accommodations that members of the Philharmonic made with the regime have something in common with those who today play instruments of dubious, unexplored provenance – such as those loaned to the thirty-odd musicians who refused to turn them in to the German state between 1951 and 1953. Both situations present opportunities to question, beyond the bell jar, an individual's relationship to power. The violinist Becker-Bender remarked to me how listening to the testimonies of apolitical wartime Philharmonic musicians provokes contemporary questions. Why did so many Nazi-era players remain in their assigned seats on the stage of the Alte Philharmonie, not wanting to see further than the scores on their respective stands? For the same reasons many collectors and musicians, even today, might not face up to the origins of their instruments, when they make such a beautiful sound. Not wanting to know one's position in a chain of exploitation, from which one profits, is a continuity that extends well beyond the Nazi era.

Hans Bastiaan playing the 1761 Guadagnini, in 1970

A Cotton Pouch

Rushed Choices

At the end of October 1944, Katalin Lőrincz made a cotton pouch large enough to hold a couple of small photographs.

'It was just a little sack,' she tells me. 'I made it from two pieces of fabric, which I sewed on all sides, except the one side left open.'

Katalin was 20 years old, had trained to be a seamstress, and found herself in a crowded room of a Budapest house designated for Jews. Outside this 'yellow-star' house, members of the Hungarian fascist regime – the Arrow Cross – waited for the occupants to line up in rows. They had come to power in October 1944, with the help of the Nazis, and knew that they were going to lose the war. Nonetheless, they took steps to kill as many remaining Jews as possible.

Katalin had only a few minutes to decide what to take with her.

'How do you know what to bring in such a situation?' I ask.

She replies without hesitation. 'It's easy. You bring food. And I brought the photographs in the pouch.'

'Which photographs did you choose?'

'You see, there wasn't much time. I couldn't really choose. I just sorted around in a box that contained many and I chose a couple of my family.'

Once the photographs were in the pouch, she cut open the lining of her coat.

'It was my uncle's winter coat, which I had modified so it would fit me. It was a fine wool coat. But it only had a simple lining. The inside was dark grey, and the outer layer was chequered. It wasn't very warm.'

Katalin sewed the photographs flat inside the coat, accessible through a pocket, before going downstairs to the waiting men.

Already around 440,000 Hungarian Jews had been deported to Auschwitz earlier in the year, most of whom were gassed on arrival. But as the Russian army approached the death camps in Poland, the agents of the Final Solution had to rely on camps far from the Eastern Front. The Jews of Budapest – among the last to be deported in the Axis zone – were to be sent the opposite direction, west, to Germany and Austria, to Dachau and Mauthausen and its subcamps, in what would be the final phase of the Holocaust.

Around 50,000 of the remaining Budapest Jews had resided in the yellow-star houses since the summer. Forced down into the street by the Arrow Cross, they were then ushered by the Hungarian gendarmerie, on orders originating with Adolf Eichmann, into the cold of a death march. Young and old walked over 100 miles from the Hungarian capital to Hegyeshalom at the Austrian border. The trek claimed a fifth of their number due to exhaustion and exposure.

Katalin carried only a few belongings with her – some food, her wedding ring and the clothes she was wearing, including the coat with the cotton pouch and its photographs – during her deportation. Although she would find replacements, not one of these objects remained with her following the war and its immediate aftermath.

This story, a variation on the theme, considers what it is like to go into the future without belongings from your past life.

From Strange Lands and Places

Growing up in Edmonton, Canada, I had next-door neighbours who were Hungarian. A husband and wife, they were both chemists at the university close to retirement. As a boy, I got to know the wife better and soon she was like a third grandmother I would visit once a week.

Our houses, with their peaked roofs, were located at the top of the river valley of the North Saskatchewan. There was plenty of snow in winter that I had to shovel. Our neighbours' drive was always neatly cleared, which I thought was strange because I had never seen them outside.

I saw them instead behind the picture window, with its lace curtains, which felt like a portal to a living room far away in Central Europe. At the age of 15, I was romantic about *Mitteleuropa*. And although I had already read Tadeusz Borowski and Elie Wiesel, I somehow did not associate them with the region. Instead, when I visited my neighbours, I had piano scores of Chopin and Schumann tucked under my arm.

Katalin was a polite and careful person. At first glance, this politeness made her seem hesitant. But I recognise her manner now as a form of elegant hospitality. And when it came to individuals, she would rarely say something negative. Rather, she'd point out what was better.

The house was full of beautiful objects, evidence that she had travelled places I would someday like to go. I remember, in particular, a Persian carpet, petal blue. It was aligned, on the combed wall-to-wall carpeting, to the Murano glass in a cabinet, an intricate ivory sculpture from China, porcelain, Vladimir Horowitz albums, and chemistry books.

Katalin made me careful little pastries in her immaculate kitchen: rounds of strudel with poppyseed bristling from the seams and crumble squares set with sour cherries, plums, apricots, or cottage cheese. After eating the pastries from flowered china in her living room, we would venture downstairs to the electric piano. It was located in a guest bedroom. Katalin played the piano like me, but with headphones, as her husband was in the upstairs window solving equations.

Katalin pronounced the names of the Schumann pieces I played – '*Von fremden Ländern und Menschen*' ('From Strange Lands and Places') – very well for someone I didn't think had ever lived in Germany. I would always ask her to play but she said: 'Oh no, I couldn't. I'm not very good.' And I would play another Chopin piece – quite badly in retrospect – but she was happy to have such a young person in her house who loved music too and enjoyed eating her pastries. Young people, after all, are allowed imperfections.

After an hour, she would gently touch me on the arm (wishing me to go with 'the old love', by way of farewell) and upstairs I'd thank her, before departing into the winter cold, never taking a short cut across the lawn, leaving tracks on the untrodden snow.

I also did not ask the questions I had on my mind – about the conversations I overhead from my parents, about camps and typhus – because the day was about beautiful things, like desserts and music. And because Katalin never talked about her past.

History was always next door. I grew up with a Holocaust survivor without ever knowing her story.

Change of Heart

Thirty years later, when she was 96, Katalin changed her mind and decided to speak.

She had moved from Edmonton in the west of the country to a nursing home in Toronto, to be close to her stepdaughter and her grandchildren after her husband passed away. Every few months, I recorded piano music for her and emailed the mp3s: an off-kilter Chopin waltz, a halting Schubert impromptu. In return, she sent me recipes for the pastries I had eaten as a child.

In January, she fell and broke her hip in nearly a dozen places. She said that the music I sent helped her. After the accident, I started communicating with Katalin more often. I discussed the situation with my mother, who asked, 'What happens if no one ever records her story before she dies? Maybe I can ask her? Maybe she will tell it to you?'

Katalin replied, 'Many friends say: why don't you write your life? I never wanted to. Before, there were so many who experienced what I did, so I didn't think it was a big thing. I changed my mind: it's good if more people know stories like mine.'

In 2021, Katalin is one of the last survivors. A recent poll suggests that two-thirds of Americans under 40 now do not know that 6 million Jews died in the Holocaust. Katalin is getting older, and memory is retreating.

I began calling her – at midnight Berlin time, 5 p.m. in Toronto – to record her stories for this book. It was difficult to ask her the hard questions to which she responded so matter-of-factly. I was torn between keeping my historian's hat on, and remaining scientific, and responding as a friend, with my heart. I hoped I could do both. I was touched to have grown up next door to someone who carries so much experience, hardship, but also resilience, in her. But as I interviewed her, numerous times, I didn't know whether I reacted sufficiently to all the tragic events that happened in her life. I retreated, like a snail, to my historian's reserve when confronted by horror.

The very first question I asked was: is there an object that tells your story?

A Field of Wheat

Katalin tells me about the photographs in the cotton pouch. 'I lost them.'

'Perhaps that's not the worst thing,' I venture. 'Haven't you had the experience of remembering the photograph but not the person?'

'I think everyone has that experience,' she replies.

'Did you take a picture of your parents with you to the camp?'

'Yes. One of my mother when she was young, with my two older brothers and my grandmother. They were all nicely dressed. It was a professional photograph,' Katalin tells me, matter-of-factly. 'I did not bring one of my father.'

Her parents Ödön and Gizella Lőrincz were Jewish bakers in the town of Ózd, north of Budapest on the border with Slovakia. They kept kosher, high holidays, but Katalin tells me that they were otherwise not very religious, although their names were recorded on the Orthodox synagogue's lists when they were transferred to the ghetto. Lőrincz is an unusual name for a Jewish family. Katalin's great-great-grandfather was the supervisor of large estates. His elegant name came with an elegant status.

'You could get rich in that position,' she tells me, 'but that wealth didn't fall on my father.'

Ödön had served in the Austro-Hungarian army during the First World War and returned with an inoperable bullet in his liver. He could no longer work, and so the family grew poor. But they had a beautiful field of wheat behind the house.

'It's one of those views', says Katalin, 'that you never forget.'

'Did you learn to bake from your mother?'

'The bakery made everything close to bread, but not real pastries, although my mother made the most wonderful ones, and cakes. If there was a wedding, she'd make the cake. She liked to help others more than cooking and doing other things at home. She made all sorts of cakes, designed them also, putting in a lot of effort. She didn't save on the ingredients even though she was very cautious about money and had to be.'

Meanwhile, the kids walked barefoot in the street. The parents could not afford to care for their daughter, Katalin Irma Lőrincz, born in 1924 – known to friends as Kati or Kató – so they sent her to Budapest at the age of 4 to live with her aunt, Etel. The aunt knew nothing about child-raising and Katalin was isolated from the other children – Etel was terrified Katalin would catch an infectious disease. At a young age, Katalin trained to be a seamstress and a caregiver, and she worked menial jobs.

As Katalin tells me what follows during the war years, I am impressed by her clarity of mind at the age of 96. I've compared all her dates against the record. They all correspond. And she remembers from conversation to conversation what we spoke about: I find she repeats herself less than I do.

In 1942, Kató, at 18, saw her parents for the last time. Hungary was a collaborationist power during the Second World War and instituted a series of antisemitic decrees. Although many Jews were sent into forced labour, especially to the Eastern Front, it was only in March 1944 – when Germany invaded to prevent Hungary falling to the Allies – that the Hungarian government began its deportations to the death camps.

'Things were reasonably normal in Budapest until 1944,' Katalin tells me, of the capital that had a Jewish population of 200,000. 'It never occurred to me that something like that could happen. Not too much was known. We had secret radio stations: but it was hard to know what was real or otherwise. And if you listened, you could be punished.'

Katalin's family in Ózd moved first to the ghetto. In May 1944 they were sent to Auschwitz.

'Do you have a photograph of your mother? Any copies that were kept by family?'

'No, I lost everything I owned. I don't have pictures of my parents any more. I did have a poor one and in the hope of improving it, I spoiled it completely. And I don't have a photograph of my father.'

'Do you remember your parents?' I ask. 'Even if you no longer have any photographs of them?'

'It's unfortunate that I only lived with them when I was very little. My mother didn't come very often. Every two years she came. My father came only once, in all those times, until I was fourteen years old. I was taken home two or three times during this time. It was two hundred kilometres roughly distant from the capital and it was expensive, and neither my aunt nor my family could afford it. My mother couldn't leave: she had to bake.'

Without answering directly – which perhaps would be painful – she has nonetheless replied, in the negative.

Volotovo

'What other photographs did you take with you in the cotton pouch?'

'One of my first husband.'

I did not know that Katalin had been married more than once.

She laughs. 'He said that photograph made him look like a fly that had fallen into a glass of milk!'

'Why is that?'

'Because, in the photograph – which was a photo ID, the kind used for a document – he was wearing a white suit and was quite tanned.'

Katalin met Artúr Landau (born on 14 July 1916) in 1941, when she was 17. Artúr was handsome and a snappy dresser, with a good salary as an accountant. He also spoke excellent English. She may never have crossed paths with him in his social world, except that Artúr was a friend of her employer's husband, and so he visited very often at the house where Katalin worked.

'How did he let you know he liked you? Did he flirt?'

She laughs. 'No, he didn't flirt. But he came to visit more often! I'd become friendly with the lady and she said to me: pretty soon Artúr will be coming every day! He impressed me because he was so well-spoken and interesting. Then one day, the lady told me that he wanted to take us out – my boss, her husband, and me – for dinner, at Gundel. With a carriage, with flowers … '

Gundel is a Budapest institution, in a free-standing building located in the City Park, known for its soaring interiors, French influences and refinement of Hungarian cuisine. It is one of the capital's most lavish addresses and I can imagine Katalin's face lighting up at the invitation.

'I had nothing to wear! But my lady said to me: we have to sew a dress. So, we sewed a dress. And she said: you must buy a pair of shoes. So,

I bought a nice pair of shoes, even though my salary was very low. Anyway, when I went out, I looked decent.'

Given Katalin's habit of understatement, this means she looked amazing.

'What colour was the dress?'

'The dress was red. And it had a slim skirt at the bottom that was white. It wasn't complicated: a nice simple dress. The shoes were red but with narrow toes, with white heels – the kind that was very much in style then. I never wore my heels too high.'

'Bright red?'

'No, a gentle red.'

Of course!

'Oh, and the food was good, very good. And there was space for dancing. Although I had almost never danced in my life because I never met anyone to dance with. The last time had been the night Hitler and Stalin made their non-aggression pact when my relatives took me out with six boys. That was the one time I'd been dancing before.'

It was not long before Katalin and Artúr were engaged. As a Jewish man, he was taken into forced labour in 1941, with only occasional breaks back to the city. This allowed them to organise the medical exams – part of a 1941 racial degree – that had become mandatory to marry. He took her to his parents for their wedding night and the next day left for the Eastern Front, where he served with a labour battalion composed of other Jews.

Thinking Artúr must be cold, Katalin bought him a coat, and sewed money into it. But in the end, she did not know where to send it. Finally, she received an official postcard saying he had disappeared near Volotovo, near Kursk, in Russia. According to the files of the Holocaust Museum at Yad Vashem in Jerusalem, he is presumed to have died of exposure and hunger.

'You lost your only photograph of him?'

'Yes, but I was lucky that my aunt, who survived the war in Budapest, had a copy of it.'

While searching the files at Yad Vashem, I came across the same photo of Artúr in a white suit. He is very handsome, with large sad eyes. I can imagine Katalin liking a man who was so self-deprecating.

He is not at all like a fly soaked in milk.

Hegyeshalom

The yellow-star house had a 5 p.m. curfew but Katalin went out regardless to retrieve provisions she had hidden in the attic of her former residence. She concealed the star she was obliged to wear on her chequered coat. On the way home, the bag she carried split open. She called for help to a woman nearby who was talking to a policeman. The woman gave her some string to bind her package.

'I was different during the war,' Katalin tells me of the risk she took with the police officer. 'I did things like that.'

Katalin brought the food back to the room. She shared it with a long-time friend, Anikó Gondos, and her two small children. These provisions may well have saved Katalin and Anikó on the death march. An ex-housekeeper and friend of Anikó, meanwhile, managed to hide the children.

Early November was a bitter time to walk for a week through the countryside on what historian Randolph L. Braham has called a 'veritable highway of death'. From 8 November, 30,000 women from Budapest would make this journey. The march was designed to pick off the weak. Katalin's chequered coat, containing the photographs, was too thin. But the bag of food – chocolate, cured meat, high-calorie foods – helped them through the march, until it was stolen by Polish forced labourers, who had been long imprisoned by the Nazis and were ravenous.

Along the way, Katalin was struck by the kindness of a woman who allowed her and Anikó to sleep in her house. She nabbed them randomly from the long line of marchers, and invited them in. She gave them food and left them alone when she went to work. But the women decided to leave after just one night, realising that, if caught, their host and her two children would be severely punished.

'It was the biggest thing that anyone did for us. You can imagine how grateful we felt,' she tells me. 'I still regret I didn't ask her name.'

Leaving the house, they simply rejoined the line of marchers, which was continuous, and proceeded to the border town of Hegyeshalom, where they slept on the unheated floor of a brick factory. They dug trenches outside the town for a few days, then walked more in the rain, slept in the rain and in the mud, where Katalin lost a shoe and continued with one foot bare. Then, one day in December, they marched to a train depot, where they were loaded on to carriages.

Another witness of the moment, Judith Konrad, whose recorded testimony I found in the archives of the US Holocaust Museum, stated that she felt relief to be put on a wagon, and into the hands of the Germans: 'Because we were optimists, we thought even the Germans must be better than the Hungarian Arrow Cross, which was almost true, because these Arrow Cross youngsters were really brutal and cruel, and they must have known they had no future. So, they thought this was their very short heyday and they wanted to make the most of it. We were actually pleased to be put in those wagons; it relieved us from walking and we had very sore feet.'

Katalin tells me: 'I don't know how long we were on the train. It felt like weeks. The train moved so slowly. I could have walked more quickly.'

The journey was not far: some 50 miles as the crow flies from Hegyeshalom, across the border into Austria, to an industrial suburb of the city of Wiener Neustadt, called Lichtenwörth, where a subcamp of Mauthausen was located.

'You must have heard of it,' says Katalin.

There, in the cold of an Austrian winter, she was given a pair of wooden shoes, in which she could hobble around.

Lichtenwörth

A troubling aspect of this story is that I had not heard of Lichtenwörth. I had studied Austria's most notorious camp, Mauthausen. But its many subcamps, scattered across Austria, are largely unknown to most historians. Some were not commemorated until decades after their closure and many not at all. The files of Lichtenwörth's commandant's office – including the prisoner files – were destroyed by the SS in 1945. The few surviving documents are scattered, mostly in Russian archives. Lichtenwörth was later mentioned, during the 1961 Adolf Eichmann trial, as a 'starvation camp' or a 'typhus camp'.

This forgetting is not atypical in Austria where, post-war, the country claimed to be the 'first victim' of Nazi annexation – despite the enthusiastic Viennese street crowds that welcomed the Anschluß of 1938, 10 per cent membership in the Nazi party, and Austrians holding key positions in the SS, such as Holocaust organiser Adolf Eichmann. In the 1970s, the Austrian victim narrative was reformulated as 'Austrian resistance' against the Nazis. It was only in 1986 that the war record of Austrian former UN Secretary-General Kurt Waldheim brought international attention to Austria, dubbed 'Naziland' in German-speaking press outlets. The country's co-responsibility finally became part of public discourse. Nonetheless, rhetoric of forgetting, reminiscent of the 1950s, typifies today's memory culture in the Freedom Party, which regularly garners a fifth of the Austrian vote.

It was only in 1975 that a small memorial plaque was erected at a town intersection in Lichtenwörth, close to the now disappeared location of the *Lager*. Online, there is almost no information about the camp. In Lichtenwörth, the far right won almost a quarter of the vote in the 2019 federal election. In short, despite the existence of this small memorial, the collective memory of the camp is under threat.

Some 40,000 Hungarian Jews found themselves in Austria at the end of the war, put to work on the *Südostwall*, a series of defensive positions ordered by the *Wehrmacht* to hinder the Red Army arriving from the south-east. Lichtenwörth was known in 1944 – using Orwellian language – as an *Erholungslager*, or 'recreation camp', because its mostly women inmates were not considered capable of this hard work. It was intended as a holding facility. 2,500 were interned in the industrial building in December 1944. Another camp named Felixdorf was located nearby.

At Lichtenwörth, there was the old factory hall, divided into two large rooms, holding thousands of women. But the experience was atomised: the camp also contained smaller rooms, at least one reserved for the very ill. Latrines were unroofed ditches outside. Katalin was in one of the small rooms for more than four months, through the winter of 1944–45, until the liberation of the camp by the Red Army on 2 April 1945.

'Lichtenwörth was a village,' she tells me. 'I had no idea which part of it we were in. We had no contact with the local people. I saw a mountain far away, called the Schneeberg. That's all. The camp wasn't very large: the building was an old factory. Nothing indicated what it had been used for. It was empty and dirty and maybe two hundred metres long in both directions, divided into maybe three or four sections, with a glass roof. The glass squares of it would jump up and down when there were bombings. We were about a hundred men and two hundred women in the small room we shared. But I can't tell you how many were in the whole facility. There was only straw on the floor and so little space that we could not sleep lying down but had to pull up our arms and knees. We sat up back-to-back and side-to-side and remained that way day and night for months. We had physical pain from that. Of course, pretty soon we had lice.'

The straw is referred to in every testimony of the time in Lichtenwörth: how it would disintegrate into powder, become filthy, and provide a breeding ground for vermin. The inmates preferred to sleep on the hard floor.

'You were kept in that same position for the whole winter?'

'We could hardly get up. But my friend Anikó would stand up in the morning to go around and console people, help them mentally. She was like that. And then they fed us. In the beginning, we got one large slice of bread and soup that had a little something in it. That was the beginning. The bread got smaller until there was no bread at all, just the water with spices.'

From other testimony, I read that in the mornings they received so-called 'salty coffee', or black water that the inmates joked was from washing black uniforms. The bread tasted of mud, and prisoners did not know whether to keep their tiny portion and eat it slowly or gobble it up.

'Didn't they have you work?'

'Sometimes they took us out to work. But we only worked at the beginning, maybe only five times, and that was unnecessary. We were digging ditches, but I don't think those ditches were ever used.'

Indeed, I later read that they only were required to do clearing work until 3 January 1945; after that, they had to occupy the endless time they spent simply in confinement, with activities like word games.

'There were German guards: police. But they also had Jewish people who had to guard us. We called them *Jupos* or *Juden-Polizei*. Some of them were worse than the Germans, I must say.

'From the digging, we came back in rows. One thing I will never forget is that there was one decent man, a guard, who had accompanied us, who came to me and gave me a cooked potato. I remember that. I thought maybe he had a daughter my age. There were a lot of people he could have given it to. I never saw him again.'

'Could you wash?' I ask her.

Katalin replies, 'Yes. Once a week, we got a small amount of water to wash.'

I later read that the camp had a shower for eighty persons, used by thousands of prisoners. Another witness, Hedvig Endrei, said, 'we stood in line there at six in the morning in order to get in, one had to go on time because they often turned off the water after a while. We washed our clothes there … Men, women, we bathed together, there was no time for us to look at each other, to be ashamed. We were happy that we got in. After we had washed, we started searching for lice.'

Katalin continues: 'The water was ice cold. Men and women were forced to wash in the same place and the camp commandant watched us.'

'What was he like?'

'This *Lagerführer* was a good-looking young man. He would bring his girlfriend and the two of them watched us wash. Maybe he thought he was being kind but he would call us "children". He'd say: "Isn't it good to have a bath, children? Do you like it, children?" as we used a tiny bowl to try to get clean.'

'Were you cold?' I asked.

'It was a cold winter. But inside the *Lager*, we were never cold because we were pressed so close to one other. Our sides were always covered with the others. We had body heat. And then my coat didn't come off me in the *Lager*.'

'Weren't you given uniforms? Didn't they take away your possessions?' I think about all the many belongings that people packed with them to the death camps, only to have them seized on arrival: the piles of shoes and suitcases and silver that now fill the spaces of Holocaust museums.

'No, we weren't touched. They didn't try to take anything from me, not that I had much. Even when the *Lagerführer* saw we were washing he never came close or touched anybody. You see, in the beginning, they thought they were going to win the war. By then, they were afraid. They treated people differently at Lichtenwörth. They were more lenient because of their fear of how they'd be judged. People weren't shot. They died instead from hunger or from typhus.'

One day, Katalin walked a little too far in the yard and saw what had originally been intended for them in the camp: 'They had three crematoria ready, but they never used them. It was too late for that. There was a pile of people. Fifty dead people. And I saw the doors of those crematoria.'

Other witnesses remember a speech by the camp commandant, who said that he was planning an enormous bath for the prisoners, in a tent, in the courtyard, which they did not know at the time probably referred to a mobile gas chamber.

The attitude towards prisoners' belongings had changed by December 1944. Depleted of resources, and knowing they were going to lose the war, the SS's strategy in Lichtenwörth was the passive elimination of Jewish prisoners – through overcrowding and disease – so that officers might later escape accusations in post-war trials. It's also called 'systemic starvation'.

'I had my engagement ring, and one of the Polish girls – one of the workers who had been suffering in Lichtenwörth before we arrived –

came to me and said that she could get a loaf of bread for it. Of course, I didn't want to give it up. There was lots of snow in the yard. She begged so much that I took off my ring. But I dropped it in my excitement. It took her a very long time searching through the snow, but she managed to find it. She bought the bread. She wanted half of it, of course. Then I shared the other half with Anikó. A quarter of a loaf of bread is what I got for my engagement ring.'

'If you still had your coat, you must have still had your cotton pouch and the photographs in the camp. Did you take them out? Could you look at them?'

'I didn't look at them very often because I couldn't move. I couldn't reach the pocket, because my neighbour was pressed up against it. Those few times that we could go outside, I would take them out. But it is interesting that I don't remember very much about what happened in the camp because it was always the same. But I do remember that I always had a Schubert song in my head ["*Frühlingsglaube*"]. Those lyrics: "*Nun muss sich alles, alles wenden*." They're still in my head. I wanted to sing them then. But I couldn't sing them there. But I thought of that song. I sang it in my head and it helped me. "Soon everything, everything must change."'

Epidemic

On 24 January 1945, the camp recorded its first case of spotted typhus.

'There are many forms of typhus,' Katalin tells me. 'None of us knew what it was at the time. When the sickness begins, you don't see anything. Then after a couple of days, tiny red dots appear on your chest. Only on your chest, nowhere else. And then I noticed after a while I had those. We were so close together, pressed together all the time. And it spread quickly. Then one day I couldn't get up any more. I was unconscious almost, very sick. I wanted to go home at any price. All this happened at the very end of my time in Lichtenwörth, maybe three weeks before the end.'

Epidemic typhus, *Rickettsia prowazekii*, is spread by human lice. First, there is a fever, then there is the rash that appears after approximately five days, then severe muscle pain and delirium, which leads to death in two-thirds of untreated cases. Typhus swept through the unsanitary conditions of the Nazi camps. Anne Frank and her sister both succumbed to the disease. Tragically, there was a prevention that was unavailable to them: an effective vaccine available shortly before the war and given to American troops sent overseas.

'Typhus was more deadly for healthy people, somehow,' Katalin observes, anecdotally. 'There was one guard: a woman, a *Jupo*. She was very healthy and well fed until the end. Then finally she got typhus fever and quickly died. She was quite cruel. Very mean. Not with me, but everyone complained that she wouldn't allow people to do basic normal things. And then she died because she was in better condition than we were.'

The remains of 232 bodies, who had suffered from 'catastrophic living conditions' such 'as lack of hygienic living spaces, hunger, and poor clothing', were exhumed from a mass grave in Lichtenwörth on 5 May 1946 and taken to be buried in a Jewish cemetery in Budapest. The total number of dead at Lichtenwörth is unclear, but testimony from the Eichmann trial and other documents estimate that only 400 of 2,500 prisoners survived.

On 2 April 1945, the camp was liberated by the Red Army, as they marched through Wiener Neustadt, as part of the Vienna offensive, whose denouement occurred two weeks later. Austria was on the front line when the gates of Lichtenwörth's camp opened.

Katalin describes what happened. 'I only remember seeing a single Russian soldier standing at the door to our cell. I was somehow able to get up when I heard that we were free. I went to the door. He was so nice. And interestingly, I didn't look very bad. Or at least I didn't seem to be just skin and bones. He was not at all like what I heard later about the Russians. He asked me what he could do to help. "Can I bring you something?" he asked. And I told him: "Don't come close to me. Be careful, we are all infested!"'

'We found the Germans' kitchen that they had abandoned. "Can I bring you something to eat?" he asked. I said, "Can you bring me a chicken?" I thought maybe I could make some chicken soup. He brought the chicken and he brought a sack of flour and sugar. It was an accident that the Russians went so far west. They made a well-equipped hospital in a nearby castle – that never happened anywhere else to my knowledge – I maybe would have ended up there but we didn't know. I just wanted to leave the camp with my friend Anikó because now we could. We walked probably a few miles. I have no idea.'

Together, Katalin and Anikó walked through the war zone in a delirium. Many of the other camp people started dying; the prisoners' bodies could not handle the sudden food intake and died from 'refeeding syndrome'. The camp's storage room had been raided, and a *Jupo* was trampled in the rush for sugar, margarine, and marmalade. Katalin was so ill that she couldn't eat, so she survived. She does not know where the energy came from, to walk, at the beginning. But eventually, she could not go on.

She recounts, 'It was war all around us. I remember standing in front of a tank asking them to stop and take us. Finally, we saw that there was a small house next to the road. Anikó and I went to it. The door was open and it was empty and there I fell unconscious in the bed. I do not remember very much. Only that I was given something to drink. I couldn't drink very much. Sometimes I woke up for short periods but, in between, I had terrible dreams, vivid dreams – this happens with typhus. I still remember them.

'I was never religious: nor was my family. Many of my siblings had married Christians. And occasionally, I would go to a Christian church. Maybe that is why I dreamt about Jesus. It never came into my mind to think of Jesus. Even when I was seven years old, I asked: who made God? And I was told you shouldn't ask such questions.'

Finally, Katalin fell into a coma. When she woke, she did not know where she was: 'I was in a bathtub and a man was bathing me. He was a nurse. I was in hospital. Then I woke again, and I was in a hospital bed, sharing it with my friend. The pain in my side was my friend against me.

Then I remember the doctors speaking, telling Anikó that I would not make it. I had more terrible dreams. But, somehow, I got better. There was a beautiful young nurse. But she caught typhus from us and died. They took everything from me when I got to the hospital. My clothes, my coat, the photographs. They were full of lice. They shaved my head.'

Katalin's condition improved and she knew, after some weeks, she did not want to stay in the hospital. Although everyone told her she was too weak to travel, she decided to try to get home to Budapest.

'I was in a very strange state of mind. I've read that young people, after a very severe illness, can suddenly be struck with this happiness. My emotions were quite alive. And it was in this state, when I was leaving the hospital, that the nurses came and gave me some food – some potatoes for my trip – '

Then something astonishing occurred.

'I don't know who had saved it, or how it happened – but they gave me back the cotton pouch with the photographs inside it. I was so happy. I couldn't believe that it had survived, after everything that had happened.'

Katalin and her object had something in common; was their survival a sign that she could return to her old life?

The Theft

Katalin left the Austrian hospital in a wretched state. 'The return was impossible in my condition,' she recalled. 'I don't know how I did it. I thought: I have to get home. I thought of Artúr and my aunt. For them, I wanted to get home.'

She found an operable train to Budapest and boarded it east. It stopped and started along the way. The countryside was destroyed by war. At one point, Katalin needed to disembark to use the toilet. When she returned to the station, the train had departed without her. She waited on the platform for the next one, full of Russian soldiers – 'so strong, so acrobatic, I couldn't believe what they were capable of'. On it was a Hungarian Katalin recognised from her regular tram journey before the war. He did not recognise her but gave her some soup. After pulling into Budapest's Eastern Station, Katalin found her weary way to the Red Cross. Her aunt, who had been hidden in the ghetto and survived, found her there.

'She cried when she saw me! I was only forty kilograms when I got to Budapest. My face was like an egg. Of course, my head was shaved. I went back home with her and it took three months for me to get better.

'I got the notice in 1943 that Artúr disappeared in Volotovo. But I hoped for more news of him after I came home. But I never got any more information. That was all. I talked to a soldier, not a Jewish person, who had been in Artúr's group, but he didn't know anything. Or he didn't want to tell me. I never saw Artúr again.'

And then – of a family of eight – one sister and one brother of Katalin's survived Auschwitz. She learned how her parents were gassed. How the two small children and the wife of her brother were also gassed. Her two siblings survived only because they were put to work.

Katalin explains: 'My sister was fed better, producing goods that the Germans never used. My brother peeled potatoes in a kitchen, so he could eat the peels. Anikó had left the hospital before me and we saw each other again. It was important to have someone with me – from the beginning to the end – but we did not speak about it afterwards.'

After the three months of convalescence, when Katalin was strong enough to go outside, she put the cotton pouch, with the photographs that had survived the camps, into her purse, and she went into the street to take a tram. But having miraculously survived the camp, the pouch and photographs were abruptly lost.

She explains the tragedy, matter-of-factly: 'Someone must have thought I kept money in there because that person on the tram stole the pouch from my purse. I cried, of course.'

I find I cannot bear to listen to Katalin. I want to cry as she tells me that she has lost the last possessions from her former life. Katalin's aunt was able to replace the photograph of Artúr. And she also gave her a picture of Katalin, taken in July 1943. But the photo of her family was gone.

'I was lucky that my aunt had a copy of the photo of Artúr. That is how I still have that picture. The one of me from 1943 is a very sad photo. In it, I wondered what would happen to Artúr. But I did not dare to begin to hope that I would see him again. I do not have a single picture of my parents any more. I have almost nothing from before the war.'

Crutches

The war had only just ended, the photographs promised a continuity with life before the war, but then Katalin was left without them. The few, fortunate facsimiles from her aunt only partly filled that void. What is it like to be separated from the past that way?

In Berlin, the floor plan of the Jewish Museum, seen from above, looks like a shattered star of David. It is made of straight lines that end abruptly (I think of Katalin's family, whose lives were cut short in Auschwitz). There are spaces that are voids (I think of the empty cotton pouch). There are also unlikely continuities – hallways that stop then continue after a gap (I think of reprints of photographs that returned to Katalin by chance). Daniel Libeskind's 2001 building is a metaphor for Jewish history in Europe in the twentieth century: out of the catastrophe, there are nonetheless continuities.

Isn't it natural for us to leave some objects behind? And then for others to come back to us by chance? Proust, in his *In Search of Lost Time*, speaks of the great power of memories that are lost and then retrieved by surprise. Imagine that you find an old box in the basement and it reveals a child's toy or a letter you have not thought about for a long time. Proust says this is the most powerful kind of memory-discovery: 'Habit weakens everything; what best reminds us of a person is precisely what we had forgotten …'

I asked Katalin whether an object like a photograph replaces the memory of a person. Is there not something unrewarding in holding on to old photographs, because their habitual memory replaces more complicated ones? I think about the lost, posed image – taken in a photographer's studio – of Katalin's mother, with her two older brothers and her grandmother. Was this photo a poor memory in comparison to, say, the scents and flavours of Katalin's parents' bakery that – if she were to taste them again – might surprise, and open 'the last treasure of the past' and 'make her weep again'?

You might never find the right ingredients or technique to recreate them on your own, so their lost flavours become powerful triggers. I yearn to taste Katalin's poppyseed swirls. There are similar desserts everywhere in Berlin, but I have not yet come across those from my childhood. Perhaps the problem is that I am looking too hard. Perhaps I will stumble over one and have that powerful moment of Proustian memory, the way the taste of a madeleine brought the author back to his childhood, evoking that word that connects memory to the senses of smell and taste: redolence.

Taste suggests, in its impermanence, too the flimsiness of memory. It feels the opposite of the photograph, which is different from many other objects in that it draws a fixed likeness from the past with light. The metonymy of photographs is curious, in the sense of how they stand in for a missing person or thing. We keep photos as souvenirs. But with their habitual, unsurprising, flat stasis, aren't they also the enemy of memory? I think again of how holiday photos replace holiday memories.

In Plato's *Phaedrus*, Socrates recounts the problem with those who use prepared notes when giving a speech. He calls notes a 'crutch' that makes people forget their ability to memorise and understand long pieces of prose. The crutch lets memory go slack. Wasn't the cotton pouch, and the photographs inside, a crutch?

There is a problem with this theorising. No matter how much I indulge in these analogies and references, I cannot escape one fact. What power is left in a memory if, in the end, it cannot be retrieved? What happens if the thread is lost and you cannot remember your family because you no longer have that image of them? Is there not a reason why the only other things, apart from food, that Katalin brought with her for her deportation were pictures? Did she understand, even then, the importance of the document, of evidence?

Today, I cannot find a single photograph of the Lichtenwörth camp. I continue to look in the archives and come up with nothing. Evidence is disappearing and we need it. Katalin's grasp of her family's faces faded; so is the story of Lichtenwörth – and certainly the role of the Hungarian collaborators who enabled the deportation there.

People collect objects precisely to defy the great abstractness of the past, to prevent authorities from playing games with memory. Some objects are our anchors, not our crutches.

Post-War

'How can you talk so matter-of-factly about this history?' I ask Katalin.

I had trouble absorbing that someone I had grown up next to – for whom I played the piano badly as a child in a peaceful Canadian city – had been exposed to a death march, the crushed conditions of the camp, the illness, the trial of the return home, losing her husband, her family. So many of the worst excesses of the war were bound up in one person's biography. How did she live with these scars?

'Because I had so many good memories later, seventy-five years of them,' she replies. 'I made myself not so sensitive to these things. It takes time and I try to live as best as I can. But I am overcome with emotion sometimes. I paint three times a week and this focuses me.'

'Do you think the war changed your character?'

'My character hasn't changed. But the war made me more inventive. After Lichtenwörth, I got good at making tools, for example if I needed to reach a high shelf. I didn't need to buy these tools, suddenly I could make them. I think this resourcefulness comes from having to get by. That's about it. Except, I was also braver during the war. But that bravery isn't with me any more.'

I discovered that a recipe book was found in Budapest, sixty-two years after the liberation of the camp. In Lichtenwörth, a group of women wrote down what they used to cook every day, at home in Budapest. This was a survival technique, to keep alive the continuity with their past lives, a time when they did not subsist on hunger rations. Most of the recipes recorded were, unsurprisingly, sweets and cakes. So, I ask: 'Did the camp change your attitude to food?'

She laughs, 'People wanted to eat more after the war! But in the long run, no. But maybe they paid more attention to food.'

'But how then did you go into the war on course to become a seamstress, and then after the war you become an accomplished scientist, a provincial analyst in Canada?'

'I never wanted to be a seamstress. But I had given up hope that anything else was possible. That was one good thing the communists did in Hungary. Schooling was paid for by the state. Yes, it was still very restricted. Only sympathisers of the government would be taught. But as a survivor, I went in 1946 or so to an institution where they appraised my ability. And interestingly, I was told that I could do anything I wanted to. I could choose a profession. But I had to finish *Gimnázium* [high school granting a qualification for university] first and work at the same time, because I needed food, which was the only thing that had value at that time. I would work a whole day for a bottle of oil. But then I got an education. I started in 1948 with high school, and then from 1950 to 1954 I went to university and obtained the equivalent of a Master diploma, as a technical engineer.

'Until the end of 1947, I was still hoping that Artúr would come back. But then I gave up and I met my future husband Ottó at a friend's place. He had also been in a camp, in Mauthausen. Before then, he had been put to work in Budapest, clearing rubble of bombing raids, and was traumatised by the body parts. It's strange to think that I always prayed that planes would destroy the city. In Hegyeshalom, the Allies flew above us, and I wasn't scared, because I thought: they're the Allies! I hoped that they would end the war.

'In Mauthausen, Ottó had also caught typhus, and when he was in the care of the Americans, convalescing, he had wild dreams and delirium and would wander the grounds, with other patients, and the Americans would drive around with their truck and pick them up. Ottó, when he came back, was in quite bad shape. He couldn't start right away working, only as soon as he could. Ottó was so understanding about Artúr, so sympathetic. He felt my loss. We started to go out. And then we married. But my thoughts often return to Artúr now that Ottó is gone. This makes me feel guilty, after seventy years with Ottó.'

We speak long about the post-war years. Katalin was unable to have children after her illness in the camp. She and Ottó left in December 1956 after the uprising against the Soviets. Strangely, they took the same route of her deportation, via Hegyeshalom, into Austria. They had relatives in the United States who said they would care for them, but they were sent instead to Canada. They moved west, to Edmonton, and made a new life there together.

'I finally got to work in a laboratory in Canada, at the University of Alberta. The Department of Agriculture took over and they built me a beautiful new laboratory, with the latest equipment, on the sixth floor of a big building. I was able to design the lab myself, the best-equipped lab in the province; Ottó helped me a lot. I was appointed the Director of the Provincial Laboratory, or Provincial Analyst. We did toxicology and forensic work and water analysis. We checked blood for alcohol, stomach contents for toxic substances. I often had to go to court to testify. Sometimes, the lawyers kept me on the stand for three hours. It wasn't an easy job as a woman, as I was the only woman in such a position, but the men respected me.'

It was only in 1979 that the couple returned to Hungary. She tells me, 'Hungary then was a strange place. But I remember – and will remember forever – how behind our house in Ózd there was a big field where wheat was growing. Somehow, I never forgot that. And as soon as I could, I went there with Ottó. I wanted to show him. As I said, there are some sights that you never forget. Huge fields. It was so free there. And it was still there.'

There is something I have been meaning to ask Katalin. I hesitate on this question: 'What do you think of me now living in Germany, Katalin? Is it something that you cannot understand?'

'I never hated the Germans despite what happened. They were just as bad and good as any other people. Hungary was also extremely antisemitic even though the Hungarian Jews were very talented and gave a lot to

Budapest. My nephew married a German woman. At first, her parents objected. But she had a heart of gold.'

'Did the Holocaust change how you feel about humanity?'

She considers, 'I was touched by all the kindnesses that often came despite the dangers during my deportation. Eighty per cent of people go along with things. I would include myself among them. But some people don't and that makes me feel better about humanity.'

Indeed, her story is marked by the kindnesses, very basic ones, when some exceptional people took care of her, sheltered her, and gave her food. I hope I am one of the 20 per cent but I recognise that one never knows until put under pressure.

'But I am worried about the rise of the far right and Europe returning to the situation before World War Two,' she says.

I reply, 'What can we do about this? How can young people learn from what happened in the past? Through your story?'

'It depends on their personality. Some would need to experience war themselves to understand it first of all, others would need to experience it just to believe.'

Vrtoch

One detail of Katalin's testimony needles me, and it is the description of the camp commandant watching the inmates wash, when he calls them children. I grow determined to find more about this 'good-looking' man, one Wilhelm Vrtoch. I plan to go to Austria to search through the archives for documents of his post-war trial before a *Volksgericht* ('people's court'). This proves impossible in the months leading up to submitting my book, as the Austrian coronavirus lockdown obstructs not just borders but also access to the archives.

You can imagine then how grateful I was one day – after having sent several desperate emails to the archive of the Documentation Centre of the Austrian Resistance – when a saintly archivist sends me a surprise email with the scanned court documents attached. The fourteen typed pages from 1948 are torn in places at the margins and scrawled with the illegible angular hand of perhaps the judge. But from them, I can both corroborate Katalin's story and fill in aspects of the camp's brutality. It's one of the few primary documents left about camp life, apart from the survivors' testimony.

Born on 12 June 1920 in Vienna, Wilhelm Vrtoch trained as a plumber and joined the SS as a volunteer at the age of 18. After an injury that made him unfit for combat, he first became a clerk in a concentration camp in Hungary, before becoming the commandant of Lichtenwörth and Felixdorf camps in late 1944, at the age of 24. The court affirmed that the twin camps were not 'recreation camps' as described but rather places of mass extermination. Trial witnesses – and Vrtoch's own confession – show he committed inhumane acts and was guilty of abuse of power leading to extreme suffering and scores of deaths. But the wanton cruelty of his acts emerges in the details. Vrtoch usually carried a poker with him that he would use to beat the prisoners at 'every opportunity' when he was not ordering his men to do so. He frequently fired shots in the air as a scare tactic; unsurprisingly there were victims. He purposefully knocked over a latrine bucket from the sick ward onto women prisoners. He beat an old man so hard that he fell into a pile of glass and smashed his face. Abuse at roll call is also documented. One witness tries to explain this cruelty, testifying that Vrtoch, because of his youth, 'was not able to cope with the task he was given'.

It is frustrating that almost all the twenty witnesses called to testify were men, with German names. It is unlikely that the surviving women of Lichtenwörth would have been able to travel to Vienna from Soviet-occupied Hungary. Had they been there, however, they would have been able to add even worse crimes to the record.

The *Lager* chief is described by Judith Konrad: 'I remember him very well. We were, by that time, in bad condition, rather dirty, and underfed. He looked radiant, beautiful, very very handsome, tall, a young man with typical German looks, blond and blue-eyed, very very cruel, icy blue eyes. I remember his eyes more than anything else, always wearing his smart uniform, with a stick in his hand … One of the most terrible experiences was when I saw a pregnant woman whipped in this way and she never got up and died.' He had, apparently, a fascination with pregnancy, as he watched a woman giving birth while holding a bright light over the delivery, according to the testimony of Aviva Fleischmann at the Eichmann trial in 1961, because 'he wanted to see how a human being is born into this world'. Neither the woman nor the baby received any medical attention, according to the trial transcript, and so both died. Konrad further describes how he had the prisoners line up for roll call in the courtyard over Christmas 1944, where they were forced to stand for two days and watch him eat his holiday meals.

The court records conclude Vrtoch was the 'archetype of the SS-man: blindly obedient, brutal and reckless'; his behaviour was against 'the natural principles of humanity and international law'. It is perhaps no surprise that the court was disposed to impose the death penalty. Instead, the extenuating circumstances of his youth, and his need to care for his wife and old mother, saved his life. Vrtoch was sentenced on 13 January 1948 to eighteen years of hard labour. Again maddening – given the severity of his crimes – is to learn that he was released prematurely in 1953. This was at a time when the Austrian government was keen to emphasise its status as the 'first victim' of the Nazis – a revisionist narrative that forgave many homegrown war criminals like Vrtoch. He died, perhaps after a comfortable post-war life, in 1993.

But I do not yet have a photograph of him. Somehow a photograph would peg him, make him coalesce from the air. Is this the same reason why photographs were so important to Katalin? Of course, I am also curious and intrigued that even the prisoners thought he was beautiful – an inversion of the classical view that there is virtue in beautiful faces. And what of this object: his poker? Is it the belonging that tells his story?

In the early summer – months after I wrote the previous section – an envelope arrives from the German Federal Archive containing Wilhelm ('Willy') Vrtoch's SS file. I am about to go for a run when I find the thick packet in the downstairs mailbox. I climb back up the eighty-eight steps instead to read it on my kitchen table in my trainers.

Soon I realise – it's a heart-quickening coincidence – that the documents have arrived on the Nazi's 101st birthday. I think about how easily the camp commandant and his atrocities could have been forgotten, slipping through the net of history.

The file corroborates the court documents: Vrtoch was born in Vienna to a labourer and only remained in school until he was 14, when he began training as a plumber. He joined the SS on 12 May 1938, just three days after his 18th birthday. He fought in Poland, France, and Russia until, on 10 September 1941, he took a direct hit to his left hand. Removed from battle, he worked in camps in Hungary and Austria. In a letter from June 1942, he also refers to service with the Gestapo. He was 184cm (6ft) tall and had blue-grey eyes, and ash-blond hair, just as Judith Konrad described in her testimony.

I wonder whether anything in the file can illuminate his cruelty. The Federal Archive suggested I might save on photocopy costs by omitting the parts of Vrtoch's file concerning his attempts to gain permission to marry his girlfriend. But everyday details that are overlooked often prove the most revealing. The approval process through the SS Race and Settlement Main Office, charged with the racial purity of the SS, constituted some forty pages of his sixty-page file. Vrtoch's fiancée, three years his junior, came from a family with a history of mental illness: her maternal grandfather had been incarcerated for quackery (he used forbidden herbs to cure an amputee) and was sent to a mental hospital for 'congenital psychopathy'. A maternal aunt also lived with an unspecified mental illness. A maternal uncle was born with a disability and forcibly sterilised. Nazi Germany, of course, systematically 'euthanised' (read: murdered) disabled persons. The SS office's inquiries and research into the case began in earnest in May 1942 for three months, until permission was finally granted on 15 July. I cannot help but wonder whether this long investigation into a loved one's suitability for an SS officer influenced Willy's role, as a man charged with overseeing others designated as eugenic inferiors. Was he especially cruel because of an insecurity closer to home?

The file also contains what I was missing before: photographs of the man. I stare at them, somehow thinking they will provide explanations. In profile, Willy looks like a meathead, a brute. But would I have thought so, not knowing his role in the fate of thousands? Straight-on, he looks more elegant. He might be holding a glass of something sparkling, like Sekt, and – if it weren't for the SS on his collar – I might accept an invitation to dance.

I shake my head: I'm projecting, doing what the Nazis do, attaching fantasies to physiognomy – treating Vrtoch like … an object.

Raum zum Aufkleben der Lichtbilder.

The Future

Sachsenhausen was the 'model' concentration camp on which all other work camps were designed, including Lichtenwörth. In Austria, there is nothing left of Katalin's camp – only a plaque – while Sachsenhausen has a comprehensive documentation centre and acted as the central inspection office for the Germans' concentration camp system. What happened to Katalin was coordinated twenty-five minutes from today's Berlin Central Station, followed by a walk to the camp. The site also has an important museum of objects. It is a gruesome place that bundles together many aspects of Katalin's story.

I had been avoiding the camp, to be honest, and had never visited despite living in Berlin for more than a decade. Early in my time in Germany, I visited a handful of camps: Auschwitz-Birkenau and Dachau. Their horrors did not make me want to confront one so close to where I live. Sachsenhausen remained just outside the circle of my life. But after the first night interviewing Katalin, I decide I have to go.

Like Lichtenwörth, Sachsenhausen was not a purpose-built death camp, although many tens of thousands of people died here. It was built primarily as a holding pen for prisoners of war, homosexuals, political dissidents, the mentally ill, and Jews. Sachsenhausen experimented on its inmates, overworked them, tortured them, and killed them. Compared to Lichtenwörth, the camp was older, enormous, and sophisticated. But here too was a place where things were done to appear by the book. The victims got autopsies, even though they were faked. The veil of officialdom was draped over the lies.

I am always surprised to find houses abutting the perimeter fence of such camps – to walk through neighbourhoods of buoyant trees, a trampoline in a yard, cars well washed in driveways. I think again of Lichtenwörth and how the locals lived alongside horrors.

Through the gate, with its bars twisted to the words '*Arbeit Macht Frei*', one enters a great field, with the barracks fanning out from the yard used for roll call and the gallows. Behind a wall is the death facility Station Z, where the SS tried out, or 'test-labbed', various ways to kill: shot through the neck from behind during a fake medical exam (too many bullets, too much time), herded into a ditch and shot (too many bullets, too much panic), being gassed (no bullets, no panic). More than 10,000 Soviet soldiers were killed here in a matter of months. The doors of the crematoria ovens still hang loosely, makeshift. There are fields and fields of ashes and mass graves from forced marches. Like in Lichtenwörth, the Jews were crowded into immobile, airless squalor, in Barracks 37 to 39 of the so-called 'small camp'. Altogether, more than 200,000 people of eighteen nationalities passed through Sachsenhausen.

Sachsenhausen's museum of objects is housed in the former kitchen. The exposition, explaining key events in the history of Sachsenhausen and the everyday life of the prisoners, is tactile and expository. There is a wooden device on which people were whipped until they lost kidney function; it requires little commentary. There is an elaborately carved cigarette case made in secret by a prisoner in a workshop; it has the flags of the Allies on it. There are blue metal discs used to identify Soviet soldiers to be shot. A prisoner counted them, giving us a number of deceased. Each object brings individuals into relief out of the enormous statistics.

Neither Sachsenhausen nor Lichtenwörth were systematic death camps like Auschwitz. They remind us that 'the concentration camp universe' of the Nazi system, as Primo Levi called it, extended to many forms of degradation. The visitor who feels that these camps are like gruesome rides – and that Auschwitz was scarier – might be disappointed. How is it that suddenly 'the worst' is the measure of all things – the Nazis having pushed the bar so high for atrocity, even comparatively within their system of camps?

There is something useful in visiting camps that are not like Auschwitz. Struggling to understand the camp on its own terms – its function, its particular horrors – tears one out of the popular imagination of the Holocaust, one of the transports leading directly to the gas chambers, as happened with Katalin's parents. When one struggles with the unexpected, one sees the camp again, demystified. That is what the objects in the Sachsenhausen museum do as well. Each object presents snippets of unique, and not habitual, humanity, which is the way into the tragedy. There is the temptation to dismiss Sachsenhausen – or Lichtenwörth – because they are not the classic 'movie image' of Auschwitz, which is a disservice to the thousands who suffered in these places, and camps like them.

Katalin said that young people might need to experience the horror themselves to understand the worst of history. But with witnesses like Katalin, these well-documented places of remembrance, and objects of individual suffering, I think we have a fighting chance. They all hold back a scenario of no more pictures, the hollow somewhere of a cotton pouch.

Frühlingsglaube

It's a summer day in Berlin and I have recorded the piano part of the Schubert song *Frühlingsglaube*, or 'Faith in Spring', and emailed it to Katalin. In return, she sends me a recipe for *Gyümölcsös kocka*. 'Kids enjoy something fruity. Everyone's liked it so far,' she writes. Neither the music nor the tray cakes will last very long.

The evening I am preparing for will also go by quickly. My cellist friend – Jewish, recently moved to Berlin from London – has invited me over. Her small children also play instruments and already speak much better German than either of us. In the other room, they play. I bring out Katalin's pastries, sunken nectarine squares. Next time I will bring desserts from the new continent to the old: oatmeal cookies and Nanaimo squares. I feel like I am passing something on, at least I am trying.

Perhaps the smell of something baked will surprise one of these children decades from now, a flavour they thought they had forgotten. But I take pictures of the evening just in case.

A Way Without Words

In One Room

I imagine putting all my witnesses together in a room, each holding their belonging. Some attention to detail might help avert a disaster: don't serve tea but something stronger. Instead of cooking and inviting them home, meet somewhere neutral, like a café where no one feels trapped. Even the country is a loaded choice: I have trouble seeing Katalin – polite but uncomfortable – in Germany, or at the same table with Erna. A shared love of cooking would hardly bridge the gap. I don't relish Katalin's reaction on seeing my grandfather's knife. The Canadian soldier would happily exchange war stories with Karl. But my grandfather was not one to put his own feelings down on paper. He'd find the German's diary moody and self-indulgent. Erich would speak equally with all of them, even Katalin. They'd talk about music. He'd play. Perhaps, after all, it would be the double bassist who'd hold the group together, as long as the others didn't start asking him too much about his time fighting on the front. No, the gathering – no matter if we drank camomile tea or whisky, or met in Banff, Alberta or Banff, Aberdeenshire – would be a tense, courteous affair, with everyone eyeing the door.

This is a thought experiment, but similar situations – bringing together the war's victims, perpetrators, 'victors', or fellow travellers – have happened countless times in the past, just as they are unlikely to take place in the future. Such a meeting is not even difficult to imagine, now that we've met each individual and told each story.

What's left to consider, stepping back?

In this last chapter, I will speak about why objects provide such an opportunity to unlock hidden stories from the past. But I also argue how Nazi-era objects, especially, can be dangerous. How do we reconcile the opportunity with the danger? Let's see how these seemingly conflicting elements fit together and connect to the larger themes of 'everyday history'. A dozen new objects will help us along our way.

'She-Nazis'

If you love object histories, as I do, you might have fallen over yourself excitedly reading Neil MacGregor's *History of the World in 100 Objects*. He suggests we should look at objects creatively, with starry eyes even: 'A history of things is impossible without poets,' who should make 'the object under discussion their own and in consequence make their own history'. How many of us have had the experience of wandering through a space like the British Museum, examining past mysteries, heart pounding, imagining history come to life?

With respect to Dr MacGregor, and museums wishing to engage a wider public, 'making the object your own' is bad advice when it comes to Nazi-era objects. In 2010, the German Historical Museum mounted an exhibit called *Hitler and the Germans: Nation and Crime.* It was the first-ever comprehensive exhibit on Hitler shown in a federal German museum since the war and it presented everyday objects from the Nazi period. Some were playthings. Others were board games, uniforms, elaborate weapons with Nazi insignia, and banners. The toys became a particularly popular news item precisely because they linked intimate family life with images of the Nazi leadership (through figurines of Hitler and his ministers). One wondered if many of the older people wandering the exhibit might have even played with them.

The inclusion of fascist paraphernalia – 'Nazi relics' – caused enough panic that the director of the museum made a public statement: 'We are not haunted by neo-Nazis because we are a place of enlightenment. They don't read books and they don't go to exhibitions.' (This is both wishful thinking and an underestimation of the adversary!) Luckily, neo-Nazis did not show up in numbers big enough to make the news. The German Historical Museum's guardedness, however, was understandable: the curators were terrified visitors would approach everyday objects from the Nazi regime at best poetically, and at worst as fetish objects. Their solution was masses of contextualising text by historian Ian Kershaw.

Neo-Nazis, and others who admire the era's perpetrators, do not have a monopoly on fetishisation. The fascination of victims and their descendants with the luridness of Nazi objects, their symbols, and their protagonists, is complex territory. A disturbing example is Stalag comics, which circulated among Israelis, including the children of camp survivors, before being banned in 1963. They are Nazi-inspired objects rather than strictly Nazi objects, but they illustrate the point. The comics typically depict Jewish prisoners sexually abused in camp environments by 'she-Nazis', wearing the regime's symbols. The comics portray a male fantasy-inversion of the documented cases of female prisoners forced into prostitution at camp brothels, or *Lagerbordelle*. However, the fantasy is not a true inversion, as Jewish women were not used as sex workers in these establishments, because of rules of 'racial hygiene'.

Despite their historical inaccuracies and unlikely pornographic plots, the Stalags are thought to have formed a generation in their perceptions of camp life and the sexual trauma occurring there. In fact, they became the most popular circulating publications in Israel before the court's ban. A Hebrew University study establishes that Stalags were the most read publications among 18-year-olds, with the most popular title, *Stalag 13*, selling 25,000 copies (bought by one in sixty-five of the total population of the country at the time). Nazi evil was laced with the erotic, a powerful chaser, making these objects all the more marketable and alluring. Stalags, meanwhile, muddled the documentary record, replacing suffering with sadomasochistic pleasure. A revisit of the comics' fabrications and their legacy only began in 2008, when Ari Libsker's documentary *Stalags* returned the subject to public debate.

Both examples – the toys and the Stalags – distil the problem: aren't Nazi objects, and the stories told about them, mostly dangerous because they are useful screens for projection, for assumptions, fabrications, even titillations, about the Nazi past? In what circumstances might they be instructive and useful?

I grow more and more mistrustful of the belongings in this book. In the best case, objects are useful tools to unlock the past. Take, for example, the recipe book chapter, where the virtual belonging is a strategy to open up subjects for discussion (or its flip side: the absence of photographs makes Katalin's past almost inaccessible). But in the worst cases, the objects quickly acquire new community meanings – such as those that glorify Nazi fetishes. The knife becomes a manifestation of evil. Expectations for the diary romanticise the past. Meanwhile, the double bass and its music even shield perpetrators. The objects are easily misleading and misused in the absence of careful detective work and their original owners' testimony. I do not see how one could come away from this material celebrating the poeticising of the objects' narratives.

Hiding the Swastika

One reason these objects are so enticing is that their solidity imparts an aura of fact. As the French poet Francis Ponge put it in 1961, 'Objects … convince me. By the very fact they don't need to.' We are more likely to believe what we see. Objects suggest this certainty, like the murder weapon whose discovery is a long-awaited proof, the solution to the mystery. They appear more reliable than witnesses, who are transient and vanish over time like fingerprints. With this disappearance – when only durable things, like messengers from the past, remain as evidence of the monumental evil of the Nazi regime and the crimes of the Holocaust – the desire intensifies for the material object, on its own, to tell the whole story. Except, it cannot.

I asked in the first chapter whether my grandfather's knife could go on public display. Imagine the following scene: a visitor to a war museum sees the bayonet sporting its swastika exhibited. He approaches it creatively and tries to 'make the object his own'. If he knows nothing about the Third Reich, this will be difficult. But chances are he has read a good book on the subject or seen an Indiana Jones film. The small label on the museum's glass case suggests that all you need to know are a few details. And grasping just a little-bit-about-something is enough for some suddenly to become experts!

Assumptions about the past attach to the object, as if to a magnet. Any object with a swastika on it draws an immediate reaction, cinematic in scope and fashioned by pop culture, stereotypes, and superstition, alongside historical facts. The object is considered forbidden, rather than everyday, only increasing its allure. Primed to read popular stories into Nazi objects, one follows fancy down a rabbit hole of projection, as occurred with the popular reception of the sexist 'she-Nazis' of the Stalags. Some will temper these reactions. But you can be sure that most will follow my path, except without the subsequent research, spinning legends around the gruesome object. When shown in public, the knife risks becoming a nexus for the exchange of false stories. I imagine a miasma of such narratives hanging from the ceiling of the museum, a mist of lies.

Will the object itself correct those museum visitors' projections? Of course it won't. The knife is voiceless (we speaking creatures can hardly imagine its state of blank!), which is why it is so susceptible to manipulation. It is the ideal subject for projection. The self-appointed expert need never fear being contradicted!

The risks of such facile and dangerous projection are not abstract. They are the subject of contemporary, urgent, public policy. The problem is felt acutely in Germany, where Nazi objects circulate, represent power, create community, and become devotional for far-right groups. The state's response is a ban of the swastika, along with other far-right and white-supremacist symbols, under section 86a of the *Strafgesetzbuch*, or Criminal Code. Certainly, there were moments writing this book when I had to be mindful of the law, such as when I unwittingly imported the swastika. Germany's solution is to push the Nazi knife out of view, nipping projection in the bud.

The hesitations of the curators of *Hitler and the Germans* are widely shared among their German colleagues. As theorist Chloe Paver remarks, 'The graveness of the topic tends to militate against experimentation.' The use of objects in exhibits is what she intends by such 'experimentation' and museums of the Nazi period in Germany and Austria are indeed shy of Nazi things. They favour flat exhibits instead, such as poster reproductions or written panels, which are less likely to be considered relics. The German Historical Museum in Berlin has close to a million objects in its collections, but you would never know while visiting its permanent exhibit on the Nazi period. It is only recently, in 2020, that the educational centre at Obersalzberg – Hitler's 'Eagle's Nest' in Berchtesgaden – began to experiment with object-oriented displays. Swastikas, however, often remain hidden.

This strategy is unlikely to be effective. The Nazis themselves often obscured the swastika. They understood that a partial view increased its power – such as in this Hitler Youth propaganda postcard from 1932 – forcing the viewer to take the extra step to engage with the symbol and conflate it with the image of the idealised Greco-Roman youth and his bird of prey. Inaccessible objects can increase devotion and reinforce hierarchies of power. The Crown Jewels are iconic precisely because we cannot touch them.

What happens, then, when the symbol is completely hidden, as is the requirement under today's German law? Is the swastika, as an object for projection, really that dangerous? Do the laws increase its forbidden aura?

Neo-Nazi groups circumvent, and even profit, from the extrusion of the symbol from public life, by creating ersatz, transformed symbols, employing cloak-and-dagger strategies for community building. Clothing brands – such as Thor Steinar or Lonsdale – are appropriated by neo-Nazis to identify each other in public space. The shared decoding fosters the cachet of belonging to a secret sect. The brand 'Consdaple' on a hoodie, in Germany, for example, communicates the letters NSDAP (the acronym for the *Nationalsozialistische Deutsche Arbeiterpartei*, or Nazi party) at its heart more effectively than an uncoded graffito could ever manage, forcing a ban by a district court in 2010 on wearing the logo, after seven years of use.

I sometimes speculate what it would take to resuscitate the swastika and its long history. At home I have a set of Rudyard Kipling books, published in London in the 1920s and '30s, with the swastika embossed on the spines of every volume published until 1929, evoking its use in religious contexts in India. *The Jungle Book* of 1926 has swastikas but on *Wee Willie Winkie and Other Child Stories* of 1929 they disappear. Already before the Nazis came to power, they had usurped the symbol from popular use. I wonder whether this is a victory that they will continue to win, or whether it might be possible to put the detoxified symbol one day back on the books (with the understanding many find Kipling objectionable – Orwell, after all, called him a 'jingo imperialist').

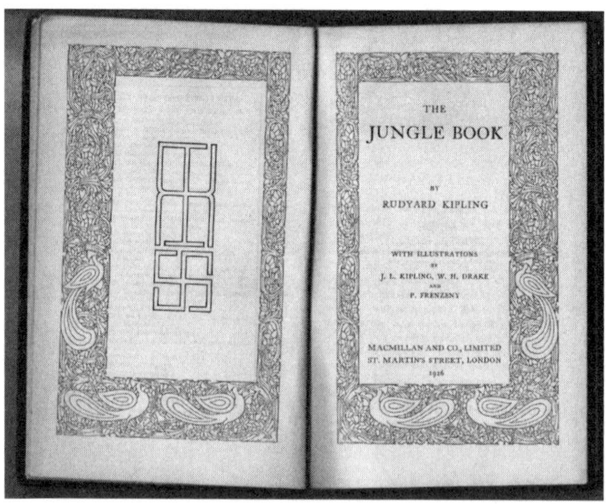

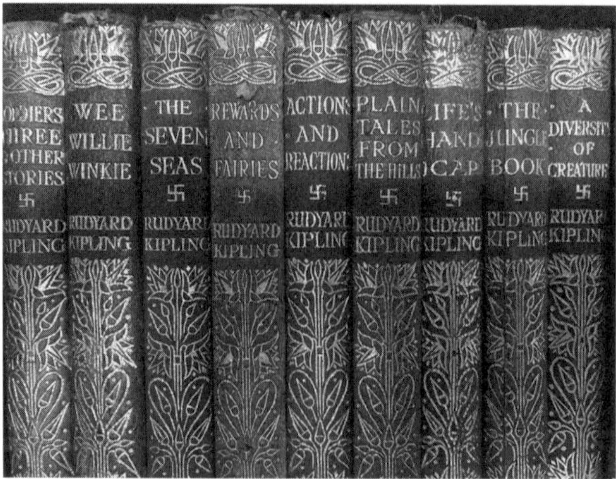

For now, everyday objects from the Third Reich, and their descendants, cause fear and panic. They engender, too, a debate that pits freedom of speech and enquiry against the need to contain extremism. Strategies of suppression weigh against the risks of creating more powerful, lurid fascinations. This discussion also frames the problem at hand: do we too push back against the inclusion of Nazi objects in museums and material history, because of the risks of projection? Or are there methods to make these objects illuminate the darkness of the past like little else? What does it mean to say: Nazi-era object history, if it's done, needs to be done extremely carefully?

'Handled Carefully'

In the late 1990s – when I was working on my doctorate at Cambridge – students of modern history were not encouraged to use objects as evidence in research. We were instead dispatched to the archive, to furnish our dissertations with written primary sources. It didn't take much to be a radical – all you had to do was gather oral history. There were reasons why traditional historical training did not stress material culture, those everyday things surrounding people in the past. The first was disciplinary: we weren't archaeologists, who (we thought flippantly) relied on objects only because they didn't have any other information to go on, from their nearly lost civilisations. We also considered evidence from objects to be too subjective. Objects were vaguer than written sources. They often weren't at hand for verification. They were hard to footnote. Our methods were shaped instead by a tradition of political, economic, and diplomatic history, and their dependence on government sources, and, arguably, disinterest in the things of everyday life. Already in the 1980s – in other disciplines like anthropology – the 'material turn' had already happened. But history is the last door of the humanities corridor on which theories knock.

Today, material history is sexy. Most historians have digested the fact that precisely because we can provide more context – than, say, many archaeologists – we can make our objects 'speak' more, giving them a better chance of enriching our work. I know that by not examining belongings, I would never have arrived at the findings in this book. That is, in itself, an argument for looking at objects.

Perhaps objects have even become a little *too* sexy. When asking my witnesses 'which object tells your World War Two story?', I did not expect that their belongings had to be the focus of each story. But, given the current public fascination with object-centred history, there was the expectation that the objects should be front and centre. In the end, I resisted the temptation to coax the tools into the spotlight and was instead delighted, even dazzled, by how the objects illuminated what each witness had to tell. Objects change the way we see history. They make us explore hidden themes and ask new questions.

Now, allow me to discuss two categories used by material historians mentioned briefly in the preface: 'object-centred' and 'object-driven' histories. The former category makes the belonging the focus of an owner's story (think of Pandora's box in Greek mythology – the character is inseparable from the object). The latter uses objects to throw light on other subjects, such as context and people's lives (Paris' golden apple is arguably peripheral, but its shiny surfaces reflect all the goddesses' whims). Of the belongings in this book, which stories were 'object-centred' and which ones 'object-driven'?

In the first category, certainly, was my grandfather's knife. The bayonet was the protagonist and we even asked if it could tell its own story. The diary was also mostly 'object-centred', even as it transformed from object to document. The recipe book, however, operated differently: it drove a story instead of being at the centre of it. While it began as an imagined belonging (Erna knew which ingredients to use off by heart but never wrote them down), it went on to reveal concrete aspects of the Goebbels' story that would otherwise have remained hidden.

As so often happens with strict academic categories, they blur. This is no bad thing: multiple perspectives are more useful than a single method. The story of the string instruments falls into both camps. The double bass is at first peripheral, a tool used for asking Herr Hartmann questions. Ultimately, however, we are brought to an object-centred story of stolen instruments. Meanwhile, the cotton pouch was an entrée to ask questions about identity, leading to a more fundamental question about what it means to live without belongings from one's past. A void of 'no belongings' stands at the centre of Katalin's story.

Regardless of whether the story was 'object-centred', 'object-driven', or a little of both, the objects remained strategies, or catalysts, to bring each witness's experience into relief. Some historians of material culture get peevish at what they call the partial embrace of the 'material turn' (they complain that there are too many 'object-driven' as opposed to 'object-centred' histories out there – 'historical material culture studies have been more about culture than about material', grumbled one critic). But I don't think this a lamentable state of affairs. It's instead an inevitable one when objects are tools and not subjects.

What, then, does it mean to handle objects carefully and avoid pitfalls of projection? I wish I could provide here a systematic, agreed method; unfortunately, one doesn't exist – historians have tried. Nonetheless, I think that I've given, in the preceding paragraphs, one answer to this question. We handle objects carefully when we use them as tools. The more an object is the very centre of fascination, the more likely it is to be imbued with misplaced importance. The knife lost its fetishistic qualities the more it was anchored by the details of its production and circulation. As a child, I felt some amorphous negative feeling from the knife. As an adult, I know where it was made and its specific purpose. Likewise, the diary was no longer so pliable the moment it could be read. The vague romance Flora and I attached to it soon dispelled with the story of a particular individual and his heartache.

I am happy to defend 'object-driven' histories and what we might call 'object-possibility' – the multiple ways objects can be used as tools to unlock hidden stories. What it means to handle objects 'carefully', as they are vulnerable to projection, is ultimately to dispel their aura. Otherwise, in the absence of context, 'object-centred' history, again, risks being a receptacle for fantasy.

Jam

By way of illustration, let me tell you a story. When I was in Görlitz, a small town at the edge of Saxony, a few years ago, I stumbled across a framed photograph in a second-hand store. My German friends were aghast because the man in the frame, whom they assumed was a soldier, wore a uniform and cap with a swastika. The merchant had put a piece of

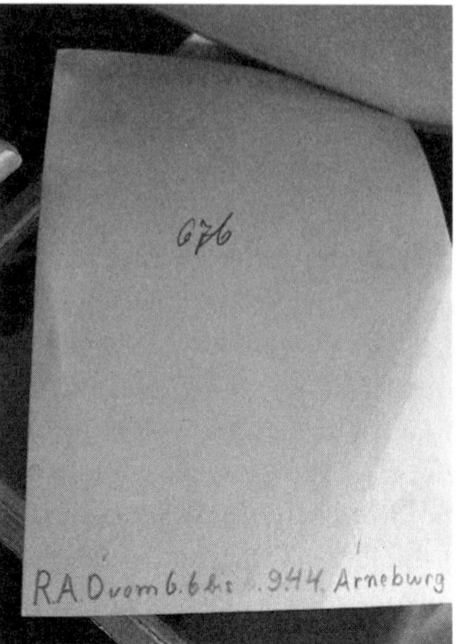

masking tape over the symbol in order legally to sell the object. Because Görlitz is in the hands of the far-right party, the AfD, or Alternative for Germany, my left-wing Berliners were quick to conflate the sale of the photograph with a problematic relationship to the past there. With their approval, I bought the photograph, to take it out of circulation and investigate it for this book. It's one of the many belongings that did not make the final draft, partly because it did not seem to tell me much on its own. It connected only to the contemporary political associations intimated by my friends.

It was only while finishing my draft that the obvious occurred to me, that I should open the frame, to see if there were clues hidden inside. Had I done this earlier, I would have uncovered a surprise. On the photograph's obverse, I found written in pencil a number, '676' (perhaps an identifier?) and then at the bottom, 'R.A.D vom 6.6. bis [ ].9.44, Arneburg' ('R.A.D. from 6.6. until [ ].9.44, Arneburg'). Some digging led me to the *Reichsarbeitsdienst* ('R.A.D.'). A make-work project for the unemployed, the Reich Labour Force became a training ground during the war for young men before they were sent to the front. I found there was one such camp in Arneburg, in a jam factory near the town on the Elbe 60 miles west of Berlin. The photograph simultaneously shows how an object can propel the investigator in an unexpected, and neglected, direction in everyday history. Certainly, I would never have been compelled to write about a jam factory on the Elbe. Also, the moment the object becomes a tool, and connects, through writing, to a larger context, its initial lurid aura is dispelled. It makes way for jam – for the banal, which as Hannah Arendt argued, is the domain in which we can best understand the operations of evil.

'Things-in-motion'

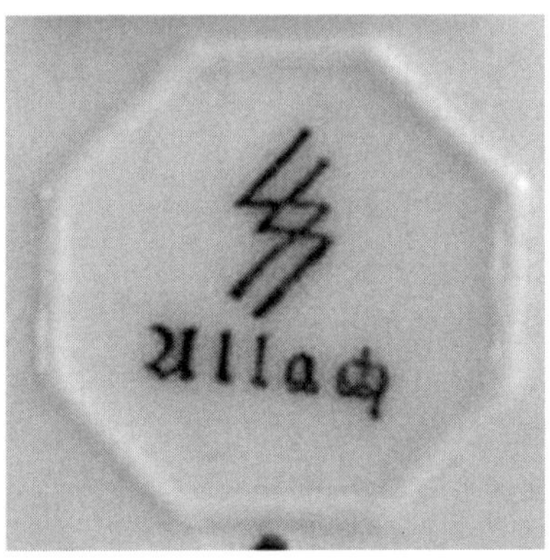

Imagine a historian finds a porcelain plate during her research on the history of forced labour in German concentration camps. It might strike her as an unusual piece of evidence for her project. If she turns the plate over, she will find a factory mark, 'Allach', and she will be correct in seeing an 'SS' in the symbol. By following the object, the researcher might be forced to pose questions she might not have otherwise been primed to ask about the history of the camps. Who made this plate? Where were the factories? Where did the materials come from? Who bought this porcelain? Who still owns plates like these? These are similar questions to those I asked of the knife, the diary, the violin.

The researcher will soon discover that Allach was a commercial enterprise of the SS. Production began in 1935 in the Dachau concentration camp, using slave labour, and the porcelain factory was closed with the liberation of the *Lager*. More than 30,000 died in Dachau. The researcher might then discover that Allach's best-selling items were candle-holders, or *Julleuchter*, ornamented with German runes. They were popular with SS

officers and their families, to light on the winter solstice. Their runic ornamentation is closely connected to Nazi mysticism. Here, I am reminded of Goebbels' anti-Christianity. I wonder also if Wilhelm Vrtoch, the camp commandant of Lichtenwörth, owned one of these lamps.

What then does it mean to find an Allach plate or an Allach candle-holder in a cupboard of a descendant in Germany or Austria? Or an immigrant German family in Melbourne? A *Julleuchter* could well illuminate a family history, providing tangible evidence of a chain of complicity, leading right back to the notorious camp. How has the perception of such an object changed in the history of memory, from the perspective of an SS officer, for whom it had symbolic value, compared to his great-granddaughter who abhors it? Would she eat off SS porcelain, knowing its story? Light a candle in an Allach *Julleuchter*? How many more questions still need to be asked, those that might never have occurred to the researcher without having first discovered this object?

The candle-holder's illumination over time is not just literal, casting its rays on some unsavoury, quasi-religious, SS-adopted festival. It shines light too on the dark corners of a historical investigation. The anthropologist Arjun Appadurai (in his 1986 edited volume, *The Social Life of Things*) also speaks in terms of 'things-in-motion' that 'illuminate their human and social context'. How convenient for our coming metaphor that the object in question is a light source!

What has the *Julleuchter* illuminated over time? Sit back and imagine the past as a long gloomy tunnel. Up ahead of us in the passage is the *Julleuchter*, casting its rays. It is much more useful to us here in the dark, as we make our way, rather than in a glass case in a museum! We follow the 'thing-in-motion', discovering that the tunnel is lined with witnesses from the past and their testimonies. The relationship between the torch and the witnesses is two-way. Balletic, in movement, it is always changing. The lamp shines light on the faces of the SS and their victims, but the witnesses also give meaning to the object. We view the object differently depending on the people who ordered it made and those who died making it.

Many of these witnesses might never have otherwise appeared in the historical record had we not followed this object towards them. A journey that follows the 'thing-in-motion' is often to untrodden parts of the cave of human experience. Because objects don't 'speak' like the traditional documentary record, they are more likely to make us engage with the unwritten, the undocumented, which is often the territory of the powerless, those who are overlooked. We discover prisoners who never wrote down a word about their experiences because they perished. We come into contact with everyday people who perhaps ignored the conditions in which their consumer goods were produced. At a certain point, deep in the passage, the light will blow out, and we will stumble our way back: but the journey has changed how we see.

One might tell the *Julleuchter*'s story in another way, which is to ask whether it has a biography, the way a person might.

Let's conduct a little experiment. Look around the room where you are reading or listening to this book. Choose one of your belongings. Now, write the biography of the thing, asking it exactly the same questions you would a person: about the thing's origin, who made it, what its career has been, and – as Igor Kopytoff suggests in his contribution to Appadurai's volume – 'what people consider to be an ideal career for such things'. What then happens over time to it, and what happens when it is no longer useful?

The questions that help us write the thing's 'cultural biography' – even those you cannot answer – already open up a world. The knife and its Nazi iconography reveal in Canada a different biography from the same object in Germany, just as a 'selective biography' of a stolen violin makes it acceptable for a young musician to play, unaware of the truth of its circulation. A cotton pouch, meanwhile, might have no proposed 'ideal career' but it gains enormous value when put into a context in which a victim has no other possessions. Each object's biography tells us what the respective society fears or values, just as the changing meanings over time of a *Julleuchter* do.

Objects that Change Us

Let's take these ideas one step farther. Remember, in our tunnel of the past, that the exchange between object and witnesses went two ways? Kopytoff writes that 'societies construct objects as they construct people'. This is a curious idea: that the belongings themselves can change their owners over time. Maybe they aren't just tools, but agents of change.

After all, perhaps it was the diary that pushed Karl's romance forward. Maybe he saw himself as a lover in the tradition of Goethe's young Werther. Were his romantic choices then in some part motivated by a desire to generate material, that he would later write up? And didn't having to carry a very large musical instrument physically change how Erich Hartmann went through a city at war? And don't the musical possibilities of such an excellent Guadagnini shape those who play it?

Objects can also change the historian. Let us consider for a moment the etymology of the word 'object'. It comes from the Latin *objectum*, which suggests an obstacle. An 'object' is literally a 'thing thrown before' – something flung in our way. It's not difficult to find examples of objects as obstacles for historians conducting research on the Second World War. A Holocaust revisionist or denier finds the piles of shoes discovered at

Auschwitz to be such an obstacle. Difficult to get around, they are rather inconvenient when you are trying to make arguments that ignore or relativise the past. These shoes have a way of rendering one speechless. They might even push the doubter onto a completely different track, one that recognises the pain and suffering of millions. Objects, in this sense, are not just things we use. They can also shape us.

For each witness, and in each chapter, of this book, their belonging has a different, changing, relationship to memory, something – to return to the image I mentioned in the preface – like an attractor, dipped into the solution of history that then forms crystals. I am even more satisfied with this metaphor because unexpected shapes can form. I found that using objects as strategies to explore witnesses' testimonies yielded surprising results and I was forced to ask questions I otherwise would never have asked. Isn't this the object at work? Its action on the historian?

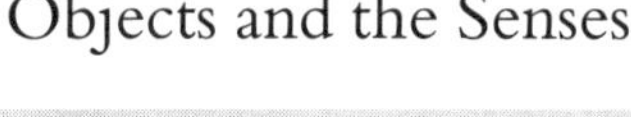

Objects and the Senses

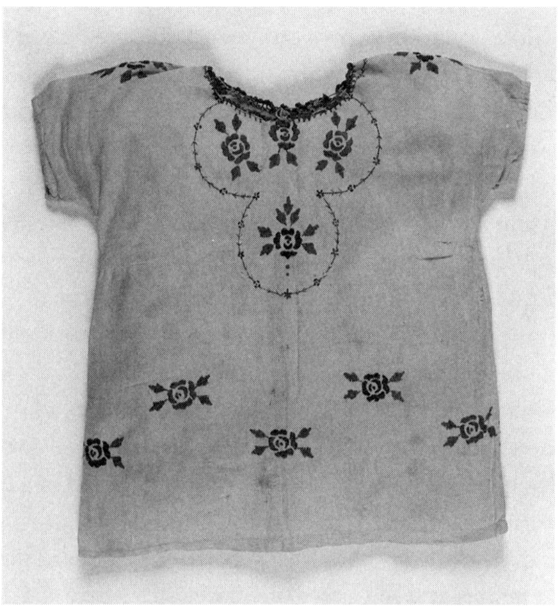

The dress of Lola Rein (born 1934) might not provide much information to the historian on its own, but the many aspects of the dress evoke the vulnerability of the child and her discomfort far more strongly than any written account. She wore the thin fabric from May 1943 to March 1944, in a hole in a barn in Czortkow, Ukraine, as a small child in hiding. The red and blue floral embroidery was stitched in the ghetto by her mother, before she was shot on the way to work on 21 March 1943. Rein kept the dress until 2002, when she donated it to the United States Holocaust Memorial Museum, giving her account of survival.

The story of the dress is especially poignant, touch being such a fundamental part of empathy. I recall how difficult it was for Katalin to describe to me in words the pain of being crushed in with other prisoners in the camp. This proximity prevented her from reaching the photographs in her pocket. And yet, perhaps because it was a sensation, this memory is vivid in her memory even after seventy-five years. I think too of better memories: of Erna's kitchen on Bogensee, or the Lőrincz family bakery in Ózd, and the conjuring of the sensual engagement in these spaces. It is not at all surprising that food, or its absence, so frequently recurs in this book as an evocation of the everyday experience of the war.

Indeed, it is a constant – in my experience of interviewing – that events return with more precision many years later if they are related to the senses. This is in stark contrast to the many non-sensual, weary, rehearsed stories (we have all heard them), which tend to become 'improved' with overtelling.

It's not easy to put the nonverbal into words but the struggle to do so scrapes deeply into the recesses of memory. Imagine you are meeting Katalin. Will you ask her: 'Can you tell me about your parents' bakery?' or will you ask 'What did a loaf of bread taste like in your parents' bakery?' The second question – about an object, the loaf of bread – requires an extra effort on the part of the witness to transform her feelings, perhaps never yet articulated, into words. Not only does the historian get around stiff ways of retelling, but the memories – thought dead – can awaken with a richness and freshness, because they are conjured for perhaps the first time. This happens when an object is posed (instead of a question that avoids a material example).

I am no cognitive scientist but I am sure that objects lead new directions because the physical and sensual relate closely to memory. Researchers at Harvard have shown how odours, for example, take a direct route to the limbic system, parts of the brain associated with memory. Objects conjure precisely what much text cannot: scent, touch, colour. Redolent, they unlock the nonverbal world. There are reasons why humans hold on closely, emotionally, to objects: they help us remember, are used to mark important moments of life (such as birthday gifts), are continuities from loved ones they have lost, are means to deal with mourning or separation. Just think of the investment that a child has in a blanket, which is a lifetime association, or a lover has in wearing the shirt of a beau when he is away. Wearing ancestors' jewellery marks family continuity over time.

The future of sensual objects is in doubt as digitalisation takes over from material traces. What if Karl had written his diary on his phone? What if Löfflerin's recipes were an e-book? Or the double bass DJ software? How much of our era will be more transient than previous ones because its objects are often virtual and easily deleted? A degraded floppy disk, of inaccessible image files, found seventy-five years from now is obviously less productive for the historian than a much older cotton pouch of printed photographs. With an ache, I noticed during my research just how well made so many of my objects were – meant to last and not planned for obsolescence. Concern for our footprint makes a good case for minimising our junk but this also poses a problem for material historians of the future in a world with fewer or less durable things. And how will witnesses in future remember their interactions with screens, social media? Or virtual reality (VR) projections, where we can literally walk through our obstacles? What consequences will there be when we depend on the recall of people with 'flat memories' or 'screen memories', stimulated by fewer senses? Proust's madeleine – at least with current technology – is not quite so redolent on Instagram.

Value

As obstacles, objects too show and test what we value today – again, they reveal. Few battles over history have such material repercussions as debates of provenance. The object forces actors to take sides, and to act in their self-interest and abandon principles, or to rise to the occasion of what they believe is just, especially when thousands, or even millions of euros, are on the line. There is perhaps no better crucible to gauge the true extent of *Vergangenheitsbewältigung*, how well countries have worked through their problematic Second World War guilt.

Because art objects are often exhibited in spaces where they can be subject to scrutiny, and their unique qualities are easier to identify, the intensity of this debate has been stronger in the fine art museum than in collections of musical instruments. A violin only rarely will be familiar from as far away as the audience. Often a specialised inspection in a workshop is needed to verify its maker. But what stolen objects in the gallery, and those on the stage, share is their value and their challenge for institutions struggling with murky provenance, often when owners cannot be found.

It is not uncommon for art objects to be excluded from fine art collections if their provenance is at all questioned. The Bern Museum of Fine Art's struggle with the provenance of the Gurlitt collection (valued in the tens of millions, partly looted by the Nazis from Jewish owners) led them to announce in November 2016 that they would not accept works that are 'not clean' in provenance. As Ronald Lauder, the World Jewish Congress president, quipped that year: 'Good faith doesn't make these paintings clean.' The E.G. Bührle Collection in Zürich – one of the world's most important collections of Impressionist and post-Impressionist paintings in private hands – also remains the subject of frequent criticism. Even though the collection has been investigated, there are frequent demands that it be rejected from public exhibition, because Emil Georg Bührle made his money selling arms to the Nazis and bought Nazi-looted works. Art historian Roger Fayet argues that the objects specifically in Zürich's collection 'are neither legally nor ethically problematic' but are 'contaminated', either 'by association or contagion as part of the entire complex of the collection'. Fayet's assessment of mere 'contamination' is perhaps premature, as the Bührle Collection currently faces renewed calls by historians for independent provenance investigations.

I was impressed by the matter-of-fact, and forthcoming, cooperation of the German state to recognise their 'unclean' collection. But it has responded to the contamination of the collection (and, let's be clear, any object obtained by the Nazis at the height of the war is contaminated) with a much softer policy than the standard being set by fine arts institutions, by deciding to allow string instruments with problematic provenance to be lent out to young musicians. It also has not faced the ongoing public scrutiny of, say, the E.G. Bührle Collection.

Yet, instruments are not like paintings. If they are not played, they deteriorate. But is it fair to the young musicians who might not be aware of their instruments' origins, and who become part of a tainted performance history? When the provenance is not made public at every opportunity, the instruments also escape scrutiny and opportunities for restitution, despite even the best efforts to investigate their origins. The German state, though – it must be said – is a more desirable partner for restitution claims, when compared to some private foundations or traders of instruments, who are happy to leave the provenance of their goods unquestioned or obscured.

Nazi-era objects proliferate online, where they have disturbing market values. A crude example is simple wooden coat hangers allegedly from Adolf Hitler schools, painted with the leader's name, which can be bought online for approximately 100 euros each. How a state treats stolen property tells us, again, what a society values, how it treats its history, and what it is willing to lose. Likewise, the sale and purchase of Nazi paraphernalia by private individuals, for reasons other than those such as research, tells us all we need to know about these communities of trade.

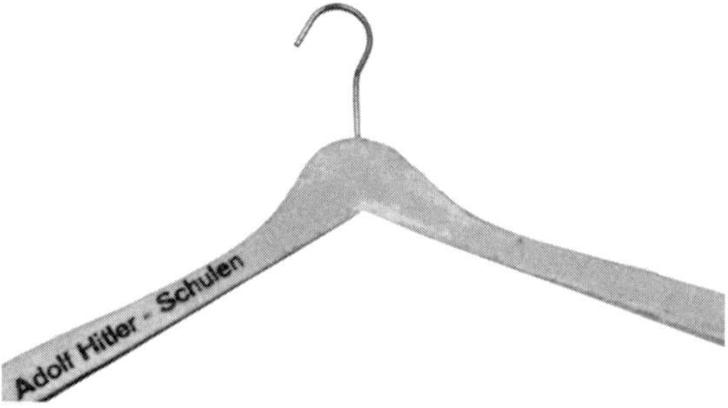

Objects are usually more durable than we are. When they are lost, we usually assume they still survive and we wonder where they are. The restitution of such belongings is an acknowledgement of the injustice – a recognition of the state's failure to protect their owners. Professor Leora Auslander provides the example of French Jews who were given the opportunity, after the war, to reclaim their stolen property. But, as a safeguard, they needed accurately to describe their belongings in advance for the authorities. This was done through restitution petitions. Victims were asked to re-imagine their apartments in the state they were before in their possessions were confiscated by the occupying Germans. Such petitions included inventory lists, drawings, written descriptions of walking through spaces. They were literal memory palaces, or imagined spaces where we keep our memories. The operation was a work of mourning and provides a picture of loss that other forms of documentation of the Holocaust do not always achieve, especially because most of the objects listed were never found. It is also a demonstration of how objects can reveal value that goes well beyond the financial.

Intersections

Let's put together the moving parts. Nazi objects pose dangers that are not just the concern of historians but also of governments challenged by the far right. And yes, such objects are easily open to abuse, as objects of this study have been. But a focus on the back of the rug also shows the salutary possibilities for object-driven history, when it takes the focus away from the lurid object and renders it an ordinary part of everyday history. When we don't see just the image, but rather the obverse with all the threads, we get past the illusion. The 'decentring', or rendering banal, of the object is the precondition for these Nazi-era objects to take us to constructive – even edifying – places. This demystification occurs precisely at the intersection of everyday and material history.

We could stop here, having told each story and talked about how objects mislead or – with some care – shine a light. But in these last pages, we can go a few steps further and recall some images that recurred. Now that we have the witnesses together in one room, let's ask what their belongings illuminate collectively, as they are set in motion.

Academics like the rule of three – *omne trium perfectum* – but we'll agree that what follows is far from complete: the individualism of my witnesses in a war of nations, the de-politicisation of everyday life in Nazi Germany, and the pressing problem of generational change.

Patriots

In Library and Archives Canada, I chanced upon a photograph of German POWs playing hockey in a camp in Canada. I compared this to another of Canadian and other Allied POWs playing curling in a camp in Germany. One group is playing with sticks and pucks, and the other with irons.

The objects bring our view right up to the individual men, the equipment cold in their hands, their feet on the ice of another country. Each man is out of context and engaged in wars that he might not understand, or to which he was deployed more or less enthusiastically. No doubt there are villains among them. Many were compromised by the Nazi project. Others were ennobled by the battle to push back totalitarianism. But they were also all young men playing on the ice. It is the ordinary objects that make clear that these men share something despite being from opposing sides of a terrible war, and I suspect that they would rather have been playing sport together than shooting one another.

The Second World War is usually told as national history, a conflict that pits broad categories of people called Germans against British or Americans or Canadians. Diverse individuals become members of each group in war. Some of my witnesses appeared to have uncomplicated relationships to their nationality, such as the cook. But my grandfather fought against the army of a man related through marriage to an English family. Karl struggled to redefine himself as an individual and not as part of the German navy. With Erich Hartmann, I did not discuss national self-definition, but I would not be surprised should he have defined himself as an artist before any national title. Katalin had an identity imposed on her by her persecutors when she had no religious affiliation; her internationalism is clear when she rebuilt her life on another continent.

The risk in disassociating individuals from their body politic is to avoid placing blame where it is due, especially at the feet of soldiers who carried out war crimes, or citizens who focused on their private lives, ignoring the persecution of others. But it is more consistent to give weight to a humane and civic responsibility, rather than one that was racial and national, which were the criteria on which the Nazis based their system.

In this vein, if we stand by absolute moral categories based on nationality, Canadian soldiers can risk appearing as irreproachable agents of the good war, while German soldiers like Karl will always be considered tainted, more akin to Wilhelm Vrtoch. It was sobering for me to revisit my grandfather's Second World War service as a litany of horror, of burning bodies.

The Allies fought a defensive war in Europe, against a murderous regime, intent on eliminating whole swathes of people based on their identity. With there being so many victims of the Nazi regime, it can appear unseemly, or even disrespectful to those murdered, to talk in the next breath of German victims, of the fire-bombing in Hamburg, Dresden, or Solingen, or of mass rapes. Or to mention the many victims of other nationalities who found themselves between the Axis and Allied forces with the advancing and retreating front lines.

But it is an injustice for Allies to celebrate the brave acts of their soldiers abroad, without pitying the horror of the war they fought. It is especially an injustice to those Allied soldiers who returned home to be treated as heroes but in a state of praise that stifled recognition of their agonies. Patriotism is usually blind to weakness and hurt.

The Allied victors can learn something from the defeated. A critical working through the past, or *Vergangenheitsbewältigung*, is still incomplete in Germany (if it had been more successful, it would not today be so challenged by right-wing movements). But there has at least been a concerted institutional effort to recognise that the war's history is a warning, rather than a patriotic or edifying account.

Certainly, there are many unturned stones in the long history of, say, British and Canadian military misadventures abroad. My grandfather did not own just the knife, but also an elegant sword owned by his grandfather, from the Boer War. I ascribed nobility to this sword as a child, despite its use in a ghastly conflict in Africa. There is room for a different, post-Colonial, story of Canadians – or British, Australians, and New Zealanders – in war, whose service is often still too sacred to question.

My grandfather and his grandfather in 1940

Everyday

A leap from these individual stories to the broader picture might appear a difficult manoeuvre. Most historians, when they write Second World War memories, record the reminiscences of prime ministers, generals, or spies, with the conviction that the affairs of state drive history. What to do then with the next-door discoveries of this book and ones that come from contexts as diverse as Berlin, France, Budapest, and Edmonton, Canada? Together, can they tell us about the big picture?

Anton Chekhov is still one of the world's most performed playwrights a century after his death. One explanation for his popularity might be something that is unusual about a Chekhov play: its plethora of everyday details. Even when specifically rooted in a moment of Russian history, these still resound with contemporary publics, even those from different cultures. One does not need to talk in terms of universalism to explain why audiences feel a sense of recognition, or verisimilitude, in – say – family dynamics, everyday concerns, persecution, and grief. By focusing on the mundane details of lives, Chekhov illustrates something larger. We all have a cherry orchard about to be cut down.

Yet, many of my witnesses lived in a particularly isolated corner of the woods. And having spent time there, when listening to the everyday of its inhabitants, one begins to create an image of life under the Nazi regime. It's a little like assembling details from a visit to a foreign country, which the past, of course, is.

In the previous section, I celebrated the individuality of each witness and their detachment from national characteristics. Allow me here a counter-argument, because I did observe national variation in this study, in the *Weltanschauung*, or worldview, of my three German witnesses. The commonalities in their stories result from their education and the organisation of their work in the Third Reich.

The bell jar of everyday concerns is the salient aspect. Albert Speer, in his *Erinnerungen*, takes time to describe it. Hitler's chief architect is worth quoting at length on just how apolitical Germans were encouraged to be under the regime:

> I felt myself to be Hitler's architect. Political events did not concern me … Nazi education aimed at separatism thinking: I was expected

> to confine myself to the job of building. It is true that as a favourite and later as one of Hitler's most influential ministers I was isolated. It is also true that the habit of thinking within the limits of my own field provided me, both as architect and as Armaments Minister, with many opportunities for evasion. It is true that I did not know what was really beginning on 9 November 1938, and what ended in Auschwitz and Majdanek. But in the final analysis, I myself determined the degree of my isolation, the extremity of my evasions, and the extent of my ignorance ... No apologies are possible ...

> The whole structure of the system was to prevent conflict of conscience from even arising. The result was a total sterility of all conversations and discussions among these like-minded persons. It was boring for people to confirm one another in their uniform opinions. Worse still was the restriction of responsibility to one's own field. That was explicitly demanded. Everyone kept to his own group – of architects, physicians, jurists, technicians, soldiers or farmers. The professional organisations to which everyone had to belong were called chambers (Physicians' Chamber, Art Chamber) and this term aptly described the way people were immured in isolated, closed-off areas of life. The longer Hitler's system lasted, the more people's minds moved within such isolated chambers ... What eventually developed was a society of totally isolated individuals.

In these two quotes, Speer shows a commonality between the experience of everyday Germans, in the specialisation of their professions, and his own at the apex of the German leadership. He brings together parts and wholes to draw a general portrait of depoliticised German society under the Nazis, which is entirely consonant with the testimonies of this book: the sailor whose everyday tasks and love affair were central to his concerns; the cook who stayed in the kitchen, who never talked about politics; or the orchestra musician who couldn't see past the notes on the page to observe the audience. I began by thinking that my German witnesses were simply not forthcoming, or strategically evasive in their testimonies. But I emerged thinking they were bred to be apolitical, to be wholly absorbed with their particular duty. (It must be said I observe the imprint of this culture of specialisation in German work life today – in details as banal as its distrust of freelancers – though not the depoliticisation.)

As Speer argues, this does not exonerate them from the duty of active citizenship, in the face of mass murder by the state, regardless of how they were determined by their educations. Despite their conviction that they were not political, each one of these witnesses was. One need only look at the very specific institutional overlaps in their stories to show how politics connected their everyday to the highest levels of leadership. Goebbels' Propaganda Ministry, for example, appears not only in the cook's testimony but also in the management and purpose of the Berlin Philharmonic. It was present in the knife's story (as the Ministry had their hooks in the working-class image of Solingen). The imprint of that Ministry is also evident in the education of Karl and the fate of people like Katalin. One sees how a presumption of a depoliticised everyday was self-deception. The Nazis pulled off a feat: politicising all levels of society, which did not admit to being political.

The feat – the synthesis – necessary for each one of these individuals shaped by the Nazi system was to experience a breakage that might de-nationalise them and push them into individual action. For Karl, that rupture was falling in love.

War in Our Time

I think about my grandfather's purpose in bringing the knife back to Canada. Why did he put it on the wall of his basement? Was it simply a curiosity? A macabre souvenir? Why did he want me to look at it? Why did he then leave such a gruesome thing to me? I think for the same reasons he privately recorded the horrors of his regiment. The war was the central event of his life and he wanted to project his memories into the future. He chose an object to do that.

With the passing of his generation goes the lived understanding of the costs of war. This loss is incalculable. Many Germans then may have thought themselves apolitical, but they also understood viscerally what it meant to lose their homes and loved ones. Allied soldiers, demobbed, woke up in the night reliving the horrors of the front. Soon, we can no longer ask what frightened them and what they never told anyone. We soon will not be able to look into the faces of the victims, who suffered most.

These individual recollections connect to collective memory, an unravelling gossamer, which touches each of us. It is like a fabric, which connects us with neighbours and family members. Tragically, we might not even notice once it wears away, even though it was shielding us.

I asked Katalin how young people could learn from what happened to her. She replied that some would need to experience war themselves to understand its cruelty. Others would need to experience it just to believe it happened in the first place. Those whose safety is ruptured by war, who have had the dome of peace shattered over their heads, who have seen their houses destroyed or their parents killed, have zero desire to revisit such conflicts. They will do anything to keep themselves and their families safe.

But those who have never suffered war themselves can be curious, vicarious, even cavalier about its dangers. It is difficult to force into our brains the reality that war is not abstract, the stuff of films or video games, accompanied by soaring soundtracks; clothed in talcum blues and fog that rolls through forsaken French villages; furnished with sweethearts who part in train stations, German soldiers who speak in monotone and only smile maliciously, or Allies in the ruins who pour their scotch fireside before the sniper appears. The war is not chocolate offered to enemy children. It is rather a crevasse around which to step delicately unless we wish to tumble into the substructures of European history. More Americans might have died from Covid-19 than in all of the Second World War. But the awfulness of a virus, whose victims suffer, often silently, behind hospital doors, has been a much more hidden affair for most than the agonies of air war and mass murder. But let's consider how unbelievable the post-2020 pandemic lockdowns would have seemed to us even a few months before coronavirus spread across the world. This gives us perhaps a sense of how the summers of 1914 or 1939 felt to those who also could not anticipate the future.

At the time of writing, in the third decade of the twenty-first century, the loss of memory of the most violent moment in global history, claiming the lives of 85 million people, is real. As previously mentioned, two-thirds of Americans under 40 do not know that 6 million Jews were killed in the Holocaust. Europe and North America have seen the spectacular rise of right-wing populism in a way that would have been unthinkable generations earlier, in forms as various as Orbanism, Proud-Boy Trumpism, Zemmourism – which wield power, have held power, or could easily seize it. It is no happenstance that we see the strength of virulent and anti-democratic nationalism, isolationism, and bully-politics on both sides of the Atlantic, not to mention Down Under, precisely at this moment of generational change. Facile formulations that make us fear and blame neighbouring countries and foreigners are more attractive to generations when we have not endured wars initiated by such hateful ideologies. The news, meanwhile, often too blithely reports confrontations between superpowers in the South China Sea, South Asia, Iran, North Korea, the Baltics, or Ukraine.

We have lived through the longest period of European peace since the *Pax Romana*, which ended in the second century. War has been more of a constant in history. Is 'war in our time' inevitable? Or – a better question – what do we need to remember so it is not? How to activate a greater awareness of the risks of violence in the quotidian of the atomic age?

Narrative might just provide a few more strands to keep this instructive gossamer of collective memory intact, a barrier between us and the power-hungry, racist, and extreme. True stories play a part in slowing this unravelling. Most young people have never had the opportunity to speak with a survivor in her home, surrounded by belongings that anchor her history. Ordinary, even banal, stories nonetheless make clear that atrocities happen in the quiet of a kitchen or at work or in a residential street – that war is everyday. As we lose witnesses, and our defences are depleted, what else do we have but the power of verisimilitude and the invitation to summon our empathy for those no longer with us?

In the Montreal Holocaust Museum is a spoon. Looking at it, one might think it's a little crude. Since it is in a museum about the Shoah, one expects it was used by a prisoner – a correct assumption. But the spoon was also *made* by the prisoner, named Jacob Chaim, as a response to the guards who would not provide him with one in order to dehumanise him.

Without its owner, the spoon does not have a story, the same way that the cotton pouch is just cloth that disappointed the thief, the recipes are a catalogue of ingredients to be bound together by heat and mixing in specific ways, and the string instruments are wood, steel, varnish and glue. Meanwhile, only a handful of people are left who can read the forgotten script of the diary, and a knife is only an amalgam of metals. Unless we speak for them.

References

My Grandfather's Knife

The Knife

Hitler and the Germans: Nation and Crime was the exhibition of the German Historical Museum, Berlin. Curators: Prof. Dr Hans-Ulrich Thamer, Dr Simone Erpel, Klaus-Jürgen Sembach. 15 October 2010 to 27 February 2011. Particularly useful texts on Berlin's memory culture, and the obsession and panic surrounding fascism, include Brian Ladd, *Ghosts of Berlin: Confronting German History in the Urban Landscape* (New Haven: Yale, 1997 and 2018), pp. 127 ff.; James E. Young, *At Memory's Edge: After-Images of the Holocaust in Contemporary Art and Architecture* (New Haven: Yale, 2002). For example: Brian Ladd critiques (pp. 132–3) how the Berlin city government obliterated an SS bunker – and its traces of everyday history under the Third Reich – in a fit of panic in 1990. James E. Young (pp. 4–5) quotes Saul Friedlander, who wonders whether the obsession with Nazism is 'a gratuitous reverie, the attraction of spectacle, exorcism, or the need to understand; or is it, again and still, an expression of profound fears and, on the part of some, mute yearnings as well?' Friedlander, *Reflections of Nazism: An Essay on Kitsch and Death* (New York: Harper and Row, 1984), p. 19.

The Makers

Sources on the blade-making history of Solingen include: Jochem Putsch, *Solingen: Industriekultur, 1880–1960* (Erfurt: Sutton Verlag, 2016), p. 9. See also Stefan Gorißen et al., eds, *Geschichte des Bergischen Landes: Band 2: Das 19. und 20. Jahrhundert (Bergische Forschungen / Quellen und Forschungen zur bergischen Geschichte, Kunst und Literatur)* (Bielefeld: Verlag für Regionalgeschichte, 2016).

For discussion on the 'stumbling stones' see Joseph Pearson, *Berlin* (London: Reaktion Press, 2017), pp. 173–4.

Both Coppel's letter and the testimony of his fellow prisoner Emil Kronenberg are taken from a memorial website, produced by the City Archive, City of Solingen ('Stolperstein Dr Alexander Coppel', www.solingen.de). For the history of the Coppel family: Klaus-Dieter Alicke, *Lexikon der jüdischen Gemeinden im deutschen Sprachraum* (Gütersloh: Gütersloher Verlagshaus, 2008); Kay Ganahl, 'Der 9. November 1938 – Pogrom in Solingen'. Student thesis submitted January 1989, Universität-Gesamthochschule Duisburg. Of particular interest is the chapter 'Arisierung im Reich und der Coppel-Unternehmung in Solingen' ('Aryanisation in the Reich and the Coppel Enterprise in Solingen'). Also see Coppel's entry in the Central Database of Shoah Victims' Names, World Holocaust Remembrance Centre, Yad Vashem (yvng.yadvashem.org). Another useful text is Wilhelm Bramann, 'Geschichte der jüdischen Familie in Solingen 1770–1942' in *Anker und Schwert*, vol. 13, Solingen, 1994. Also, visit today's Alexander Coppel website, which has a historical page: www.alcoso.com. For the tragedy following Jewish acculturation in German society, see Amos Elon, *The Pity of It All* (London: Allen Lane, 2013), pp. 9–10.

For the fire-bombing of Solingen, see: Jörg Friedrich, trans. Allison Brown, *The Fire: The Bombing of Germany 1940–1945* (New York: Columbia University Press, 2008), pp. 8, 262–3.

The Iconography

Sources for zoomorphic weapons of antiquity include Frans Theuws and Janet L. Nelson, *Rituals of Power: From Late Antiquity to the Early Middle Ages* (Leiden: Brill, 2000), pp. 44 ff. See also, for a broader discussion of related 'Animal Style', Emma C. Bunker et al., *'Animal Style': Art from East to West*, exh. cat. (New York: Asia Society, 1970). For a discussion of the eagle on Roman coins, see Donald T. Ariel, 'The Iconography' in Donald T. Ariel et al., eds, *The Coins of Herod* (Leiden: Brill, 2011), p. 118.

The iconography of the statue of *Harmodius and Aristogeiton* was very familiar to the totalitarianisms of the twentieth century. At the 1937 World Fair in Paris, it was the Soviet pavilion's enormous sculpture by Vera Mukhina, *The Collective Worker and the Industrial Farm Woman*, which imitated Antenor's *Harmodius and Aristogeiton*. The weapons, however, are replaced by the hammer and sickle. Carlo Ginzburg, 'The Sword and the Lightbulb', in Michael S. Roth et al., eds, *Disturbing Remains: Memory, History and Crisis in the Twentieth Century* (Los Angeles: The Getty Research Institute, 2001), p. 115.

For Roman daggers, see M.C. Bishop, *The Spatha: The Roman Long Sword* (Oxford: Osprey, 2020), p. 21. A useful survey of the iconography of the eagle can be found in Janine Rogers, *Eagle*, in the Animal Series (London: Reaktion Press, 2015).

I refer to Friedrich Nietzsche, *Zur Genealogie der Moral: Eine Streitschrift / On the Genealogy of Morals* (1887), my translation; Primo Levi, *Se questo è un uomo* (Turin: De Silva, 1947).

Sources

Accounts of the Second World War mobilisation can be found on the Calgary Highlanders' regimental homepage: 'Mobilisation 1939', www.calgaryhighlanders.com. See also Bercuson, *Battalion of Heroes: The Calgary Highlanders in World War Two* (Calgary: The Calgary Highlanders Regimental Funds Foundation (Penguin Books, distr.), 1994), pp. 13 ff. Bercuson indicates casualties in Normandy on p. 85.

See Canada, Department of National Defence, Calgary Highlanders fonds, Glenbow Museum, Calgary, for casualty lists, inventory files M-1961-12 ff.

German Family

Source material for the account of the Calgary Highlanders' advance from France to the Netherlands (in this and future sections) is taken from the official *War Diary of the Calgary Highlanders* published by the Canadian Public Records Office and the cassette tape of my grandfather. The specific source dates should be evident from context and are referenced when not.

Letter from Charles Oakley Sanders to his son Edward Howard Sanders (Col Gilbert Sanders' father). Ingrams, Thirsk, 23 November 1866. And letter from Howard Oakley Sanders to his brother Edward Howard Sanders. Darmstadt, 14 November 1892.

The 89th Army Corps (LXXXIX. Armeekorps), commanded by General von Gilsa between 11 June 1943 and 23 November 1944, was headquartered in Antwerp and its infantry divisions were in the Scheldt, including the 165th Infantry Division in Middelburg on Walcheren. The latter – curiously made up of soldiers with stomach problems – was renamed the 70th Infantry Division in 1944 (commanded by Wilhelm Daser) and engaged in the direct fighting with the Canadians in Walcheren. For a map of the positions of these German and Canadian forces, and the chain of command, see C.P. Stacey, *The Victory Campaign* (Ottawa: Roger Duhamel, 1966), p. 396. Another source for German battle positions is the useful map in Horst Boog et al., *The Strategic Air War in Europe and the War in the West and East Asia 1943–1944/5* (Oxford: Clarendon Press, 2006), p. 501. For full orders of battle, see Richard Brooks, *Walcheren 1944: Storming Hitler's Island* (Oxford: Osprey, 2011), pp. 21–2. Brooks' book also argues the significance of Walcheren's fortifications and strategic position, p. 5.

The Swastika

A useful history of the swastika is: Malcolm Quinn, *The Swastika: Constructing the Symbol* (Milton Park: Routledge, 1994). See also Andreas Stegbauer, 'The Ban of Right-Wing Extremist Symbols According to Section 86a of the German Criminal Code', in *German Law Journal*, vol. 13, no. 2, 2007, pp. 173–84. For more on c-Base, see their webpage: c-base.org.

The Markings

I have used the following sources on German small arms: J. Goertz and D. Bryans, *German Small Arms Markings from Authentic Sources* (Marceline MO: Walsworth, 1997); L. Don Maus, *History Writ in Steel, Police Markings 1900–1936* (Galesburg, Illinois: Brad Simpson, 2009), pp. 27–8; and George T. Wheeler, *Seitengewehr: History of the German Bayonet 1919–1945* (San Jose: J. Bender, 1999).

For sources on the role of the *Ordnungspolizei* in the east, see Christopher Browning, *Ordinary Men: Reserve Police Battalion 101 and the Final Solution in Poland* (London: Penguin, 1992); Edward D. Westermann, *Hitler's Police Battalions: Enforcing Racial War in the East*

(Modern War Studies) (Kansas: University of Kansas Press, 2005). For sources on the *Ordnungspolizei* in the west, see Wolfgang Curilla, *Die deutsche Ordnungspolizei im westlichen Europa 1940–1945* (Paderborn: Verlag Ferdinand Schöningh, 2020).

For the role of Dutch Nazis, see Richard Evans, *The Third Reich at War: How the Nazis Led Germany from Conquest to Disaster* (London: Penguin, 2012), pp. 384 ff.; Michael R. Marrus, *The Holocaust in History* (London: Weidenfeld & Nicolson, 1988), p. 105. For discussion of Woeste Hoeve, see Geraldien von Frijtag Drabbe Künzel, 'Resistance, Reprisals, Reactions', in Robert Gildea et al., eds, *Surviving Hitler and Mussolini: Daily Life in Occupied Europe* (Oxford: Berg, 2006), p. 192; Antony Beevor, *Arnhem, Battle of the Bridges, 1944* (London: Viking Penguin, 2018), pp. 20 ff., 375 ff.

A Campaign in Chiaroscuro

The painting of the Battle of Walcheren Causeway, *Hallowe'en Night 1944*, is by Robert Johnson, who fought in the battle.

W.D. Whitaker's interview with Ross Ellis, 21 August 1982, is quoted in Bercuson, *Battalion of Heroes*, p. 189. See also Bercuson for a detailed description of the battle, pp. 182–9; also Terry Copp, *Cinderella Army: The Canadians in Northwest Europe 1944–1945* (Toronto: University of Toronto Press, 2006), pp. 166–70.

For casualties and numbers of battle-exhausted see Bercuson, *Battalion of Heroes*, p. 193.

For descriptions of the reception of Allied troops in the Low Countries, I draw from Peter Schrijvers, *Liberators: The Allies and Belgian Society, 1944–1945* (Cambridge: Cambridge University Press, 2009), pp. 50–9. For birth rates, see H.F. Heijmans and C.J.B.J. Trimbos, *De niet-gehuwde moeder en haar kind* (Hilversum/Antwerpen: Paul Brand, 1964), pp. 26 and 55, quoted in Dr Nelleke Bakker, 'Mother and Baby Homes in the Netherlands in the 20th century. Report for the Irish Commission of Investigation: Mother and Baby Homes and Certain Related Matters (Order 2015)' (Groningen: Rijskuniversiteit, 2015), p. 5. For Dutch people looking for their Canadian fathers, see: Machiel Horn, 'The Canadian Army and the Liberated Netherlands', in *Pro Rege* (Iowa: Dordt University, June 1991), pp. 19, 24.

The Battle of Groningen

For descriptions of the battle, see Mark Zuehlke, *On to Victory: The Canadian Liberation of the Netherlands, March 23–May 5 1945* (Vancouver: Douglas and McIntyre, 2010), p. 323; Bercuson, *Battalion of Heroes*, p. 232; Stacey, *The Victory Campaign*, p. 131.

The coffee while machine-gunning anecdote is reported in Zuehlke, *On to Victory*, p. 333; Frank Holm, *A Backward's Glance* (Sault Ste. Marie, 1989), pp. 110–11.

Descriptions of the Dutch crowds are in Zuehlke, *On to Victory*, p. 334, quoting G.B. Buchanan, *The March of the Prairie Men: A Story of the South Saskatchewan Regiment* (Weyburn and Estevan: Midwest Litho, 1957), p. 260; Stacey, *The Victory Campaign*, p. 131.

Descriptions of the post office are in Bercuson, *Battalion of Heroes*, p. 237.

For the use of flamethrowers, see Bercuson, *Battalion of Heroes*, p. 194. See also Major Jeffrey D. Noll, *Restraint in Urban Warfare: The Canadian Attack on Groningen, Netherlands, 13–16 April 1945* (Auckland: Lucknow Books, 2014); Ralf Teters interview, 2 April 1992, quoted in Bercuson, *Battalion of Heroes*, p. 235. My grandfather is interviewed on flamethrowers in ibid., p. 235. See also Zuehlke, *On to Victory*, p. 333.

For more on the challenge of returning home, see Alan Allport, *Demobbed: Coming Home After World War Two* (New Haven: Yale, 2010).

Slaves to Objects

For discussion of the cinematic spectator and atrocities, see Sophia Wood, 'Film and Atrocity: The Holocaust as Spectacle', in Kristi M. Wilson and Tomás F. Crowder-Taraborrelli, eds, *Film and Genocide* (Madison: University of Wisconsin Press, 2012), pp. 21–44. For a more favourable impression of *Schindler's List*, see Alan Mintz's chapter, 'The Holocaust at the Movies', in *Popular Culture and the Shaping of Holocaust Memory in America* (Seattle: University of Washington Press, 2001), pp. 85 ff. See also the chapter 'The Hollywood Version of the Holocaust', in Annette Insdorf, *Indelible Shadows: Film and the Holocaust, Third Edition* (Cambridge: Cambridge University Press, 2006), pp. 3–26.

For Epictetus on things, see, for example, his *Discourses*, 2.5.

A Diary in Code

Generation Z

Most of this chapter relies on primary sources, which are obvious from context. The name of the diary's author is withheld as a courtesy, explained in the final section of this chapter. All other names, dates, places, and other historical details are unchanged. Unpublished manuscripts are quoted and summarised within the bounds of 'fair dealing' and 'fair use', except when permission has been granted.

The 'Code'

On the introduction of Sütterlin script in German schools in the Nazi period, see Margarete Götz, *Die Grundschule in der Zeit des Nationalsozialismus* (Bad Heilbrunn: Klinkhardt, 1997), pp. 75 ff.

More information about the Sütterlinstube Hamburg, formed by residents of the Altenzentrum Ansgar, can be found on their website: suetterlinstube.de.

Papyrus

The German parliament provides comprehensive information online about the historical values of German currencies: 'Kaufkraftvergleiche historischer Geldbeträge', www.bundestag.de/resource.

For Sappho, see: Anne Carson, *If Not, Winter* (New York: Vintage, 2002), introduction.

Le Havre

For testimony on everyday life under occupation in Le Havre, see the exposition: *Revival 1940–45: des Havrais sous l'occupation*. Association des mutilés et anciens combattants, 19 June to 25 June 2017. See also Clesius Néofolk, Clothilde Thioux, Simon Quignard, 'Vie au Havre sous l'occupation', a video with testimony of witnesses associated with the aforementioned exhibit: compagnonshavrais.jimdofree.com. I also consulted a commercial history of Le Havre during the occupation: Claude Malon, *Occupation, épuration, reconstruction: Le monde de l'entreprise au Havre*

(1940–1950) (Mont-Saint-Aignan: Presses universitaires de Rouen et du Havre, 2013).

For a study of the deportations of Jews, and Léon Meyer, from Le Havre, see Yves Lecouturier, *Shoah en Normandie: 1940–1944* (Anjou: Cheminements, 2004), pp. 14, 218, 240.

For a study of prostitution in occupied France, including details on Le Havre, see Insa Meinen, *Wehrmacht und Prostitution im besetzten Frankreich* (Bremen: Temmen, 2002), p. 222.

Detailed research on the bombardment of Le Havre can be found in Corinne Bouillot, John Barzman, Andrew Knapp, *Bombardements 1944: Le Havre, Normandie, France, Europe* (Mont-Saint-Aignan: Presses universitaires de Rouen et du Havre, 2016).

The Grandmother's Story

Karl's military file, from the German federal archives, the Bundesarchiv, is accessed under Article 11, Section 4 of the German Archives Law, which allows for the study of individuals of contemporary history.

For women and collaboration, see Hanna Diamond, *Women and the Second World War in France, 1939–1948: Choices and Constraints* (Milton Park: Routledge, 1999), pp. 136 ff.; Peter Caddick-Adams, *Sand and Steel: The D-Day Invasions and the Liberation of France* (Oxford: Oxford University Press, 2019), pp. 41 ff.

For more information on the struggle of German deserters to gain amnesty, see Marco Dräger, 'Monuments for Deserters? The Changing Image of *Wehrmacht* Deserters in Germany and their Gradual Entry into Germany's Memory Culture' in Gelinada Grinchenko and Eleonora Narvselius, eds, *Traitors, Collaborators and Deserters in Contemporary European Politics of Memory* (London: Palgrave Macmillan, 2018), pp. 31–57.

For the execution of German deserters by Canadian troops in Holland, see Chris Madsen, 'Victims of Circumstance: The Execution of German Deserters by Surrendered German Troops Under Canadian Control in Amsterdam, May 1945', in *Canadian Military History*, vol. 2, no. 1, 2012.

Codebreaking

My great-great-grandfather's diaries are kept in the Glenbow Museum, Calgary, Alberta, Canada (Gilbert E. Sanders papers).

Lord of the Lonely

As the diary is an unpublished manuscript and the date of its author's death unknown, 'fair use' and 'fair dealing' requires limited summary, which is why more direct quotes from the diary are not provided. All translations, from the German, are my own.

A Recipe Book

A Very Interesting Story

I interviewed Erna twice in April 2014 and all quotes are my translations from the German. She repeated material (with consistency) in our second interview, sometimes almost word for word, which alerts me to the fact that some of these are stories she has grown used to telling.

A Vacancy for a Cook

Erna Jokisch is quoted about Hitler and the SS in the publication of her care home: *Kleeblatt*, no. 61, 2016, p. 7.

The mother of Magda Goebbels had her story serialised for a tabloid between 5 January 1952 and 31 May 1952. She agrees that Joseph Goebbels was repulsive but speculates on why many younger women found him 'transfixing'. Auguste Behrend, 'Meine Tochter Magda Goebbels: Ein ungewöhnlicher Lebensweg' in *Schwäbische Illustrierte*, 8 March 1952. Information about the previous cook is also noted in Behrend, 24 April 1952.

Regarding Erna's photograph: the children were frequently attired in their white dresses and white socks. Behrend, 1 May 1952, explains how the children's dresses, for photos taken at Christmas 1944, were made thriftily from old curtains: 'The [children] were not in any way spoiled.'

I am not surprised they frequently re-wore the same outfits. Another famous image is from Goebbels' 45th birthday in October 1942, where the family is in a pyramidal tableau (pictured in this chapter) wearing similar clothes. A different photograph shows them in the same uniforms, with Helga holding a box on which is written 'Sommer 1942'. In these last two photographs, the children look about two years younger than in Erna's photograph, which would match her statement that her photograph was taken in 1944.

The House at Lanke

Information on how the Minister acquired the house: Joseph Goebbels, ed. Reuth, *Tagebücher 1924–45* (Munich: Piper, 2008), entries from 17 and 18 September 1936 (also quoted in Peter Longerich, trans. Alan Bance et al., *Goebbels* (London: Vintage, 2015), p. 324). *Der Angriff* called it a birthday present in their 30 October 1936 late edition, as did Berlin officials quoted in Stefan Berkholz, *Goebbels' Waldhof am Bogensee* (Berlin: Ch. Links, 2004), pp. 11–12.

Information on the house's expenses and structure: Longerich, *Goebbels*, pp. 406 and 324. The reports about the house in the press are in *Der Angriff*, 31 October 1936. Refurbishment costs: Berkholz, *Goebbels' Waldhof am Bogensee*, p. 43. Value of the tapestry: Longerich, *Goebbels*, p. 405, quoting R 55/421, Notiz betr. Neubau Dienstwohngebäude für den Reichsminister, 28 February 1939. Pictures of the house's interior can be found in the private archive of Claudia Schweitzer, reproduced in Berkholz, *Goebbels' Waldhof am Bogensee*, p. 51. I do not reproduce these here.

The family's more permanent move to the house is described in Anja Klabunde, trans. Shaun Whiteside, *Magda Goebbels* (London: Sphere, 2001), p. 302; Longerich, *Goebbels*, p. 598; and Goebbels, *Tagebücher*, 2 August 1943. Klabunde describes the children going to school, p. 302. The pony and cart saved petrol in a time of rationing, explains Behrend, 1 May 1952.

For more on the servants' lodgings: Berkholz, *Goebbels' Waldhof am Bogensee*, p. 52. Berkholz suggests that the butler lived upstairs, but the butler had his own room downstairs near the entrance according to the floor plan.

About Magda's indecision, see: Behrend, 15 March 1952. On Magda's humble origins: Klabunde, *Magda Goebbels*, p. 6. On her changing accent:

Behrend, 1 March 1952. On her affair with the Zionist: Longerich, *Goebbels*, p. 701.

The 'first lady of the Nazi Reich' is also the approximate English-language title of Hans-Otto Meissner, *Magda Goebbels. Ein Lebensbild* (Munich, 1978) (as *Magda Goebbels, First Lady of the Third Reich*, trans. Gwendolen Mary Keeble (Scarborough: Nelson, 1981)). Meissner was in circles close to the Quandt family and his book, while fiercely critical of Joseph Goebbels, is a hagiography of Magda. I have quoted here from both language editions, indicated by the separate titles and page numbers.

Erna exaggerates only a little when she describes how Magda met Quandt: born on 28 July 1881, Quandt was twenty years her senior. In Behrend, 8 March 1952, Magda's mother claims that she met Quandt on a train between Berlin and Goslar. For the three-way arrangement, see Longerich, *Goebbels*, pp. 159–60.

Goebbels being slapped by the jealous man would have happened at Schwanenwerder and before Erna's time employed by the family. But both Baarová and Fröhlich state, in their memoirs, that it was a rumour: Baarová, *Die süße Bitterkeit meines Lebens* (Koblenz: Kettermann u. Schmidt, 2001), pp. 112 ff. and Gustav Fröhlich, *Waren das Zeiten. Mein Film-Heldenleben* (Frankfurt: Ullstein, 1989) (original publication: Munich: F.A. Herbig, 1983). See pp. 352 ff. of the latter for a description of the affair.

About Magda's desire for a divorce, see: Meissner, *Magda Goebbels. Ein Lebensbild*, pp. 210 ff. For Magda's agreement with Goebbels and Hitler for a marriage of convenience, see: Longerich, *Goebbels*, p. 524; Meissner, *Magda Goebbels. Ein Lebensbild*, p. 236 ff. Lída Baarová fled that winter to Prague.

The 'passionate love affair' with Hanke is according to Annemarie Kempf, in Gitta Sereny, *Albert Speer: His Battle with Truth* (London: MacMillan, 1995), pp. 133 and 192. Klabunde describes his role in finding the house: Klabunde, *Magda Goebbels*, p. 250. More details about Hanke's list detailing the affairs of Goebbels can be found in Meissner, *First Lady of the Third Reich*, p. 187. Ello Quandt tells Magda how much Hanke is in love with her in Meissner, *First Lady of the Third Reich*, p. 194.

Is Hedda the daughter of Hanke? Let us take seriously, for just a moment, this piece of 'upstairs-downstairs' gossip: the likenesses of the potential father and daughter are strikingly similar. The set of Hedda's forehead and brow match Hanke's to a tee, though obviously we are not in a position to ask Hanke for a paternity test! Hanke is the person with whom Magda had the most public affair in the period around Hedda's conception in August 1937. Her affair with Kurt Ludecke was back in 1933. The affair with Hanke may have only gained visibility in October 1938 (Longerich, *Goebbels*, pp. 394 and 420), but it was certainly active before the summer of 1938 (Meissner, *First Lady of the Third Reich*, p. 201). Albert Speer, who describes Hanke as an 'old friend', writes that they both 'to the horror of everyone in the know, wished to marry', approaching Hitler with the idea, but that Hitler refused (Albert Speer, *Inside the Third Reich* (London: MacMillan, 1970), p. 149. The affair ended in the summer of 1939 after Magda confessed it to Goebbels (he called Hanke 'a first-class rogue' in his diary on 23 July). Hanke was dispatched from the Propaganda Ministry and later became Gauleiter in Lower Silesia in 1941 (which would not have precluded him from reporting back in Berlin and visiting Magda at Lanke). Hanke then married in early 1945, the same year that Magda became infatuated with Hanke's replacement, Dr Werner Naumann (Meissner, *First Lady of the Third Reich*, p. 236). A rapprochement between Magda and Goebbels only occurred in the winter of 1944–45. I cannot prove that Hanke was Hedda's father, but I do suspect the cook knows more than simply the ingredients of the soup.

Apfeleierkuchen

Meissner mentions Magda's frozen nerve: the 'pain in the right side of her face, in the Trigeminus nerve', when writing about her reaction to the 20 July plot on Hitler's life (Meissner, *First Lady of the Third Reich*, p. 228), and he tells of the operation that became necessary in August 1944 (ibid., p. 234, also in Petra Fohrmann, *Die Kinder des Reichsministers* (Swisttal: Fohrman Verlag, 2005), p. 47). It affected Magda's salivary glands, which may account for Erna's testimony that special separate food needed to be prepared for Magda at dinners.

Descriptions of Harald are in Paul Gathmann, *Narziss Goebbels: Eine Biografie* (Vienna: Böhlau, 2009), p. 162. I am reluctant to cite this source as it is badly sourced.

The importance of physiognomy to Goebbels: Gathmann, *Narziss Goebbels*, p. 165.

Descriptions of Hilde may be found in: Goebbels, *Tagebücher*, 14 April 1934. Behrend also mentions Goebbels' disappointment in the sex of the child, 24 April 1952.

Was Goebbels an affectionate father? See Sereny, *Albert Speer*, p. 509.

Descriptions of Holde may be found in Meissner, *First Lady of the Third Reich*, pp. 143–4; Behrend, 5 January 1952.

For descriptions of Heide as the 'reconciliation child', see: Meissner, *First Lady of the Third Reich*, p. 209. Behrend describes her as a 'beast', 5 January 1952.

Longerich doubts Goebbels' affection as a father (*Goebbels*, p. 362), quoting a number of entries between April and October 1937.

Descriptions of Goebbels as a caring father also appear in: Goebbels, *Tagebücher*, 4 December 1944; 3 August 1935 ('Played with both children, they are so sweet and kind like never before'); 15 February 1937 ('I am so happy when I have these small beings around me'); 24 October 1938 ('The children are especially funny and cute. Helga and Hilde kiss me without interruption and are happy to see their father again'). Meissner interviews the children's governess, Frau K., who also said that at meals an 'unforced atmosphere' prevailed at home, 'the children were allowed to chatter to their hearts' content', and that the Minister was 'much loved by the household staff' and that he had 'excellent table manners' and 'was at his best at mealtimes', *First Lady of the Third Reich*, p. 245.

On Goebbels and religion, see: Longerich, *Goebbels*, p. 26. Quoting 'Erinnerungsblaetter', in *Die Tagebücher von Joseph Goebbels. Sämtliche Fragmente*, ed. Fröhlich, p. 27; Meissner, *First Lady of the Third Reich*, p. 147.

Magda's mother also briefly mentions the French prisoner of war: 'Jean-Marie who kept the garden in Lanke in order.' Behrend, 31 May 1952.

Joseph Goebbels wrote that the children attended mass rallies in: *Tagebücher*, 14 February 1943, 3 February 1943, 21 March 1943, quoted in Longerich, *Goebbels*, p. 561.

(False) Whipped Cream

About the children's butter rations, see Fohrmann, *Die Kinder des Reichsministers*, p. 23.

On Magda's extravagant gifts to her staff: Behrend, 26 April 1952. On the extravagant refurbishment: Berkholz, *Goebbels' Waldhof am Bogensee*, p. 52, quoting the papers of the architect in charge of the renovations. On Magda returning to her spending habits after an abstemious period: Meissner, *Magda Goebbels. Ein Lebensbild*, p. 252. On the extravagant Mercedes purchase: Longerich, *Goebbels*, p. 525, and Goebbels, *Tagebücher*, 23 October 1940, and (quotes) Klabunde, *Magda Goebbels*, pp. 300–1. The stocked wine cellar and Magda's 'bell jar' are quoted from: Meissner, *Magda Goebbels. Ein Lebensbild*, pp. 275–6.

Returning the expensive ham is recounted in: Behrend, 8 May 1952. The order for shoes and hats is from an official document quoted in Klabunde, *Magda Goebbels*: Zentrales Staatsarchiv Merseburg, Rep 90, Go2, vol. 2, incorporated since 1993 in the Geheimes Staatsarchiv Preußischer Kulturbesitz.

Duck and Vegetable Stew

Hanke's December visit is recorded in Goebbels, *Tagebücher*, 31 December 1944, quoted in Longerich, *Goebbels*, p. 664.

The children's nanny remarks on the tense relationship between Auguste and the Minister in Fohrmann, *Die Kinder des Reichsministers*, p. 26, while Magda's breakdown is in Meissner, *Magda Goebbels. Ein Lebensbild*, p. 304.

For the 'bloodlands', see Timothy Snyder, *Bloodlands: Europe between Hitler and Stalin* (New York: Basic, 2012).

Hitler's Last Visit

Joseph Goebbels records this visit: *Tagebücher*, 4 December 1944. Hitler's bad state is in: Klabunde, *Magda Goebbels*, p. 306, quoting Behrend, 1 March 1952.

The staff of the house at Lanke only remained until the end of January. I wonder whether Erna did not want to tell me she lost her job?

Hot Chocolate

The firm that built the bunker, Hochtief, still exists and is worth 14 billion euros.

Drug use in the bunker is documented in Norman Ohler, *Der totale Rausch: Drogen im Dritten Reich* (Cologne: Kiepenheuer & Witsch, 2015), pp. 292–3.

Magda's letter of 28 April 1945 to her son Harald is reproduced in many collections, here from Meissner, *Magda Goebbels. Ein Lebensbild*, pp. 337–8. Helge begging not to die is recounted in Meissner, *Magda Goebbels. Ein Lebensbild*, p. 324.

Accounts of those wishing to save the children: Sereny, *Albert Speer*, p. 531, and Klabunde, *Magda Goebbels*, pp. 314 and 317; Meissner, *Magda Goebbels. Ein Lebensbild*, pp. 314 ff.; Erich Kempka, *Die Letzten Tage mit Adolf Hitler* (Pr. Oldendorf: K.W. Schütz, 1975), pp. 100–1.

Goebbels' postscript quoted in Anton Joachimsthaler, *Hitlers Ende: Legenden und Dokumente* (Munich: F.A. Herbig, 2004), p. 185. Registry Office certificate published in *Domarus II* 2234, 2241.

Magda's mother recounts how her daughter said to Hausintendant Rohrßen that hot chocolate 'will be our last ever drink' in Behrend, 31 May 1952.

Kempka testifies to the role of the doctor (*Die Letzten Tage mit Adolf Hitler*, p. 104); this was corroborated in a 1950s court case testimony by Dr Helmut Kunz (source: Allan Hall, 'Court papers shed light on killing of Goebbels children', in *The Telegraph*, 8 October 2009).

For the deaths of the children, Sereny, *Albert Speer*, quotes Rochus Misch's testimony on pp. 540–1. Kempka's testimony is the same, *Die Letzten Tage mit Adolf Hitler*, p. 106.

Cyanide Soup

The number of rapes, extrapolated from medical records, is quoted in Barbara Johr, 'Die Ereignisse in Zahlen', in Helke Sander and Barbara Johr, eds, *BeFreier und Befreite: Krieg, Vergewaltigung, Kinder* (Munich: Kunstmann, 1992), p. 59. See also Antony Beevor, *Berlin: The Downfall* (London: Penguin, 2007), p. 410. The republication of Marta Hillers, *Anonyma – Eine Frau in Berlin* (Munich: btb Verlag, 2003), reignited the debate in the press.

Innocent Recipes
The building risking demolition may be found in: 'Bogensee bei Wandlitz. Berlin prueft abriss von ehemaliger Goebbels Villa', in *Berliner Zeitung*, 10 September 2018.

A Trick
The fact that there is no mention of the quality of Goebbels' meals can be read about in: Longerich, *Goebbels*, p. 291, quoting Semmler, *Goebbels*, p. 77; Wilfred von Oven, *Mit Goebbels bis zum Ende, vol. I* (Buenos Aires: Dürer, 1949), pp. 56 and 277 ff. See also Goebbels, *Tagebücher*, 16 August 1926, 4 January 1926, 1 December 1926; Oven, *Mit Goebbels*, pp. 277 ff.; Goebbels, *Tagebücher*, 6 June 1944.

A String Instrument

Flowers
The violinist Hans Bastiaan appeared, along with the double bassist Erich Hartmann, in Enrique Sánchez Lansch's 2007 film *Das Reichsorchester* about the Berlin Philharmonic during the Nazi period. The film was made between 2004 and 2006. Hartmann's story receives only a smattering of quotes in Misha Aster's book (*Das Reichsorchester* (Munich: Siedler, 2007)). I quote from the English edition: Aster, *The Reich's Orchestra* (London: Souvenir Press, 2011), pp. 66–7, 74, 217–18, 226. My chapter is the first time Hartmann's story is told in detail.

Youth
Thank you to Ulrich Wolff, double bassist at the Berlin Philharmonic, for his insights on Saxon music education. Hartmann also describes his experience of his audition in the film, *Das Reichsorchester.*

The Double Bass
Hartmann describes many of his experiences – and confirms much of what he tells me in interview – in his memoir, published locally in Berlin,

Die Berliner Philharmoniker in der Stunde Null: Erinnerungen an die Zeit des Untergangs der alten Philharmonie vor 50 Jahren (Berlin: Werner Feja, 1996). See also his biographical details in Gerassimos Avgerinos' compendium of Philharmonic musicians, *Künstler Biographien: die Mitglieder im Berliner Philharmonischen Orchester von 1882–1972* (Berlin: Avgerinos (self-published), 1972).

A Nazi Orchestra

A useful chronology is provided in documents in Peter Muck, *Einhundert Jahre Berliner Philharmonisches Orchester, Band I* (Tutzing: Schneider, 1982). Also useful is a text by a Philharmonic percussionist from the period: Gerassimos Avgerinos, *Das Berliner Philharmoniker Orchester, 70 Jahre Schicksal einer GmbH* (Berlin: Avgerinos (self-published), 1973).

For the founding of the *Reichsmusikkammer* in the Philharmonic, see exh. cat., *Die Alte Philharmonie, ein Berliner Mythos – Katalog zur Ausstellung* (Berlin: Stiftung Berliner Philharmoniker, 2016), p. 7. For documentation on the Reichsmusikkammer, see Joseph Wulf, *Kultur im Dritten Reich* (Frankfurt, Ullstein, 1989), pp. 119 ff. Wulf's book of documents has also been useful to chart Richard Strauss' involvement in the Nazi project (pp. 194 ff.) and the prohibitions against Felix Mendelssohn (Anhang, pp. 447 ff.).

For a list of *Kraft durch Freude* concerts and those for the arms industry, see Stiftung Berliner Philharmoniker, *Variationen mit Orchestra, 125 Jahre Berliner Philharmoniker, Band 2* (Berlin: Henschel, 2007), pp. 310 ff.

See Alex Ross, *The Rest is Noise* (London: Picador, 2008), p. 314, for an eloquent account of the orchestra and its tastes under the Reich. I have also used Fred K. Prieberg, *Musik im NS-Staat* (Frankfurt: Fischer, 1982) and Pamela Potter, 'The Nazi "Seizure" of the Berlin Philharmonic, or the Decline of a Bourgeois Musical Institution', in Glenn R. Cuomo, ed., *National Socialist Cultural Policy* (New York: St Martin's Press, 1995), esp. pp. 53 ff.

For the Philharmonic's appearances at Nazi events, see Aster, *The Reich's Orchestra*, pp. 117–22 and 135. Hitler's request that his men attend opera concerts is discussed in Speer, *Inside the Third Reich*, p. 103. See also Richard J. Evans' invaluable *The Third Reich in Power* (London: Penguin, 2005), pp. 187 ff. I also refer to the first volume of his series:

Richard J. Evans, *The Coming of the Third Reich* (London: Penguin, 2003), pp. 399–402.

The orchestra's financial benefits under the Third Reich are summarised in Aster, *The Reich's Orchestra*, p. 110. Furtwängler's salary is on p. 97. For Nazi programmes of procurement, see Willem de Vries, *Sonderstab Musik* (Amsterdam: Amsterdam University Press, 1996); and Aster, *The Reich's Orchestra*, pp. 68–9. I am grateful to Aster for having found a number of pertinent documents such as Dr Drewe's contracting of agents and the RMVP note stating that one instrument originated from a certain Graf Hartig, who was Jewish (both in Bundesarchiv files R 55/853).

The RMVP document is quoted by Aster, *The Reich's Orchestra*, footnote 141 on p. 69. See also Carla Shapreau, 'A Violin Once Owned by Goebbels Keeps Its Secrets', in *The New York Times*, 21 September 2012. Erich Hartmann explains reactions to *Uk-Stellung* in his memoir, p. 7. *Uk-Stellung*'s relationship to the essential service of propaganda is discussed by Herr Bastiaan in the film *Das Reichsorchester*, when he examines a primary document related to the topic.

Speer, *Inside the Third Reich*, pp. 191 ff., explains the relationship between musical taste and Nazi racial policy. Stresemann's Mendelssohn query comes from *The New Yorker*, 24 June 1945, quoted in *Die Alte Philharmonie*, p. 10. Herr Bastiaan states, in the *Reichsorchester* film, that the image of Mendelssohn had been removed from the Alte Philharmonie. On regularly playing Beethoven's 9th in 1942, see: Aster, *The Reich's Orchestra*, p. 141.

Playing for Furtwängler

Hartmann's first concerts with the Philharmonic are described in his memoir, p. 13. A list of concerts in his first months is in Muck, *Einhundert Jahre Berliner Philharmonisches Orchester*, pp. 308 ff. Speer says Hitler was not often in concert attendance but other sources disagree; see also Aster, *The Reich's Orchestra*, p. 116, for concert attendance by Nazi officials. The bombings of those times are in ibid., p. 149.

I have relied on Herbert Haffner's *Furtwängler* (Berlin: Parthas, 2003); and Fred K. Prieberg, *Kraftprobe, Wilhelm Furtwängler im Dritten Reich* (Munich: Brockhaus, 1986). The latter text, however, is highly problematic; Prieberg's first chapter inverts the scapegoating of Jews to describe

Jewish emigrants' scapegoating of Furtwängler. Prieberg describes camps which held Jewish Germans in Allied countries as 'differing little from German concentration camps' (p. 11: '"feindlichen Ausländer" [wurden] oft Seite an Seite mit den Parteigenossen der deutschen Botschaften, Konsulate, oder Handelsvertretungen in Lagern, die sich kaum von den Konzentrationslagern der Deutschen unterschieden'). The viciousness of the debate surrounding Furtwängler is intimated by the author's tone. Furtwängler's relationship with the Nazis is also summarised in Evans, *The Third Reich in Power*, pp. 195 ff.; Michael Meyer, *The Politics of Music in the Third Reich* (New York: Lang, 1991), pp. 329 ff.; Sam H. Shirakawa, *The Devil's Music Master* (Oxford: Oxford University Press, 1992); and Aster, *The Reich's Orchestra*, p. 10. Thomas Mann's quote comes from *Tagebücher* (Frankfurt: S. Fischer, 1977) (1993, third edition), vol. 3, p. 47.

For a documentation of the Hindemith controversy, see Wulf, *Kultur im Dritten Reich*, pp. 371 ff.

Nazis and Jews

Hartmann's memoir, referring to the 'human feeling' of Nazi orchestra members, is quoted (p. 9).

Aster, *The Reich's Orchestra*, pp. 57 ff., describes the Nazi sympathies of various musicians and how they represented the community of musicians through their advisory board and service contract.

For the purging of Jews from German stages and cultural institutions, see: Evans, *The Coming of the Third Reich*, pp. 394 ff. and Ross, *The Rest is Noise*, p. 314. The antisemitism of Furtwängler is documented in Evans, *The Coming of the Third Reich* (p. 400) as is the fate of Jewish musicians after the Nazis came to power (p. 402). On Jewish musicians losing their jobs, see Ross, *The Rest is Noise*, p. 314, and Evans, *The Third Reich in Power*, p. 196. The experiences of Jewish wives of musicians, and patrons is described in Aster, *The Reich's Orchestra*, pp. 51–4.

Alte Philharmonie

For the history of the Alte Philharmonie, see *Die Alte Philharmonie*, pp. 13–18. The musical life of the war years is described in Hartmann's memoir, p. 13.

Destruction

Description of the bombing of the Alte Philharmonie can be found in Aster, *The Reich's Orchestra*, p. 72; Avgerinos, *Das Berliner Philharmoniker Orchester, 70 Jahre Schicksal einer GmbH*, p. 65; and is documented in Muck, *Einhundert Jahre Berliner Philharmonisches Orchester*, pp. 174 ff.

For information on the detonation of the remains of the Alte Philharmonie, see: *Die Alte Philharmonie*, pp. 7–8, 18.

Herr Hartmann describes playing in the dark in the film *Das Reichsorchester.*

Tours

Hartmann describes the propaganda role of the orchestra in his memoir (pp. 7 and 15). Buchholz describes the orchestra 'conquering countries' in *Das Reichsorchester* film. For foreign reviews, see Aster, *The Reich's Orchestra*, p. 187. See also Potter, 'The Nazi "Seizure" of the Berlin Philharmonic', pp. 57–8, who argues that the Philharmonic under the Nazis is reduced to a 'public relations vehicle outside the Reich' that at home promoted 'the music created for and by the *Volk*'.

For the use of military trains and interactions when abroad, see Aster, *The Reich's Orchestra*, p. 203. For accusations of spying, see ibid., p. 213. Smuggling, and the conditions of the voyage from Spain through France, back to Germany, is recounted in Hartmann's memoir, pp. 19 ff., as is the stay in Baden-Baden, p. 27. Other details, such as dates of the tours, concerts and the premiere of the *Philharmoniker* film are taken from Muck, *Einhundert Jahre Berliner Philharmonisches Orchester*, pp. 176 ff. Herr Bastiaan's comments about coffee are from the film *Das Reichsorchester.*

The propaganda purpose of playing until the end, and in a *Wehrmacht* hospital, is elucidated in an interview with Herr Bastiaan in the film *Das Reichsorchester.* For suicide pills, see Ross, *The Rest is Noise*, p. 338. See also *Variationen mit Orchestra, 125 Jahre Berliner Philharmoniker, Band 2,* p. 313.

Avgerinos quotes his diary of 16 April 1945 in *Das Berliner Philharmoniker Orchester, 70 Jahre Schicksal einer GmbH*, p. 68.

Stunde Null

See the section 'Stunde Null' in Hartmann's memoir, esp. pp. 31 ff for descriptions of the Battle of Berlin and its aftermath for the musicians.

The image of the double bass in a baby carriage is on p. 36. On pp. 34 ff., he recounts the first meetings of the reunited orchestra. This meeting is also recounted in Avgerinos, *Das Berliner Philharmoniker Orchester, 70 Jahre Schicksal einer GmbH*, p. 70.

On Borchard, see Aster, *The Reich's Orchestra*, p. 222; and Hartmann's memoir, p. 41. On Celibidache, see Hartmann's memoir, pp. 43–5. On Klemperer, see ibid., p. 49.

For the number of musicians forced out and denazified, see Aster, *The Reich's Orchestra*, pp. 224 ff., and Abby Anderton, *Rubble Music: Occupying the Ruins of Postwar Berlin 1945–50* (Bloomington: Indiana University Press, 2019), pp. 47 ff. Anderton's numbers on p. 47 differ a little from Aster's: she counts seventeen former party members of whom nine were dismissed. Neither Avgerinos, in *Das Berliner Philharmoniker Orchester, 70 Jahre Schicksal einer GmbH*, p. 70, nor Muck (*Einhundert Jahre Berliner Philharmonisches Orchester*) makes mention of the orchestra 'cleansing itself'; Avgerinos mentions only the question of finding scores and instruments; Aster reports that the events at the meeting are unknown, *The Reich's Orchestra*, p. 223.

For documents on the Allies having interviewed both Hartmann and Bastiaan, see Bundesarchiv files, R 9361-V 139087 and R 9361-V 143318. I found no transcript of the interviews of these investigations. Further research on the Allies' denazification efforts, and remaking of the orchestra, is in Abby Anderton, '"It was Never a Nazi Orchestra": The American Re-Education of the Berlin Philharmonic', in *Music and Politics*, vol. 7, no. 1, 2013.

Hartmann's thoughts on his Nazi colleagues are recorded in his memoir, p. 9. Herr Bastiaan remarks on the musicians being 'children' politically in the film *Das Reichsorchester*.

For the Philharmonic's work schedule, see Aster, *The Reich's Orchestra*, pp. 112–14.

The Instrument

Herr Bastiaan's violin, as part of the procurement programme, is listed in the Berliner Philharmoniker *Spielzeit* programme from 1942; the image is reproduced in the chapter. Aster also notes the loan: *The Reich's Orchestra*, p. 69. The information here about the Federal Commissioner for Culture and Media's understanding of the origin of the instruments, their history as property of the state post-1945, and the current loan programmes, come from emails between me and the federal government, the Musical Instrument Museum in Berlin, and the Deutsche Stiftung Musikleben.

Looking for a Violin

Kolja Blacher's biographical details come from Avgerinos, *Künstler Biographien*, p. 15.

The Owner

I have combed the website of the Deutsche Stiftung Musikleben in March 2021 and the question of dubious provenance is nowhere to be found. For example, on the entry regarding the bestowing of the 1761 Guadagnini on Ioana Cristina Goicea, the history is abridged between the eighteenth century to 1994 when Isabelle Faust began to play the instrument. Websource: www.deutsche-stiftung-musikleben.de/projekte/instrumente.html. I hope that in the period between submitting this manuscript (1 April 2021) and the book's publication that the Stiftung will make more of its instruments' histories public.

Provenance

The quote on restitution requiring knowledge of looted property is taken directly from the 2009 Terezin Declaration. The full text is available as a websource: www.state.gov/prague-holocaust-era-assets-conference-terezin-declaration.

Alte Philharmonie, Again

For more on the 31 October–3 November 1943 recording of Beethoven's 7th symphony in the Alte Philharmonie, see the notes of the producer, Andrew Rose, on the remastering of the tracks: www.pristineclassical.com.

For arguments that the Berlin Philharmonic was not a 'Nazi orchestra', see Hartmann's memoir, pp. 50 ff., and Aster, *The Reich's Orchestra*, p. 220.

For Goebbels' goal of a spiritual awakening see Evans, *The Third Reich in Power*, p. 211, with Goebbels' text in note 241 (the Minister is speaking at the opening of a Reich Theatre Week in Hamburg on 17 March 1935).

For artists who left Nazi Germany, see Evans, *The Coming of the Third Reich*, pp. 412 ff.

For the return of Westermann as intendant, see Aster, *The Reich's Orchestra*, p. 233.

A Cotton Pouch

Change of Heart

For the poll of US adults, see: 'Holocaust Knowledge and Awareness Study'. Conference on Jewish Material Claims Against Germany (Claims Conference) survey. Online source: 'Holocaust Knowledge Awareness Study Executive Summary, 2018', www.claimscon.org. Also reported by Harriet Sherwood in 'Nearly two-thirds of US young adults unaware 6m Jews killed in the Holocaust', *The Guardian*, 16 September 2020.

A Field of Wheat

For specific information on those deported for forced labour, see Eleonore Lappin-Eppel, 'Der Zwangsarbeiteinsatz und die Todesmärsche ungarischer Jüdinnen und Juden in Österreich 1944/45', in exh. cat., Christian Gmeiner, *Mobiles Erinnern- Gedenken: Todesmarsch ungarisch-jüdischer Zwangsarbeiter 1944–45* (Krems/Donau, 2005), p. 19.

Volotovo

I later see that the files at Volotovo relating to Artúr were submitted by Katalin herself; yvng.yadvashem.org. I wish we had information about him and regret that the facts we have rely on one witness.

Hegyeshalom

For numbers forced to march, I have referred to Eleonore Lappin-Eppel, 'Der Zwangsarbeiteinsatz und die Todesmärsche ungarischer Jüdinnen und Juden in Österreich 1944/45', pp. 8 and 32; Randolph L. Braham, *The Politics of Genocide: The Holocaust in Hungary* (Detroit: Wayne State University Press, 2000), pp. 187 ff.

For the comparison between the Arrow Cross and the Germans, I use the testimony of Judith Konrad, United States Holocaust Memorial Museum, Oral History | Accession Number: 1995.A.1285.25 | RG Number: RG-50.149.0025, part II (34:00).

Lichtenwörth

An overview of the paucity of documentation about Lichtenwörth was provided in correspondence with the archive of the Sachsenhausen Memorial and Museum. No information about Lichtenwörth is in the archive's database.

For lack of commemoration of Nazi atrocities in Austria and the politics of memory in the country, see Heidemarie Uhl, 'From Victim Myth to Co-Responsibility Thesis: Nazi-Rule, World War II, and the Holocaust in Austrian Memory', in Richard Ned Lebow, Wulf Kansteiner and Claudio Fogu, eds, *The Politics of Memory in Postwar Europe* (Durham and London: Duke University Press, 2006), pp. 40–72. The toponym 'Naziland' has been perennially evoked since the Waldheim Affair, by left and right alike in Austria, in publications such as *Der Standard* or *Die Presse*. See, for example, Paul Lendvai, 'Kontraproduktive Attacken Haider und das Ausland: Lehren aus der "Waldheim-Krise"', in *Der Standard*, 8 October 1999; or Martina Salomon, 'Das Klischee ist zurück: Österreich als Naziland', in *Die Presse*, 28 September 2009, among the many examples.

The mention of Lichtenwörth during the Eichmann trial was in sessions 61 and 62 on 1 June 1961, Film | Accession Number: 1999.A.0087 | RG Number: RG-60.2100.074 | Film ID: 2073.

For background on the Lichtenwörth camp, I have consulted: Eleonore Lappin-Eppel, 'Erinnerungszeichen an die Opfer des Zwangsarbeitseinsatzes ungarischer Juden und Jüdinnen in Niederösterreich 1944/5', in Heinz Arnberger and Claudia Kuretsidis-Haider, eds, *Gedenken und Mahnen in Niederörsterreich* (Vienna: Mandelbaum, 2001), pp. 60 ff. See also: Vera Broser, *Der Weg ungarischer Juden nach Niederösterreich 1944–5* (Vienna: Verein Kultur im Alltag, 1990). A brief summary is in Werner Sulzgruber, *Die jüdische Gemeinde Wiener Neustadt* (Vienna: Mandelbaum, 2005), pp. 361 ff.

I have cross-referenced Katalin's account with the testimony of Konrad; the testimony of Aviva Fleischmann from sessions 61 and 62 of the Eichmann trial on 1 June 1961, Film | Accession Number: 1999.A.0087 | RG Number: RG-60.2100.074 | Film ID: 2073; and that of Hedvig Endrei in Szilvia Czingel, 'Recipes for Survival: Survival Strategies in the Lichtenwörth Concentration Camp', in *SIMON* (*Shoah: Intervention, Methods, Documentation*), vol. 6, no. 1, 2019, pp. 123–32. All provide information confirming the layout of the camp, the paucity of food, how time was spent, the horror of typhus, etc. 'Salty coffee' is a phrase from Hedvig Endrei. The mobile gas chamber is referred to by Konrad, and also in the testimony (in Hungarian) of Helen Lowinger, United States Holocaust Memorial Museum, Oral History | Accession Number: 2006.70.92 | RG Number: RG-50.583.0092.

Information about the memorial in Lichtenwörth can be found in Claudia Kuretsidis-Haider and Heinz Arnberger, 'Gedächtniskulturen und Erinnergungslandschaften in Niederösterreich', in Arnberger and Kuretsidis-Haider, eds, *Gedenken und Mahnen in Niederörsterreich*, p. 34, and the appendix, pp. 527 ff. The appendix lists 2,500 Jews arriving with a transport in December 1944.

For sleeping conditions, a secondary source indicates the prisoners slept on a 'bare brick floor and were given hunger rations'. Eleonore Lappin-Eppel, 'Der Zwangsarbeiteinsatz und die Todesmärsche ungarischer Jüdinnen und Juden in Österreich 1944/45', p. 19.

That the work outside the camp ceased in January is recorded in Eleonore Lappin-Eppel, 'Erinnerungszeichen an die Opfer des Zwangsarbeitseinsatzes ungarischer Juden und Jüdinnen in Niederösterreich 1944/5', p. 73.

Additional report of locals giving the women in Lichtenwörth something to eat can be read in Szabolcs Szita, *Verschleppt, verhungert, vernichtet: die Deportation von ungarischen Juden auf das Gebiet des annektierten Österreich 1944–1945* (Vienna: Eichbauer Verlag, 1999), p. 180. Konrad also states that the elderly German guards were kinder than the SS officers or the *Jupo*.

For the recipes that Jewish women wrote down in the camp and the phenomenon of 'systemic starvation' see Czingel, 'Recipes for Survival', pp. 123–32. The testimony about washing from Endrei can be found in ibid., p. 126.

Epidemic

Information on the mass grave, with the names of those exhumed, is indicated in the appendix of Amberger and Kuretsidis-Haider, eds, *Gedenken und Mahnen in Niederörsterreich*, pp. 527 ff. Lappin-Eppel refers to approximately 300 dead in the camp in her work but I believe this refers to the mass grave, rather than the total number who died: Fleischmann says only 400 of the 2,500 survived and Konrad witnessed fifty dying per day from malnutrition and disease. Their numbers are more consistent with a typhus outbreak and are consistent across the survivor testimonies. These numbers are corroborated by the Vrtoch court documents.

The raiding of the camp food storage is also recounted in Czingel, 'Recipes for Survival', p. 127.

Crutches

The quotes come from Marcel Proust, trans. C.K. Scott Moncrieff and Terence Kilmartin, 'Place-Names: The Place' in *Within a Budding Grove* (New York: Modern Library, 1998), p. 300; *Phaedrus*: 275a-b in Plato, trans. Harold North Fowler, *Plato in Twelve Volumes, Vol. 9* (Cambridge, MA: Harvard University Press, 1925): 'Their trust in writing, produced by external characters which are no part of themselves, will discourage the use of their own memory within them.'

Post-War

For the recipes that Jewish women wrote down in the camp and the phenomenon of 'systemic starvation', see Czingel, 'Recipes for Survival', p. 124.

Vrtoch

The Wilhelm Vrtoch *Volksgericht* court documents were obtained from the Dokumentationsarchiv des österreichischen Widerstandes (Documentation Archive of the Austrian Resistance), who hold the archive, with the following catalogue number: LG Wien Vg 12 Vr 7552/46. The Vrtoch trial is mentioned briefly in Fritz Plasser, *New Perspectives on Austrians and World War II* (Milton Park: Routledge, 2017), p. 291. The SS service file of Vrtoch at the German Federal Archives, which I obtained, has the catalogue number: R 9361-III/215429, 'Rasse- und Siedlungshauptamt SS' (Berlin Document Center/BDC).

A Way Without Words

'She-Nazis'

In discussing 'making the object your own', I quote Neil MacGregor, *A History of the World in 100 Objects* (London: Penguin, 2010), preface and introduction.

Parts of the exhibition *Hitler and the Germans* at the German Historical Museum can be visited virtually: www.dhm.de/archiv/ausstellungen/hitler-und-die-deutschen/en. I also refer to press reactions at the time: Frank Hornig and Michael Sontheimer, 'A Visit to Germany's First-Ever Hitler Exhibition', in *Spiegel*, 13 October 2010; Stephen Evans, 'Hitler's Relationship with Germany Explored', in *BBC News Online*, 15 October 2010.

A history of prostitution facilities in German concentration camps, which documents the exclusion of Jewish women, is Robert Sommer, *Das KZ-Bordell: sexuelle Zwangsarbeit in nationalsozialistischen Konzentrationslagern* (Paderborn: Verlag Ferdinand Schoning, 2018).

The Hebrew University-led research on Stalags is published here: Amit Pinchevski, 'Holocaust Perversions: The Stalags Pulp Fiction and the Eichmann Trial Critical Studies', in *Media Communication*, vol. 24, no. 5, December 2007, pp. 387–407. The work is in Hebrew and I have relied on automatic translation. For a contemporary perspective on internet regulation of pornography in Israel, see Matt Lebovic, 'When Israel banned Nazi-inspired "Stalag" porn', in *The Times of Israel*, 17 November 2016. See also Ari Libsker's 2008 film *Stalags*.

Hiding the Swastika

Francis Ponge, 'My Creative Method', *Méthodes* (Paris: Gallimard, 1961), pp. 12–13. Translation: Robert Melançon, 'My Creative Method', in *Maisonneuve*, 18 November 2002. See also discussion in B. Brown, 'Thing Theory', in *Critical Enquiry*, vol. 28, no. 1, 2001, p. 2. Ponge's text is responding to concerns in twentieth-century literary theory that are not exactly our own (the Mallarmean relationship between poetic language and reference) but his observations can also be useful to this discussion.

For the museology of Nazi objects, see Chloe Paver, *Exhibiting the Nazi Past* (New York: Springer, 2018), pp. 2 ff. Observations about obscuring the swastika are on p. 100.

George Orwell writes in an essay that 'Kipling is a jingo imperialist, he is morally insensitive and aesthetically disgusting'. 'Rudyard Kipling', *Horizon*, September, 1941.

'Handled Carefully'

History was a latecomer to the 'material turn', despite the influence of cultural history, such as the *Annales* school, which encouraged historians to look at everyday life. In the 1980s, it was the anthropologists, mostly, who were exploring how the circulation of commodities revealed cultures. I'm thinking here of the 1986 publication of Arjun Appadurai's edited volume, *The Social Life of Things: Commodities in Cultural Perspective* (Cambridge: Cambridge University Press, 1986). For a contemporary cultural and media studies perspective on objects, the essay and book series *Object Lessons* (edited by *The Atlantic* and Bloomsbury) has studies dedicated to classes of objects from remote controls to refrigerators to dust.

My definitions draw from Bernard Herman, who writes about 'object-centred' versus 'object-driven' research in *The Stolen House* (Charlottesville: University of Virginia Press, 1992). See also the discussion in Karen Harvey, *History and Material Culture* (Milton Park: Routledge, 2013), pp. 2–3. I have also drawn from Leora Auslander, 'Beyond Words', *American Historical Review*, vol. 110, no. 4, 2005, p. 1025.

Also thinking of 'object-centred' versus 'object-driven' histories: Jules D. Prown sets up a curious opposition as between the 'farmer and the cowman'. See Jules D. Prown, 'Material/Cultural: Can the Farmer and the Cowman Still be Friends?', in W. David Kinger, ed., *Learning from Things* (Washington DC: Smithsonian, 1996), pp. 19–30, also quoted in Auslander, 'Beyond Words', p. 1025. The farmer is a realist who sees the thing before him, while the cowman is the dreamer who attaches metaphors and explores context. The cowman is sometimes disparaged as talking about 'objects with stories', and not 'stories from objects'. Both, however, are needed, as Thomas J. Schlereth observed already in 1985: 'Few scholars would argue with the claim that material culture evidence of the past should be used in historical research when it is the only evidence available ... we must remember that it is always the culture, rather than the material, that should interest the material culture historian.' Objects are necessarily housed in these cultural and temporal contexts (even if none of us can claim full knowledge of them). T.J. Schlereth, 'Material Cultural Research', in *The Public Historian*, vol. 7, no. 4, 1985, pp. 23 and 32.

For Frank Trentmann's observations (and quote) on the 'partial embrace' of material culture, see 'Materiality in the Future of History', in *Journal of British Studies*, vol. 28, no. 2, 2009.

Jules D. Prown attempted to create a method for working with material culture in 'Mind in Matter', *The Winterthur Portfolio*, vol. 17, no. 1, 1982. His brave attempt to distil an experimental design for material historians – systematic steps of description, deduction, intellectual engagement, speculation, leading to the programme of research – did not go uncontested. I am not the only one to find Prown's method to be a straight-jacket – a prescriptive method simply doesn't suit; it doesn't provide enough flexibility for the subject matter. The material object, when at the centre of a design, too easily becomes the subject of research, rather than a tool. The definition of 'material culture', after all, is not just the things themselves, but all the meanings associated with them. A critique of Prown and other perspectives on method can be found in Anne Gerritsen and Giorgio Riello, eds, *Writing Material Culture History* (London: Bloomsbury, 2015), pp. 2–5. They usefully provide us with multiple ways objects can enrich historical work: to complement other sources, to make historians ask new questions, and to explore hidden themes. In each case, the object is a way to unlock context.

'Things-in-Motion'

For *Julleuchter*, see documentation on their production in Wolfgang Benz, *KZ-Aussenlager: Geschichte und Erinnerung* (Dachau: Verlag Dachauer Hefte, 1999), pp. 122 and 132. See also: Derek Niemann, *A Nazi in the Family: The Hidden Story of an SS Family in Wartime Germany* (London: Short Books, 2018), ch. 5.

Appadurai discusses 'things-in-motion' in his introduction to *The Social Life of Things*, pp. 3–5. Appadurai urges us to think of objects as revealers of a larger system of cultural meaning: 'Commodities, like persons, have social lives … we have to follow the things themselves, for their meanings are inscribed in their forms, their uses, their trajectories. It is only through the analysis of these trajectories that we can interpret the human transactions and calculations that enliven things. Thus, even though from a theoretical point of view human actors encode things with significance, from a methodological point of view it is the things-in-motion that illuminate their human and social context.' See also the discussion in Samuel J.M.M. Alberti, 'Objects and the Museum', in *Isis*, vol. 96, no. 4, 2005, pp. 560–1. On the relation to the global circulation of goods, see Anne Gerritsen and Giorgio Riello, eds, *The Global Lives of Things* (Milton Park: Routledge, 2015).

I refer to Igor Kopytoff, 'The Cultural Biography of Things', in Arjun Appadurai, ed., *The Social Life of Things: Commodities in Cultural Perspective*, esp. pp. 67, 90. Kopytoff, when discussing the 'cultural biography' of things, uses the example of an American car ending up in Africa, revealing a 'wealth of cultural data' from how it was acquired, what journey it made, what status it afforded, who used and borrowed it, and how it was junked. 'All of these details would reveal an entirely different biography from that of a middle-class American, or Navajo, or French peasant car.'

Objects that Change Us

For a discussion of objects and agency, see Kopytoff, 'The Cultural Biography of Things', p. 90. See also Martin Heidegger, *Being and Time* (Hoboken: Blackwell, 1962); Pierre Bourdieu, *Outline of a Theory of Practice* (Cambridge: Cambridge University Press, 1977); and Bourdieu, *Distinction: A Social Critique of the Judgment of Taste* (Milton Park: Routledge, 2010). See also the discussion in Leonie Hannan and Sarah Longair, *History Through Material Culture* (Manchester: Manchester University Press, 2017), pp. 19–20.

Objects and the Senses

Lola Rein's dress is in the collection of the United States Holocaust Memorial Museum (Accession Number: 2002.54.2) and was the subject of the museum's online exhibit *Silent Witness*.

On olfaction and memory, see the work of Harvard's Venkatesh Murthy, quoted in Colleen Walsh, 'What the Nose Knows', *Harvard Gazette*, 27 February 2021.

For the discussion of objects and the senses, see Schlereth, 'Material Cultural Research', p. 25 (many objects involve 'modes of knowing that entail a nonverbal comprehension of the significance of the three-dimensional in human history') or see Brooke Hindle, 'Technology Through the Three-D Time Warp', in *Technology and Culture*, vol. 24, no. 3, 1983, p. 456, also quoted in Schlereth, 'Material Cultural Research', p. 26 (Hindle speaks of 'fingertip acquaintance and fingertip knowledge'). The importance of objects to their owners – such as children's blankets – is explored in Auslander, 'Beyond Words', pp. 1019 ff.

The paragraph on the future challenges for historians as objects become increasingly virtual is from a productive exchange with Neta Alexander, Assistant Professor of Film and Media at Colgate University, New York, and co-author with Arjun Appadurai of *Failure*. Cambridge: Polity, 2019. Alexander has forthcoming work on the role of VR in Holocaust memory.

Value

For a discussion of 'clean' museum collections, and the policies of Swiss museums, see Roger Fayet, '"Clean" Collections: On the Idea of Contamination in the Provenance Discussion', *CrossCurrents*, September 2019, pp. 278 and 286.

For the restitution of property to French Jews, see Auslander, 'Beyond Words', pp. 1036 ff. Compare to how Germans lived among stolen possessions in confiscated Jewish apartments in Carolin Dorothée Lange, 'After They Left: Looted Jewish Apartments and the Private Perception of the Holocaust', in *Holocaust and Genocide Studies*, vol. 34, no. 2 (Winter 2020), pp. 431–49. For the idea of the memory palace, see Cicero, *De Oratore*, II, lxxxvi.

Patriots

For the reference to curling, see websource: 'The Prisoners of War who Curled in Oflag IX A/H', curlinghistory.blogspot.com. The men in the photograph likely include the Canadian Major Painchaud; this information I have from a clipping of a similar photograph found by Ian Seath. See also: Peter Green, *The March East, 1945: The Final Days of Oflag IX A/H and A/Z* (Cheltenham: Spellmount, 2012), p. 28.

Everyday

Albert Speer is quoted from *Inside the Third Reich*, pp. 170 ff. and 67 ff.

War in Our Time

For the poll of US adults, see: 'Holocaust Knowledge and Awareness Study'. Conference on Jewish Material Claims Against Germany (Claims Conference) survey. Online source: 'Holocaust Knowledge Awareness Study Executive Summary, 2018', www.claimscon.org.

Jacob Chaim's spoon can be seen at the Montreal Holocaust Museum: museeholocauste.ca.

Image Credits

The author and the publishers wish to thank the below sources of illustrative material for permission to reproduce each image. Images not indicated are either copyright of Joseph Pearson, public domain, fair use, or reproduced legally under other licences.

My Grandfather's Knife

Solingen Stadtarchiv: Nazi Propaganda Ministry (RMVP) photo from 1937 featuring a worker of Solingen (p. 6); photograph of Alexander Coppel (1865–1942) (p. 8).

Franz Xavier Bartle: *Harmodius and Aristogeiton* (D-DAI-ROM-58.1789), courtesy of the Museo Archeologico Nazionale di Napoli/Deutsches Archäologisches Institut (p. 11).

Archives and Libraries Canada: photo of Hugh John Sanders Pearson from his personnel file, 6 June 1944 (p. 16), and image of his Service and Casualty Form (p. 17).

US Army: US Army Map of the Battle of the Scheldt, October–November 1944 (p. 22).

Wehrmacht postcard of General Freiherr Werner von und zu Gilsa (p. 23).

Jorge Láscar: Goa Lawah ('Bat Cave') Temple, Bali, Indonesia, CC-BY-2.0 (p. 24).

The Bancroft Library, UC Berkeley: Poster for Tag der Deutschen Polizei, 1941 (p. 30).

The Calgary Highlanders Museum and Archive: Walcheren causeway, aerial view (p. 32); Walcheren Causeway, October 1944, painting by Robert Johnson (p. 33).

Bert Kaufmann: view of the canals of Groningen, the Netherlands, CC-BY-SA 3.0 (p. 36).

A Diary in Code

Jeannette Thomé: handwritten letter.

Examples of Sütterlin script in Ludwig Sütterlin: *Neuer Leitfaden für den Schreibunterricht*. Berlin, Albrecht-Dürer-Haus, 1917, p. 54 (p. 49).

Ludwig Richter, illustration of *Der alte Turmhahn* by Eduard Mörike, 1855 (p. 51).

Archives municipales du Havre: 1930s view of Place Gambetta, Bassin du Commerce, and Bassin du Roi, Le Havre. 4Fi85, ELD (editor: Ernest Le Deley) (p. 55); Destruction of Le Havre. Photo from 4–6 September 1944. 71Fi1398 (p. 56); Le Havre, postcard of a general view. 4Fi352, ELD (editor: Ernest Le Deley) (p. 63); 1930s, Le Havre, the Beach. 4Fi27, ELD (editor: Ernest Le Deley) (p. 71).

The National Archives, War Department: shaving of French women collaborators, 29 August 1944, Montélimar (p. 62).

Erich Andres: German sailor on the beach in Le Havre, 1940. © United Archives GmbH/Alamy (p. 68).

Bundesarchiv (BArch): Details from the *Kriegsmarine* file of 'Karl Biedassek', Deutsche Dienststelle (WASt) für die Benachrichtigung der nächsten Angehörigen von Gefallenen der ehemaligen deutschen Wehrmacht, B563V/SPO (archive number redacted for privacy) (pp. 79, 84 and 86).

Bordeaux Archives: photos by Lacarin (photographer) from *La Nouvelle République*, August 1944 (21 Fi 178) (pp. 85 and 86).

A Recipe Book

Erna Mußack: photo of herself (approximately 1944) (p. 91); photo of the Goebbels children (1944) (p. 98).

Bundesarchiv (BArch): Nazi Propaganda Ministry (RMVP), Berlin, Bild 183-H13457, CC-BY-SA 3.0 (p. 95); Magda Goebbels in 1933, Bild 183-R22014, CC-BY-SA 3.0 (p. 109); Joseph Goebbels, Bild 102-01888A, CC-BY-SA 3.0 (p. 110); Karl Hanke, Bild 183-1989-1120-502, CC-BY-SA 3.0 (p. 112); Goebbels Family Portrait, 1 January 1944, Bild 146-1978-086-03, CC-BY-SA 3.0 (pp. 112 and 114); Goebbels Family and Hitler in Obersalzberg, Bild 183-1987-0724-502, by Heinrich Hoffmann, CC-BY-SA 3.0 (p. 115); Goebbels children giving Hitler salute, Bild 183-C17887, by Wagner, CC-BY-SA 3.0 (p. 119); German soldiers in Kharkiv, Ukraine, burning a farmhouse, Bild 101III-Zschaeckel-186-36, by Friedrich Zschäckel, CC-BY-SA 3.0 (p. 126).

Tim Adams: Foot of Colossus of Constantine in the courtyard of the Musei Capitolini in Rome, Italy, CC-BY-3.0 (p. 100).

Hic et nunc: Hilda Krahl (p. 103).

Haus am Bogensee (floor plan): Brandenburgisches Landeshauptarchiv, Rep. 2A I Hb 1553, CCO 1.0 license (p. 107).

Martin Wolf: Lída Baarová. © Mary Evans/SZ Photo/Knorr + Hirth (p. 111).

Dalibri: Adventskranz, CC-BY-SA 4.0 (p. 118).

Craig Franklin: German ration stamps, CC-BY-SA 3.0 (p. 120).

A String Instrument

Archive of the Berliner Philharmoniker: Erich Hartmann in the 1960s (far left) (p. 141); Furtwängler playing in wartime (p. 145); opening of the Reichskulturkammer, 15 November 1933 (p. 149); Hans Bastiaan in 1940, photograph by Alexander Schmoll (p. 154); Furtwängler with Hermann Göring, Adolf Hitler, Joseph Goebbels in the front row in 1935 (p. 155); Szymon Goldberg and Gilbert Back during a concert tour in 1931 (p. 159); 1939 Berlin, Alte Philharmonie with Wilhelm Furtwängler on the podium and in the foreground empty rows of chairs (p. 162); the destroyed Alte Philharmonie, 1944 (multiple images) (p. 165); reception after a concert in Paris: principal cellist Arthur Troester (third from left) and concertmaster Gerhard Taschner (right) with a German general and other guests (p. 168); Erich Hartmann in 1984 (p. 189); Hans Bastiaan, 1970, photograph by R. Friedrich (p. 196).

Franz Löwy: Wilhelm Furtwängler, 1912 (p. 143).

Bundesarchiv (BArch): the Berlin Philharmonic playing in the AEG Werke in Berlin, February 1943, Bild 183-L0607-504, CC-BY-SA 3.0 (p. 150); Staatskapellmeister Herbert von Karajan, 1941, Bild 183-R92264, CC-BY-SA 3.0 (p. 195).

Yivos Archives: Violins confiscated from Jews being examined in Łódź Ghetto, 1942 (p. 151).

Library of Congress: Stravinsky and Furtwängler, between 1920 and 1923, George Grantham Bain Collection (digital ID: ggbain.32393) (p. 153).

Haendelfan: Alte Philharmonie in 1888, Gottlob Theuerkauf, *Illustrirte Zeitung*, no. 91, p. 605 (p. 161).

Museuminsulaner: chair from the Alte Philharmonie (p. 163).

Imperial War Museum: an aerial (oblique) photograph taken from a De Havilland Mosquito of the RAF Film and Photographic Unit showing badly damaged buildings in the area between Friedrich Hain [*sic*] and Lichtenberg, Berlin 1945–7, C5284 (p. 170).

Collections of the Jewish Museums in Prague: plundered wartime violins in a warehouse of the Prague Treuhandstelle (Trustee's Office) (p. 180).

The National Archives: An American soldier guards looted goods in 1945 in Ellingen, Germany (p. 192).

A Cotton Pouch

Katalin Lőrincz: photo of herself, July 1943 (p. 197); photo of Artúr Landau (p. 205).

Jesus Hernandez: *Rickettsia prowazekii*, body louse with two larval young (p. 212).

IM Thayer and Günter Schneider Photography: Jewish Museum, Berlin, aerial view, CC-BY-3.0 (p. 216).

Bundesarchiv (BArch): SS file photograph of Wilhelm Vrtoch, R 9361-III/215429, 'Rasse- und Siedlungshauptamt SS' (Berlin Document Center/BDC) (p. 225).

A Way Without Words

Peter Merholz: Nazi toys (p. 229).

Ludwig Hohlwein: 1932 Hitler Youth postcard, Munich, CC-BY-SA 4.0 (p. 235).

Nicholas Weed: Allach porcelain maker's mark; Allach-style candle-holder (reproduction) (pp. 241 and 242).

Bibi595: shoes found at Auschwitz-Birkenau camp, CC-BY-SA 3.0 (p. 244).

United States Holocaust Memorial Museum Collection, Gift of Lola and Walter Kaufman: Embroidered dress worn by a Polish Jewish girl in hiding, Object | Accession Number: 2002.54.2 (p. 245).

Curling Association of Scotland: Canadian prisoners of war playing curling at camp Oflag IX, A/H, Spangenberg Castle, Hesse, Germany, reproduced from the Annual of the Royal Caledonian Curling Club for 1944–45 (p. 251).

Library and Archives Canada: German prisoners' hockey team, Directorate of Internment Operations, Camp 132, Medicine Hat, Alberta, 25 February 1946, Item Number: 3403292 (p. 251).

Musée Holocaust Montréal: Jacob Chaim's Spoon, made in Dora-Mittelbau forced labour camp, 1945. © Montreal Holocaust Museum Collection, photographer Peter Berra, 2011X.94.05. (p. 259).

Acknowledgements

Many people contributed to this project, but I am most indebted to my witnesses for sharing their stories: Erna Jokisch and Katalin Lőrincz; and 'Karl Biedassek', Erich Hartmann, and Hugh John Sanders Pearson in memoriam. My gratitude to Flora Giuliani and her grandmother, the late Madame Jeannette Thomé, for trusting me with the story of the war diary. Thank you also to the many individuals with the last name 'Biedassek', who replied to query letters and shared their family histories.

Many people have accompanied the research as interlocutors and intermediaries. Ana Senčić introduced me to Frau Jokisch. Annemarie Bastiaan, Marie-Pierre Langlamet and Klaus Wallendorf at the Berlin Philharmonic presented me to Herr Hartmann. Thank you to Jason Price for his violin knowledge. Carla Shapreau's expertise on the provenance of violins was invaluable; I am particularly grateful for her generosity on a subject of overlapping interest. My appreciation to Hartmut Dorgerloh and Thomas Köstlin, who also sent me in the right direction. Thank you to the musicians Korbinian Altenberger, Tanja Becker-Bender, Kolja Blacher, Alexander Gilman, Ioana Cristina Goicea, Michael Mücke, and Ulrich Wolff. Bob Cowan, Bruce Crawford, and Ian Seath, meanwhile, kindly shared their research on curling in POW camps.

For their transcription of the war diary, my thanks to the Sütterlinstube Hamburg e.V., especially Barbara Sommerschuh. For their expertise, thank you to Melanie Amman, Gabriella Etmektsoglou, Marjorie Lamberti, Avi Lifschitz, William Mulligan, Brendan Simms, Emery Snyder. Thank you also to L. Don Maus and George T. Wheeler.

A number of institutions and archives have been invaluable to this research: the German Federal Archive (Bundesarchiv), in particular the assistance of archivist Michael Schelter; the librarians and collections of the Free University Berlin and the Jacob-und-Wilhelm-Grimm-Zentrum of the Humboldt University; the Berlin State Library (Staatsbibliothek zu Berlin); the archive of the Memorial and Museum Sachsenhausen; the Berlin Philharmonic's archive and its remarkable librarian Katja Vobiller; Anett Sawall at the Deutsche Kinemathek – Museum for Film and Television; the Musical Instrument Museum in Berlin and its director Prof. Dr Conny Restle; Deutsche Stiftung Musikleben and its head of programming, Saskia Egger; the Federal Commissioner for Culture and the Media of the Federal Republic of Germany, especially Martin Eifler in the Department for Music; the General Secretary of the Search division of the German Red Cross; City Archives of Solingen (Stadtarchiv Solingen); Archives municipales du Havre, especially Sebastien Juteau and Thierry Vincent; Archives Bordeaux Métropole; Stichting Museum of the Canadian Allied Forces, Groningen; Library and Archives Canada; the Calgary Highlanders Museum and Archive. Thank you to Siegfried Sanwald of the Documentation archive of Austrian Resistance (Dokumentationsarchiv des österreichischen Widerstandes) for so kindly copying and forwarding court documents when travel to Vienna was impossible under a coronavirus lockdown.

I am also grateful to my students and the faculty of the Barenboim-Said Akademie, and to my colleagues at the Graduate Research Initiative of New York University.

For their general or specific advice on the manuscript (all errors are my own), thank you to: Neta Alexander, Vivian Constantinopoulos, Matthew Gaskins, Markus Hoffmann, Olivier Jacquemond, Emily Mitchell, Ian Pearson, Kit Pearson, and Josh Tyree. Additional thanks to Katherine Farris, Susan Grimbly, Anne Pearson, Will Pearson, and Eszter Sarkozi. My appreciation too to Berlin friends for their support and insights, including Julie Cartier, Guy Chazan, Leda Mureda, Aki Naito, Joe Pace, Miriam Philippe, Marc Schroeder, and Sven Taddicken. Thanks also to Robert Rinder for his enthusiasm for the project, and to Thomas Ostermeier and Gabino Rodríguez for useful conversations and ideas on presenting documentary material to an audience. Thanks to Natalie Clein for her support and advice at many stages of the project, not least the chapter about musical instruments. My apologies for any oversights.

I am especially grateful to my agent, Annabel Merullo, at Peters Fraser and Dunlop Agency in London, and to my editors Simon Wright at The History Press and Jim Gifford at HarperCollins. Thanks too to the staff of PFD and my publishers, including my project editor Alex Boulton.

Finally, a special thank you to my parents, my family, and to James Helgeson for everything.

Index

Note: *italicised* page references indicate illustrations.